ARE YOU MISSING THE
REAL ESTATE
BOOM?

WHY HOME VALUES AND OTHER
REAL ESTATE INVESTMENTS WILL CLIMB
THROUGH THE END OF THE DECADE—AND
HOW YOU CAN PROFIT FROM IT

David Lereah

CURRENCY

DOUBLEDAY

NEW YORK   LONDON   TORONTO   SYDNEY   AUCKLAND

TO WENDY, ABBEY, JEFF, AND JENNA

A CURRENCY BOOK
PUBLISHED BY DOUBLEDAY
a division of Random House, Inc.

CURRENCY is a trademark of Random House, Inc., and DOUBLEDAY is a
registered trademark of Random House, Inc.

Book design by Chris Welch

Cataloging-in-Publication Data is on file with the Library of Congress

ISBN 0-385-51434-4

PRINTED IN THE UNITED STATES OF AMERICA

First Edition: March 2005
All trademarks are the property of their respective companies.

SPECIAL SALES
Currency Books are available at special discounts for bulk purchases for sales
promotions or premiums. Special editions, including personalized covers,
excerpts of existing books, and corporate imprints, can be created in large
quantities for special needs. For more information, write to Special Markets,
Currency Books, specialmarkets@randomhouse.com.

1 3 5 7 9 10 8 6 4 2

CONTENTS

ACKNOWLEDGMENTS

I am indebted to a number of individuals who have contributed in some meaningful manner to the final pages of this book. I owe a special debt of gratitude to my Doubleday editor, Roger Scholl, who helped inspire, shape, and edit the entire manuscript. He provided invaluable direction and encouragement throughout the entire writing of the manuscript. I would also like to pay special thanks to James Wade and to his assistant, Sharon Nettles, and to Kate Anderson, who also provided valuable editing assistance. I would also like to thank Dale Mattison from the Mattison Group, Long & Foster for providing a Realtor®'s view of the book, and Brian Chappelle from Potomac Partners for providing insights from the lending community. A special thanks goes out to Lawrence Yun, my colleague at the National Association of Realtors®, whom I used as a sounding board as well as a data source for so many of the arguments and positions taken in this book. And in no particular order, I would like to acknowledge Laurie Janik, General Counsel for the National Association of Realtors®; Rick Schomo, Wachovia Securities; Cassandra Sims, National Association of Realtors; Dave Hehman, President of EscapeHomes.com; and Steve Hornburg, Emerging Community Markets, for their much appreciated contributions.

I would be remiss if I did not thank my agent, Alice Martell, who made this book a reality by introducing me to Doubleday and Roger Scholl. And finally, I would like to thank my family for their support and patience throughout what, at times, seemed like a neverending process that took me away from family time. I particularly owe thanks to my wife, Wendy, for applying her accountant's eye to most of the accounting/tax-sensitive material throughout this book.

If I have inadvertently omitted someone who contributed to the completion of this book, I apologize for the empty acknowledgment. Of course, I alone am responsible for the contents of this book and for whatever misuse I might have made of the suggestions from others.

And to all those Realtors® associated with the National Association of Realtors® and to all those lenders associated with the Mortgage Bankers Association, whom I have grown to know and admire so much over the years—thank you for putting people into homes and creating opportunities for all households to go after the American dream of home ownership. You have given them the opportunity to grow and prosper in America.

PREFACE

oday's residential real estate markets are booming, and I and many other prominent housing economists believe they will most likely climb into the next decade. Some in the media and elsewhere claim there is a housing bubble, and that it will eventually burst, similar to the stock market bubble debacle in 2000. As I demonstrate throughout this book, their reasoning is flawed, a point I have driven home time and again on major business television networks like CNBC and CNN in recent years. Nonetheless, each year the naysayers come back sounding further alarms. Fortunately, given the reaction from the marketplace, few are paying attention.

I am not suggesting that real estate prices will post double-digit growth as they have in so many of our nation's local housing markets the past several years. That is not a healthy market situation in the long run. Demand for homes needs to come more into balance with the supply of homes. The frenzied local real estate markets with 20 to 30 percent price appreciation over a couple of years' time, and with multiple bids on a house that result in a sale price significantly higher than the price for which the house is listed, is neither sustainable nor desirable. One should not equate the word "boom" with this kind of frenzied market environment. Simply stated, a real estate boom is a healthy real estate expansion. And for a variety of compelling reasons I outline in this book, this healthy expansion has endured for about thirteen years and promises to continue into the next decade. Do not think that a slowing in price appreciation (from double digits) signals the demise of the real estate boom. The fact is that residential home sales could even have a down year without indicating an end to the boom. You can't post a record-setting performance year in and year out. From 10,000 feet in the air, a one-year dip is just a blip in the long-term expansion path. Stick with real estate investing for the remainder of this decade and into the next, and you will experience substantial and satisfying wealth gains.

The contents of this book are based on my twenty-plus years as a real estate/banking economist. You'll find simple and easy-to-use information on how to successfully purchase, invest in, and maintain real estate. To learn more, I urge you to visit the following Web sites for information and insight: www.Fanniemae.com; www.Freddiemac.com; www.REALTOR.org; www.REALTOR.com; www.mbaa.org; and www.nahb.org.

Perhaps the most important message of this book is that real estate doesn't even need a boom to roar. Even when property sales and price appreciation settle back to more normal levels of activity, property returns still offer benefits that more traditional investment vehicles such as stocks and bonds cannot. I'm talking about the leveraging power of your real estate investments as well as the tax and other government benefits bestowed upon property. Such benefits give real estate a "competitive edge" over stocks and bonds and other investment rivals as long-term investments, even in a slower real estate market. In a boom, such benefits are even more powerful.

In my view, there has never been a better time to make real estate a bigger part of your long-term financial future.

THE OPPORTUNITY OF
A GENERATION

The recent U.S. real estate boom has made money for an incredible number of households in America. In fact, in 2001 and 2002, many economists (including me) claimed that real estate was the only sector propping up the economy and keeping it from a full-blown free fall. Even as stock prices tumbled and businesses faltered, the real estate market continued to soar, with home prices rising steadily in most areas of the country. For most home owners, their house is far and away their biggest investment. This great rise in real estate values meant that home owners saw their household wealth increase substantially. Moreover, the savviest real estate investors have discovered how to profit from the boom in ways other than just owning their own home—through home improvements or renovations, buying rental properties, vacation houses, Real Estate Investment Trusts (REITs), and more. The performance of real estate as a financial asset has been astounding.

What you may not know is that opportunities still abound in U.S. real estate markets. And those opportunities will continue to exist throughout this decade and into the next. What we are seeing today is a phenomenon that takes place only once every other generation: a long-term expansion of the real estate market. And that is why you need to take advantage of this once-every-other-generation opportunity *now*.

Those of you who are home owners are already participating in the real estate boom to an extent. During the first four years of this decade (2000–2004), home owners and investors in residential real estate collectively enjoyed a $4.6 trillion increase in the value of their properties! That means, on average, each home owner experienced a $42,700 gain on their home in just a four-year period. And, of course, some home owners saw an even greater increase—as much as 70 to 150 percent of the value of their house. In some high-priced areas such as Anaheim, California, households earned more than $200,000 over this period. That is a lot of wealth.

But not everyone benefited from this rise in value. Too many households do not own any real estate property. And of those who do, most do not realize the many ways they can leverage their investment and increase their stake in the real estate boom. Most home owners view their home as a place to live and have an emotional attachment (justifiably) to their homes. It is often difficult for these individuals and families to make sound, objective financial decisions about their homes. To them, home is a security blanket, a safe haven from an outside world plagued with crime and terrorism. From a financial perspective, they view their home as a large, tangible, appreciating asset, one that most expect to eventually sell and use the proceeds to purchase another home or to add to their retirement nest egg.

But there is so much *more* you can do to profit from real estate during a boom period. It does, however, require changing old habits. Home owners need to learn to separate their emotions from economics. What do I mean by that? Most home owners make home improvements that satisfy them emotionally but do not increase the value of their house (i.e., the pink carpet in a daughter's bedroom, or the wet bar in the basement). Modernizing a kitchen or installing central and energy-efficient air-conditioning, on the other hand, can be effective investments that yield a substantial increase in the long-term value of your home.

In most cases, real estate is the largest financial purchase a household ever makes. It needs to be treated as an investment similar to stocks and bonds. Property ownership should be integrated into the goals and objectives of one's long-term financial planning. And the returns from property ownership need to be thought of as a primary component of a household's investment and retirement portfolios. Real estate can improve your ability to take care of your financial health. Think of real estate as a dynamic asset, generating monthly and/or annual returns. Home owners need to factor in these returns as they review the performance of their investment and retirement portfolios.

I will argue that over the next decade, some funds currently earmarked for stock and bond investments should instead be earmarked for real estate: home renovations/additions, second homes, rental properties, real estate investment trusts (or REITs), and real estate mutual funds. In the current boom, the benefits of real estate investing vis-à-vis stocks, bonds, and other income-generating assets should be obvious. First, the stock market (as of this writing) experienced a 10-percent negative return as measured by the S&P 500 Index over the past four years. Because real estate investments are usually far more leveraged than stock/bond investments (you pay a down payment, usually a small percentage of the full price), they generate much higher returns on average per dollar invested. Real estate also creates wealth more quickly through the combination of amortization schedules, tax deductions, rental income, and price appreciation, as I will show in the chapters that follow.

Why do I believe that the real estate boom will continue into the next decade? While many real estate watchers like to attribute the boom to low mortgage rates, that is only part of the story. And even if mortgage rates notch up a percentage point or two, they will still remain historically low. What are the other factors at work? First, technological advances such as automated underwriting and Internet-driven home listings have reduced home ownership costs and simplified the process with which houses are bought and sold. Most important, a continued high level of demand for homes by baby boomers, their children, and new immigrants buying their first homes helps to ensure that the boom will continue into the next decade. There is no real estate "price bubble." The long-term fundamentals for housing remain excellent into the foreseeable future.

I believe that in years to come historians will see the beginning of the twenty-first century as the "golden age" of real estate. And I want to persuade you to take advantage of this historic opportunity. In the first part of this book, I will paint a clear picture of today's real estate boom and explain why the boom will continue well into the next decade. In the second part of the book, I will show how you can profit from real estate with or without a boom. I spell out the financial benefits of owning real estate and offer specific strategies for investing available funds into real estate opportunities. In the final part of the book, I present the tools, information, and analysis you need to become a savvy real estate investor, and show how you can integrate your real estate investments into your overall investment strategies and financial planning goals and objectives.

WHY THE REAL ESTATE BOOM HAS WINGS

I believe the real estate boom or expansion will continue into the next decade, generating trillions of dollars of additional household wealth. Usually in the forecasting business, the best we can hope for is to be fortunately right or intelligently wrong. Most of us are usually intelligently wrong. No one can predict the future with any regularity and accuracy. But I have a great deal of data and market observations to support my case.

The Japanese have a proverb: "He who can see three days ahead will be rich for 3,000 years." That is why I feel compelled to tell the story of a sleeping industry that awoke in the early 1990s and has been spreading its wealth ever since. It is the story of the Great Real Estate Boom of the twenty-first century.

A Boom Was Born

In the early 1990s, the real estate markets were just recovering from the housing contraction of 1990–91. Home sales were sluggish. Home price appreciation was relatively weak. Mortgage rates were hovering above 10 percent—double-digit territory. Mortgage origination volume (i.e., the dollar amount of mortgage loans) averaged a relatively modest $500 to $600 billion per year.

People purchased homes to live in—pursuing the American dream of home ownership. Homes were viewed as large assets that were not easily transferable but provided shelter, security, and a roof over one's head. Purchasing a home leads to pride of ownership, which in turn generates social benefits such as reducing crime and improving the quality of life in communities across America.

Real estate was rarely mentioned in the same sentence as investments such as stocks and bonds. Earning a competitive return and building meaningful wealth was just an afterthought for most households purchasing real estate. Only the wealthy—the real estate moguls—made serious money in the real estate markets. But even they had incurred large losses in the early 1990s, as a consequence of the 1986 Tax Reform Act, which literally crippled the commercial real estate marketplace and sent commercial real estate values plummeting.

But something happened in late 1991 that changed the face of the real estate markets forever. Mortgage rates began to drop. Some households called their lenders to "refinance" their mortgage loans to the lower rates. The idea was to take advantage of the lower interest rates and lower their monthly mortgage payments. If you were paying 10 percent interest on a $100,000, 30-year mortgage loan, your monthly payment was about $877 per month. If you could refinance the mortgage loan at 8 percent, the monthly payment would drop to $733 per month, saving you $144 per month or $1,728 per year. Lenders were very receptive to the increased refinancing volume, since they earned fee income for providing the "refi" opportunity in a low-interest-rate environment. By early 1992, the real estate markets were experiencing a major refinancing boom.

Falling interest rates also made homes more affordable, increasing home buying across the nation. Existing home sales grew a robust 10 percent in 1992 and 9 percent in 1993. Mortgage origination volume, consisting of both refinancing mortgage loans and purchasing mortgage loans (taking out a mortgage to purchase real estate), totaled

$800 billion in 1992 and reached the astounding $1 trillion origination mark in 1993.

But the events behind 1992 and 1993 were not solely the result of people refinancing and purchasing homes in record numbers. The other part of the story was that the mortgage lending companies, settlement service providers (e.g., title insurance companies), and real estate agents were able to process the record refinancing and home purchase volume without significant delays and bottlenecks. Somehow the real estate markets had evolved under the radar screen to service double and triple the volume of just one to two years prior. Moreover, the costs of purchasing and/or refinancing a home dropped precipitously, permitting the housing markets to expand in unprecedented proportions.

As they say, the rest is history. Some ten years later (2003), the real estate market found itself in uncharted, record-breaking territory. Mortgage originations, which began at a modest $560 billion in 1991, totaled almost $4 trillion in 2003! Similarly, existing home sales grew from a modest 3.1 million homes sold in 1991 to over 6 million homes sold in 2003, a 100 percent increase in the number of existing homes sold in the nation in just over a decade's time. Our nation's largest sector of the economy doubled in size in just over a decade. Imagine the manufacturing sector doubling in size, or the automobile industry producing 32 million vehicles rather than the 16 million vehicles it produces today. It was an astounding accomplishment.

How did this real estate boom happen? How did it get started? There were six major developments influencing the real estate markets during the past decade that jump-started the boom:

1. Mortgage rates dropped to generational lows.
2. Housing finance innovations lowered home ownership costs.
3. Home listings were centralized on the Internet.
4. Minority home ownership became a government priority.
5. Demographic influences (e.g., the maturing of the baby boom generation) strengthened housing demand.
6. Real estate became a safe haven for household wealth.

Mortgage Rates Dropped to Generational Lows

For a typical household, monthly mortgage payments represent by far the greatest cost of purchasing a home. Everyone wants to buy that "bigger" or more appealing house when shopping for a home, but eventually everyone must decide what the maximum monthly mortgage payment they can handle is, and then focus their search on houses selling at prices they can afford. However, this past decade, America experienced, and continues to experience, a prolonged period of single-digit mortgage rates for the first time in more than four decades. We have to go all the way back to the 1950s and 1960s to identify such a golden age for the financing of real estate property. Compare that with households purchasing real estate in the 1970s and 1980s; they faced rising mortgage rates throughout the 1970s, and double-digit mortgage rates throughout the 1980s.

Double-digit interest rates are now a distant memory. The last time the U.S. real estate markets experienced a double-digit 30-year mortgage rate over the course of a year was in 1990, posting a 10.13 percent average for the year. With only a few minor exceptions, mortgage rates have tumbled ever since, dropping down to a 5.82 percent average in 2003. It doesn't take a rocket scientist to make the connection between falling mortgage rates and increased home buying. Low rates make homes more affordable for everyone—first-time home buyers and current home owners looking to trade up or purchase a second home.

Lower mortgage rates also allow home buyers to get more "bang" from their buck, enabling them to purchase higher-priced homes without raising their monthly mortgage payments. In 2000, 30-year mortgage rates were hovering around 8 percent. A typical home buyer purchasing a $250,000 home with a 20 percent down payment would pay $1,467 per month on a $200,000, 30-year mortgage loan. In 2004, with mortgage rates hovering around 5.5 percent, the same home buyer could now purchase a $323,000 home at the same monthly mortgage payment by taking out a $258,000, 5.5 percent mortgage loan. With the lower mortgage rate, home buyers can get almost 30 percent more house (i.e., $323,000 versus $250,000)!

During the past two years (2003 and 2004), mortgage rates averaged

THIRTY-YEAR MORTGAGE RATES

Year	30-Year Rate
1972	7.38%
1973	8.09
1974	9.19
1975	9.04
1976	8.86
1977	8.84
1978	9.63
1979	11.19
1980	13.77
1981	16.63
1982	16.08
1983	13.23
1984	13.87
1985	12.42
1986	10.18
1987	10.20
1988	10.34
1989	10.32
1990	10.13
1991	9.23
1992	8.40
1993	7.33
1994	8.36
1995	7.96
1996	7.81
1997	7.60
1998	6.94
1999	7.43
2000	8.06
2001	6.97
2002	6.54
2003	5.82
2004*	5.90

Source: Freddie Mac Primary Market Survey

*estimate

around 5.85 percent, the lowest level in more than forty-five years. There is also a psychological lift when mortgage rates approach generational lows. They are noticed by all: consumers, the media, home owners, and housing analysts. It's like a snowball rolling downhill, becoming larger as it gathers more snow. As mortgage rates tumbled downhill during this past decade, more and more households were encouraged to refinance or purchase with each 1 percentage point additional drop.

Housing Finance Innovations Lowered Home Ownership Costs

Most home buyers need to borrow a great deal of money from a mortgage lender or bank to purchase real estate. Applying for, qualifying for, and eventually closing on a mortgage loan can be an intimidating and costly process, sometimes inhibiting households from purchasing a home. But innovations swept the housing finance markets during the 1990s, reducing costs and simplifying the processes of loan application, loan underwriting, loan approval, and loan closing.

Mortgage lending companies, with assistance from the large secondary mortgage market players—Fannie Mae and Freddie Mac—computerized almost every aspect of the lending business, from loan application to underwriting to generating the paperwork required for a closing. Fannie Mae and Freddie Mac simplified the loan approval/underwriting process by creating automated, computerized underwriting systems that enabled loan officers to input a home buyer's credit history into their laptop computers and receive credit approval in a matter of minutes rather than days or weeks, as was the case in the past. The cycle time from application to closing was shortened considerably, reducing the labor costs as well as paper costs for companies serving customers. Industry consolidation among the large mortgage companies also reduced the costs of mortgage originations and servicing through economies of scale—that is, productivity levels improved.

The real estate financing process became simple, quick, and relatively inexpensive, enabling people from all walks of life to participate in the home buying process. Fannie Mae and Freddie Mac also opened up new funding sources for the mortgage markets by tapping the global capital markets via debt issuance. Their ability to raise funds both domestically and globally helped expand access to credit among households while exerting downward pressure on U.S. mortgage rates.

As a result of the new funding sources and innovations in housing finance, a long and varied menu of mortgage products was created. Home buyers seeking ways to finance their home had lots of choices: 30-, 20-, and 15-year fixed-rate loans, 1- and 3-year adjustable-rate loans, balloon loans, FHA loans, VA loans, conventional (Fannie, Freddie) loans, low-down-payment loans, jumbo loans, and subprime loans (offered to households with blemished credit histories).

Greater choice of mortgage product made it infinitely easier for households to purchase homes in the 1990s. Households purchasing a home for the long term locked into a long-term fixed-rate mortgage product, while households purchasing homes for the shorter term (expecting to sell their house and buy another in five to seven years) took advantage of the lower-rate adjustable mortgage loan. Households with little savings for a down payment but a steady income could take out a low-down-payment loan, and so on.

Home Listing Advertisements Were Centralized on the Internet

Perhaps the greatest technological advancement was the displaying of home listings by the multiple listing services on the Internet. A multiple listing service, MLS, is an organization that gathers real estate brokerage company home listings for a local area. In the mid-1990s, Homestore began to operate and manage what is now called the REALTOR.com site, which became the centralized source for most brokers to advertise their listings nationwide. A potential home buyer visiting this site would have access to virtually every home for sale in the United States (over 2.2 million listings as of this writing).

REALTOR.com, as well as other smaller listing Web sites, empowered home buyers across the nation, giving them a wealth of home search information. Potential buyers could begin their home search without leaving their homes—during a wintry blizzard day or late at night when their children were asleep. This was a huge information coup for consumers. Home buyers were able to gather as much information as they wanted about homes—prices, house characteristics (e.g., the number of bedrooms and bathrooms), school district, and so on, with a click of a mouse. Real estate on the Internet reduced search costs substantially, while making the buying and selling of real estate simpler and faster.

Minority Home Ownership Became a Government Priority

As healthy and as vibrant as the U.S. housing markets were in the 1990s, there continued to be a wide gap in home ownership rates between minority groups and non-Hispanic whites. Overall, the home ownership rate for the nation is roughly 69 percent. However, the home ownership rate for non-Hispanic whites is about 75 percent, while the home ownership rates for African Americans and Hispanic Americans are 48.4 and 48.7 percent, respectively.

To bridge the home ownership gaps, the government launched a series of initiatives to expand home ownership opportunities for minority groups, substantially increasing the number of minority households pur-chasing homes in the 1990s and into the twenty-first century. With the government setting the tone, most housing organizations—Fannie Mae, Freddie Mac, the Mortgage Bankers Association, the National Association of Realtors®, large and small lenders, large and small real estate brokerage companies—participated in home ownership opportunity programs.

Capital became far more readily available in low-income and minor-ity communities. Home ownership counseling programs, housing fairs for minorities, and brochures on how to purchase a home or how to qualify for a mortgage loan were made available. President Bush announced in June 2002 that he wanted to boost the number of minor-ity home owners by at least 5.5 million by the end of the decade.

Demographic Influences Strengthened Housing Demand

Fueling the home buying fever were healthy increases in the overall population and household formation. Demand was particularly high among baby boomers and immigrants.

Population Growth

Population growth directly influences the demand for housing—the more people living in the United States, the greater the demand for homes. So high population growth rates are good for housing, while low population growth rates are bad. Of course, people don't purchase homes until they become adults. So we need to look at population growth within age groups to explain this past decade of housing activity. For example, the population over age fifty-nine, dubbed the "traditionalists," is about 75 million. It has one of the highest home ownership rates, approaching 80 percent (versus 69 percent for the nation as a whole). Over the past fifty years, the number of people who fall into this basket of older Americans has continually expanded due to improved health care and prolonged life expectancy.

Next, from 1946 to 1964 there was a tremendous increase in births in the United States—the so-called baby boom generation. It is not coincidence that the baby boomers entered their peak earning years in the 1990s and home sales exploded. There are about 82 million boomers, fueling the purchasing of larger homes and second homes.

After 1964, there was a leveling out in birth rates, creating what economists sometimes call the baby bust period (1965 to 1976). This population group, sometimes called Generation X, because it is a relatively small population group (about 46 million), has not made a significant contribution to the high-growth home buying market. But immigration growth surged during the 1980s and 1990s, filling the population void left by Generation Xers. Immigration totaled 7.3 million in the 1980s and 9.3 million in the 1990s, compared to only 4.4 million immigrants in the 1970s. Most arriving immigrants to the United States fall between the ages of sixteen and thirty-five years, matching the age range of the Generation Xers.

Finally, the children of the boomers, dubbed the "echo generation," born in 1977 and after, entered the home buying marketplace in the late 1990s as first-time buyers. This population group (76 million) is almost as large as the boomer group and promises to spur the housing markets for years to come.

Household Formation

Actual home purchases are determined by what we call household formation. A married couple is considered one household. If they divorce and live separately, they create two households out of one. This is important because social trends such as marriage rates, divorce rates, and the age that children leave home determine the number of households, which in turn determines the level of demand for home buying.

The 1990s delivered us the greatest economic expansion in the history of the nation. And a favorable economic climate provides more opportunities for people to become their own head of household and purchase a home.

Real Estate Became a Safe Haven for Funds

September 11, 2001, changed the world for all Americans. We have a new set of priorities and a new set of challenges. People are more frightened about possible terrorist attacks. In this uncertain environment, families justifiably are seeking a safe haven for their funds. During the twentieth century, gold served as that safe haven. As we begin the twenty-first century, it appears that real estate may be serving that "safe haven" need, because it is tangible—something you can touch and feel secure in. The values of stocks and bonds are subject to the sways of the terrorist pendulum. Investors are uncomfortable with uncertainty. Should another 9/11 type of terrorist attack take place in the United States—and I fervently hope it never does—I believe we'd see that even more funds would flow from the equity and bond markets into harder assets such as gold and real estate.

Just What Is a Real Estate Boom?

A real estate boom or expansion doesn't necessarily mean that home sales post record numbers every year. For example, existing home sales recorded an all-time record in 2004, 6.5 million homes sold (estimate). I project that number to drop to 6.3 million homes sold in 2005. Does that mean real estate is in decline? Absolutely not. The 2005 number will be the second-best year ever for existing home sales.

Let's take a look at some major measures of housing activity since the last housing contraction in 1990–91 to paint a clearer picture of today's real estate expansion.

HOME SALES ACTIVITY
Existing and New Homes, Housing Starts

	Existing Home Sales	% Change	New Home Sales	% Change	Housing Starts	% Change
1988	3,510,000	2.2	674,000	0.8	1,488,000	−8.7
1989	3,349,000	−4.6	653,000	−3.1	1,382,000	−7.1
1990	3,226,000	−3.7	533,000	−18.4	1,203,000	−12.9
1991	3,167,000	−1.8	509,000	−4.4	1,009,000	−16.2
1992	3,473,000	9.7	614,000	20.5	1,201,000	19.1
1993	3,778,000	8.8	674,000	9.9	1,292,000	7.5
1994	3,926,000	3.9	667,000	−1.1	1,446,000	12.0
1995	3,882,000	−1.1	670,000	0.3	1,361,000	−5.9
1996	4,179,000	7.7	756,000	12.9	1,469,000	7.9
1997	4,390,000	5.0	806,000	6.7	1,475,000	0.4
1998	4,963,000	13.1	889,000	10.3	1,621,000	9.9
1999	5,193,000	4.6	879,000	−1.2	1,647,000	1.6
2000	5,158,000	−0.7	880,000	0.2	1,573,000	−4.5
2001	5,290,000	2.6	907,000	3.1	1,601,000	1.8
2002	5,593,000	5.7	977,000	7.7	1,711,000	6.9
2003	6,098,000	9.0	1,087,000	11.3	1,848,000	8.0
2004*	6,540,000	7.2	1,170,000	7.6	1,934,000	4.6

Source: National Association of Realtors®, U.S. Census Bureau

*All data in 2004 are estimates.

Highlights of the 1992–2004 Real Estate Expansion/Boom

The tables on this page and the next paint a clear picture of the ups and downs of the housing markets during a contraction and an expansion. The last contraction in the housing markets occurred in the 1989–1991 period. Both existing and new home sales and housing starts fell in 1989, 1990, and 1991, while housing starts were also down in 1988. The fact that housing starts fell a year prior to home sales is not unusual, since builders cut back production in anticipation of a fall-off in home purchases. Notice that existing-home sales make up about

HOME PRICE APPRECIATION AND SUPPLY
Existing Homes

	Home Price Appreciation	Months' Supply	Mortgage Originations ($ billions)	30-year Mortgage Rates (%)
1988	4.2	8.6	NA	10.34
1989	0.2	8.4	NA	10.32
1990	2.7	8.9	458	10.13
1991	5.4	9.0	562	9.25
1992	3.0	8.2	893	8.40
1993	3.0	6.4	1019	7.33
1994	4.1	5.4	768	8.36
1995	2.7	5.7	639	7.96
1996	5.2	6.1	785	7.81
1997	5.1	6.0	833	7.60
1998	5.4	5.5	1656	6.94
1999	3.9	4.8	1379	7.43
2000	4.1	4.5	1139	8.06
2001	5.8	4.6	2243	6.97
2002	7.5	4.7	2834	6.54
2003	7.6	4.7	3800	5.82
2004*	7.0	4.5	2670	5.9

Source: Mortgage Bankers Association; Freddie Mac; U.S. Census Bureau, National Association of Realtors®

*All data in 2004 are estimates.

80 percent of total home sales, while new home sales comprise the remaining 20 percent. The number of existing home sales is also a more stable measure of housing activity, since the ups and downs of existing home sales are a great deal smaller than both new home sales and housing starts. Double-digit swings in growth rates (positive or negative) are common for new home sales and housing starts, while existing home sales experienced double-digit growth only in 1998.

What is particularly revealing in the housing data is the fact that the real estate boom has not exhibited steady, high positive growth rates every year. Existing home sales posted negative growth in 1995 and

2000. Similarly, new home sales posted negative growth in 1994 and 1999, and housing starts turned negative in 1995 and 2000. Despite these temporary setbacks, from a longer-term perspective, the housing markets never strayed from their expansion path. That is just the nature of this housing beast—the trend line is up in a real estate expansion, although there are fluctuations around the trend from time to time.

Notice in the housing data that home prices never fell. Even in the 1989–90 contraction, when there was an oversupply of homes (i.e., 9 months' supply), prices never retreated. At the worst of times, home prices flattened to a 0.2 percent appreciation rate. By the end of the period, 2004, the supply of homes (as measured by the months' supply) tightened to roughly half—4.5 months' supply. Based on historical data, it would be difficult to concoct a scenario in which home prices retreat under such lean housing supply conditions.

Recent Unsustainable Pace

In recent years, the real estate boom has been on an unsustainable pace. Real home price gains have averaged 5.4 percent during the 2002–2004 period, compared to a historical average of 1.5 percent during the past 35 years. Similarly, existing home sales growth averaged 7 percent during the past 3 years compared to a 4.6 percent historical average. These numbers will eventually come back to earth as the boom softens but continues in a more healthy manner.

Why the Boom Will Continue

During the past decade, real estate has come to be seen as a relatively safe, wealth-building asset. The so-called real estate boom has leaped over many economic obstacles and is still moving steadily ahead. It absorbed a soft landing (very sluggish growth) in the economy in 1994, an international finance crisis in 1998, a recession in 2001, and significant job losses in 2002 and 2003. For most of the real estate expansion, home prices rose and sales were strong.

Looking forward, expect more of the same—this real estate boom has got wings. Don't be fooled by any temporary pullback from the record-setting housing numbers of 2004. I predict no major contraction in the housing markets in the foreseeable future. In other words, there is no national real estate bubble. Even if mortgage rates rise, the long-term national expansion will continue.

Why do I say that? Because the market fundamentals I discussed earlier that gave birth to the real estate boom of the 1990s will still be in play for the remainder of this decade and into the next. Although there are no sure bets, a compelling case can be made that this boom will continue for another five to ten years. Nor am I alone in my predictions. Last year, the chief economists of the five leading real estate organizations in the nation (yes, I was one of them)—Fannie Mae, Freddie Mac, National Association of Homebuilders, National Association of Realtors®, and America's Community Bankers Association—provided ten-year housing projections that clearly forecasted continued healthy expansion in the housing markets for the next decade. The study projected that existing home sales throughout the 2005 to 2014 period would average 5.93 million sales per year, a 17 percent gain over the 5.06 million annual average from 1995 to 2004. The study also projected that annual home price appreciation would hover in the healthy 5 to 6 percent range during the next ten years.

The reasons for projecting a continued real estate boom are plentiful:

- Today's economic expansion is expected to create healthy job and income gains over the remainder of this decade, boosting home buying activity.
- Mortgage rates are expected to hover in the 5.5–8.5 percent range for the remainder of this decade because of low inflationary pressures, providing relatively low-cost financing for home buying.
- Home price appreciation will continue at a healthy pace due to a lean inventory of homes across the nation.
- New projections based on the 2000 Census suggest stronger household growth than anticipated, raising estimates for future home sales.
- The baby boomer population will continue to age into their peak earning and retirement years throughout the next decade, creating an even greater demand for first and second houses.

- The high growth of immigrants over the past twenty years will start to pay dividends as they purchase homes in record numbers during the next ten years.
- The baby boomers' children—the echo generation—will be entering home buying age in dramatic fashion, significantly boosting first-time home buying.
- The large retiree (seniors) population will live longer due to advances in health care. Combined with the boomer population, they will create an even greater demand for retirement homes and second (vacation) homes.
- Led by a number of government- and industry-sponsored housing opportunity (affordability) programs, minority home ownership rates are expected to rise significantly during the next decade.
- Home ownership costs (e.g., loan underwriting, approval, and closing activities) are expected to continue to fall during the next decade, making it possible for thousands of renters to afford to buy a home.
- For the foreseeable future, Americans will continue to live in a terrorist-sensitive environment. Concerns about future terrorist attacks and the economic repercussions from any such attack likely make many investors favor the safe haven of tangible, income-generating assets such as real estate property over stocks, bonds, and other more economically volatile income-generating assets.

Let me elaborate on these trends.

Prospects for Economic Growth Are Expected to Remain Favorable

The U.S. economy is projected to grow at a healthy pace into the next decade. Given that the economy just experienced a recession in 2001, it is likely that the expansion will continue for some time. A growing economy means job and income gains and rising consumer confidence, providing consumers with the financial wherewithal and confidence to purchase homes.

Single-Digit Mortgage Rates Expected to Continue

I believe the U.S. economy will remain in a low, single-digit interest rate environment for the remainder of this decade. Again, inflationary pressures remain low, and there is little indication of any serious future inflation. The only potential time bomb for the interest rate outlook is the nation's swelling budget deficit. If the federal government does not address the deficit problem in the near future, interest rate pressures will surely rise.

As the current economic expansion continues to gain strength, mortgage rates could rise a bit, but according to most forecasters, mortgage rates should hover in the range of 7 to 8.5 percent at most, providing historically low-cost financing for home buying. If the expansion slows or stalls, mortgage rates could drop back to the 5.5 to 6 percent range, as they did in the fall of 2004. Expect mortgage rates to hover in the 5.5 to 8.5 percent rate range for the remaining years of this decade.

In addition, the housing industry is less interest-sensitive to rising mortgage rates than in the past. During the past decade, adjustable-rate mortgages, or ARMs, have become very popular. Historically, adjustable-rate mortgages are roughly 2 percentage points below 30-year, fixed-rate mortgages. Looking forward, if mortgage rates were to move up considerably, there would be a significant number of households moving to ARMs to "blunt" the negative impact of a rate rise.

Lean Housing Supply Bodes Well for Home Prices

Today's real estate market boasts the leanest inventory of homes in recent memory. Nationally, tight housing supply has been associated with very strong home price appreciation. The inventory of homes, as measured by the months' supply, has hovered in the 4.3 to 5.0 months range for the past two years, tight by historical standards (5.5 to 6.0 months' supply is considered normal). A 4.5 months' supply means that at the current sales pace, the inventory of homes would be exhausted in 4.5 months' time. In the fourth quarter of 2003, there were nineteen major metropolitan areas in which the months' supply was less than 4. It is not mere coincidence that most of these metro areas also experienced double-digit price appreciation.

Housing construction is behind rather than ahead of housing demand, helping to exacerbate the tight supply of homes in the market. There are simply not enough homes to meet demand over the next 10 years. I have estimated that demand from new households will fall within the 16 to 20 million range, while the supply of homes will fall short of demand, projected to be in the 15 to 18 million range during the 2005–2014 period. And government-imposed growth restrictions in many areas across the nation have inhibited housing construction. The fact is, homebuilders got caught with their financial pants down in the last housing contraction (1989/90) and have been a bit more conservative this time around. The months' supply of inventory in 1989/90 was about 9 to 9.5 months, double the months' supply today. Because inventories are very lean, even with a serious drop in home buying, upward pressures on home prices are expected to persist. Tight housing inventories is one of the most significant fundamentals at play in today's marketplace. It gives me a high level of comfort in predicting that home price appreciation will continue at a healthy pace into the foreseeable future.

Strong Demographic Influences Are Expected to Push Home Buying to Higher Levels

The long-term prospects for real estate depend to a very large degree on the underlying demographics of the nation. New projections based on the 2000 Census suggest stronger household growth than anticipated. A greater number of households means greater demand for housing. In addition, the baby boomer population will continue to age into their peak earning and retirement years throughout the next decade, creating an even greater demand for houses. Immigration is expected to continue at the strong pace set in the 1980s and 1990s, which also bodes well for future housing demand. The boomer children—the echo generation—will be entering home buying age in dramatic fashion, significantly boosting first-time home buying. And finally, both the traditionalist (retirees) population and the boomer population will combine to create an even greater demand for retirement homes, trade-up homes, and second homes.

Household Growth Has Been Revised Upward

The Census Bureau's newly revised population counts imply that household growth over the coming decade will be as much as 1.5 to 2.0 million more than previously anticipated!

Baby Boomers Will Be a Stronger Buying Force Than Ever

The baby boomers were the primary "home buying" force behind the 1991–2004 real estate boom, and they promise to be an even stronger force for the remainder of this decade and the next. Born between 1946 and 1964, boomers were between 28 and 58 years old during the 1992 to 2004 period. A significant number of boomers entered their peak earning years—45 to 54 years old—recently, creating a greater demand for home buying. For the remainder of this decade and into the next, boomers will be between ages 41 and 68, possessing greater income and wealth potential, and creating an even greater demand for home buying.

This 41- to 68-year-old generation will be by far the most active home buyers in the nation from 2005 to 2014. Home ownership rates are positively correlated with age; as households grow older, their home ownership rates rise, as seen in the table below.

Immigrants' Propensity to Purchase Homes Is Expected to Rise

Immigration is expected to continue at the strong pace set in the 1980s and 1990s, boding well for future housing demand. Immigration has been and will continue to be an important driver of home

HOME OWNERSHIP RATES BY AGE GROUP
(2004, Third Quarter)

Under 35 Years	43.1%
35 to 44 Years	68.6%
45 to 54 Years	77.4%
55 to 65 Years	81.2%
65 Years and Over	81.8%

Source: U.S. Census Bureau

sales. Immigrants have accounted for more than one-third of household growth since the 1990s. More significant, a large number of immigrants of the 1980s and '90s probably have children who will be approaching home buying age in the next ten years. While immigrants have lower home ownership rates than do native-born Americans of comparable races, ethnicities, and ages, the immigrant home ownership rate is expected to rise throughout the next decade thanks to greater emphasis on home ownership counseling programs, cultural diversity programs, and a breaking down of the language barriers. In fact, according to the U.S. Census Bureau, immigrant home owners' rates rise significantly with their length of stay in the United States. For example, immigrants who entered the United States in the 1990s registered a 40 percent home ownership rate, compared to a 58 percent rate for immigrants entering the United States in the 1980s, a 73 percent rate for immigrants entering in the 1970s, and an 85 percent rate for immigrants entering the United States before 1970.

Approximately 16 million new immigrants entered the United States over the past twenty years, and another 5 million in the first years of this decade (no data is available yet). A percentage of these immigrants have already entered the home buying marketplace. But a significant percentage of these immigrants who have either rented or lived with extended families (it takes time to save for a down payment) is expected to enter the home ownership markets during the next decade.

The Echo Generation

The baby boomer children will have graduated to become full-time home buyers over the next ten years. The 76 million echo boomers promise to enter the housing markets in dramatic fashion, significantly boosting first-time home buying. Ranging in age from 12 to 33 over this ten-year period, approximately half of them will likely purchase a home for the first time.

Traditionalist (Retiree) Population

The over-fifty-nine crowd will continue to grow during the next decade. Advancements in health technology and health care have lengthened the average life span. This has dramatic implications for the real estate markets, creating an increasing demand for retirement homes. It also means the supply of existing homes will remain tighter than usual because a significant percentage of retirees will stay in their existing homes and, as a result, not enter the inventory of homes for sale.

Minority Home Ownership Rates Are Expected to Rise

Over time, real estate experts expect home ownership rates for African Americans and Hispanics, currently at 48.4 and 48.7 percent (2004, third quarter), respectively, to rise toward 50 to 65 percent levels. This is not an unreasonable goal. Seventy-five percent of non-Hispanic white households purchase homes. A reduction in the disparity of home ownership between non-Hispanic whites and other minority groups is expected to boost minority home buying activity for years to come. The minority share of total households increased from 17 percent in 1980 to 25 percent in 2000. It will likely reach about 32 percent by 2020. While minority households have accounted for two out of every five net new home owners since 1994, they still represent only one in five home owners, leaving plenty of opportunity for growth.

Home Buying Costs Are Expected to Drop Further

Home ownership costs (e.g., those for loan underwriting, approval, and closing activities) are expected to continue to fall during the next decade, which could make it possible for thousands of renters to afford to purchase a home. Based on U.S. Census Bureau estimates, a reduction of $1,000 in origination costs could help an additional 116,000 renters afford home ownership. A reduction of $2,000 in origination costs could make it possible for an additional 314,000 renters to be able to afford to buy a home.*

*Source: "Who Can Afford to Buy a House in 1995," by Howard Savage, U.S. Census Bureau, Current Housing Reports H121/99-1, August 1999, Table 5-3.

There Is No Real Estate Bubble

Year after year, as real estate prices achieve new heights, the media and a handful of Wall Street analysts warn us that "the bubble is about to burst." As I stated earlier, there is no bubble in real estate. Bubbles imply that prices are bloated, that they are unaccountably high. The stock market developed a bubble in the late 1990s because irrational exuberance led investors to overbuy the market. A large number of stock purchases in companies—particularly the high-tech and Internet stocks—were based on pure price speculation rather than the economics of the company. Price/earnings ratios had risen to levels never seen before—200 to 500 P/Es, compared with historical P/Es in the 10 to 30 range. An equity bubble eventually swelled and then burst in 2000, hurting businesses and individual investors alike.

No such irrational exuberance exists in real estate today. Today's real estate market is the result of rational decision making based on supply-and-demand conditions. Real estate experts learned their lesson in the devastating fallout from the 1986 Tax Reform Act, when real estate investors lost a great deal of money basing purchasing decisions on tax breaks rather than on the economics of the deal. Today, investors and households alike purchase homes based on economic sense rather than tax consequences or the desire to make a quick buck. In Chapter 12, I make a compelling case why no national price bubble in the U.S. housing markets exists today. While there can always be local price bubbles, with today's economy, home owners are in no danger of experiencing a widespread fallout of home prices.

CHAPTER 3

REAL ESTATE DOESN'T NEED A BOOM TO ROAR

The fact is, real estate is the gift that keeps on giving. It has built-in benefits that many other income-generating assets lack. First, there are the social benefits of owning a home: pride of home ownership, improved relations with family members, reduced crime in the community. Second, real estate is a highly leveraged asset generating high-yielding returns and creating significant wealth through amortization schedules and steady price appreciation on the money you put down. Third, real estate expands your borrowing/buying power, allowing you to borrow against the equity in your property. And finally, real estate brings with it tax benefits and government subsidies that no other income-generating asset can rival.

Most households are underinvested in real estate, in large measure because many Americans are unaware of all the benefits property ownership has to offer. In the past, purchasing real estate has been costly, intimidating, and downright inefficient. Households have justifiably shied away from property purchases other than their primary residence. But in recent years, as I indicated in Chapter 2, the market for real estate has become more liquid, less costly, and less intimidating, promising to expand the world of real estate investments for everyone.

Studies have shown that home ownership creates greater household stability (lower divorce rates), greater social involvement (more involvement in local politics and activities), more highly educated children (e.g., higher SAT scores), and improved individual health as well.

America's Greatest Leveraged Investment

Real estate is perhaps the greatest leveraged investment in America today. When they purchase real estate, most buyers essentially purchase the property on margin—by making a down payment and financing the remaining value. The typical down payment for residential real estate is about 20 percent, but some forms of financing are available that will let you purchase a house for 10 percent down—or even nothing down.

Assuming a typical 20 percent down payment, a $20,000 investment can buy you a $100,000 house. If the price of your property rises by 6 percent (i.e., $6,000) in the first year of ownership, the return on your $20,000, were you to sell your house, would be 30 percent ($6,000/$20,000)! Most people assume that when the price of their home rises by 6 percent, they are earning a 6 percent return. But since they have invested only their down payment in the property, the return is significantly greater. Of course, there are other costs associated with real estate purchases, such as closing costs, maintenance expenses, and property taxes, that bring the final return down a bit. But these costs are relatively small compared to the value of the property. Notice that I didn't include your mortgage payments in the calculation associated with the purchase. This is because if you didn't own a home, you would be paying rent, which is approximately equal to the after-tax mortgage payment. (With investment property, the rent you receive from a tenant will help offset the mortgage payments.)

Most real estate experts argue that the principal paid through your amortized mortgage payments should also be included in your investment. Through the money paid in principal, you are in effect paying yourself a return on the use of your own funds. (Again, if you didn't own a home, you would be paying a comparable amount to rent.) Thus, if you pay $1,100 back against the principal in the first year of the loan, then the true return on your $20,000 down payment would be the year's price appreciation, $6,000 plus the $1,100 paid in princi-pal, totaling $7,100, for a 36 percent return ($7,100/$20,000). When you pay rent, there is no return on the money you pay the landlord.

Building Wealth Through Amortization and Price Appreciation

The fact is, real estate is America's number-one vehicle for building wealth. Total home owner equity in the United States is now almost $9 trillion. The home equity *gain* in 2004 is estimated to total $915 billion. Real estate wealth is built in two ways: (1) through paying off principal in the loan payments and (2) by rising real estate values. To elaborate on what I said above, in an amortizing loan, your outstand-ing balance is reduced with every payment made. Part of each pay-ment goes toward interest; the remaining part of your payment goes to principal. As you pay off the principal balance on your loan, you are in effect increasing your equity (wealth).

In effect, an amortization schedule is sort of a "forced savings" program for most home buyers. Over the course of the loan, you build equity in your home, and at the end of the loan period, you own the home entirely. Amortization by itself can make you substantially increase your wealth. And you can decide what amortization schedule fits your needs, based on your financial situation and savings (retirement needs). Let me give you an example. A home owner would pay $289,595 in interest over the life of a 30-year $250,000, 6 percent mortgage loan, but he or she would pay only $129,595 in interest for a similar 15-year loan (saving $160,000 in interest payments). The trade-off is that the monthly payment on the 15-year loan comes to $2,100, versus $1,499 a month on the 30-year term. In essence, the difference in payments is the price you pay for building equity that much faster. But if you can afford the monthly pay-ments and are looking to retire in the next 10 to 15 years, a 15-year term mortgage loan may well be the way to go.

By its nature, real estate is an appreciating asset. Unlike other assets, such as an automobile, real estate values go up over time rather than down, unless the property isn't properly maintained or the neighbor-

MORTGAGE AMORTIZATION COMPARISONS
Principal: $250,000
Mortgage Rate: 6%

	10 Years	15 Years	20 Years	30 Years
Monthly payment	$2,776	$2,110	$1791	$1,499
Principal payments	$250,000	$250,000	$250,000	$250,000
Interest payments	$88,062	$129,736	$179,859	$289,595
Total payments	$333,062	$379,736	$429,859	$539,595

hood where the property resides deteriorates. To compare it to other investments, the value of corporate stock could plummet to zero, as we've seen recently with so many Internet stocks. The closest parallel in residential real estate is when a home owner defaults on his or her mortgage obligation or fails to pay property taxes and the house is put up for foreclosure. Even then, while the home owner loses whatever equity he or she has in the home (usually very little in a default situation), such a default doesn't affect the home's value.

Real estate property appreciates in value two ways: (1) market conditions create upward pressure on prices (e.g., demand exceeds supply) and (2) home improvements or renovations to a property, or an improvement to a neighborhood, add to a property's selling price. Home improvements/renovations alone, however, will not substantially add to a home owner's wealth, since he or she has to spend funds for improvements. So it is the supply-and-demand conditions of the marketplace that have generated steady price increases during the housing boom of the past decade. Prices across the nation rose 5.2 percent annually in the 1990s and 6.5 percent in the first half of the 2000s. (There has never been a price drop in home prices since the National Association of Realtors® started collecting price data on existing home sales.)

The table on the following page offers an illustration of how home owners build wealth via amortization and price gains. Using the national average price appreciation (for existing homes) for the years 1988 to 2002, the table shows how both unrealized price gains and amortization increase a home owner's wealth on a $250,000 home purchased in 1988. As you can see, the home owner builds wealth far faster with a 15-year mortgage than a 30-year mortgage. For example, in 1988, the home owner below paid only $2,456 in principal (which now becomes home equity) on the 30-year mortgage, compared to $8,483 in principal on the 15-year loan. By 2002, the price of the home increased to $459,410, creating a price gain of $209,410, and the entire $200,000 mortgage has been paid off to boot. The amount paid to principal using the 30-year mortgage comes to only $57,897. Net net, the wealth gain using a 15-year mortgage totaled $409,410, compared to $267,307 for a 30-year mortgage.

BUILDING WEALTH THROUGH PRICE APPRECIATION AND AMORTIZATION
($250,000 Home and $200,000, 6% 30-Year Mortgage Loan)

Wealth	Price Growth	Adjusted Price	Added $ Value	Principal Paid (30-year Amortization)	Principal Paid (15-year Amortization)
1988	4.2	$260,500	$10,500	$2,456	$8,483
1989	0.2	261,021	521	2,607	9,606
1990	2.7	268,068	7,047	2,768	9,562
1991	5.4	282,543	14,475	2,939	10,151
1992	3.0	291,019	8,476	3,120	10,777
1993	3.0	299,750	8,731	3,312	11,442
1994	4.1	312,040	12,290	3,517	12,148
1995	2.7	320,465	8,425	3,734	12,897
1996	5.2	337,129	16,664	3,964	13,693
1997	5.1	354,323	17,194	4,208	14,537
1998	5.4	373,456	19,133	4,468	15,434
1999	3.9	388,021	14,565	4,744	16,386
2000	4.1	403,930	15,908	5,036	17,397
2001	5.8	427,358	23,428	5,347	18,470
2002	7.5	459,410	32,052	5,677	19,609
Wealth Gain:			$209,410	$57,897	$200,000
Total Wealth Gain (30-year Amortization):			$267,307		
Total Wealth Gain (15-year Amortization):			$409,410		

Increased Borrowing Power

Owning real estate gives home owners and investors the added opportunity to tap into their stored wealth (i.e., the equity in their property) by borrowing against it. Borrowing against your equity permits you to make home improvements, pay off student loans, buy a new car or other goods when necessary, reduce credit-card debt, or even fund a family vacation. There are three primary ways to borrow against your home equity: cash-out refinancings, home equity loans, and home equity lines of credit.

Cash-Out Refinancings

Cash-out refinancings became very popular in a falling-mortgage-rate environment. A cash-out occurs when a home owner refinances his existing mortgage but takes out cash from the transaction. For example, suppose you put 20 percent down (i.e., a $50,000 down payment) and took out a $200,000, 8 percent, 30-year mortgage loan to purchase a $250,000 home. Five years later, you had paid off $10,000 in principal, and the home value increased by 20 percent. You would now have $110,000 in stored equity ($50,000 original down payment + $50,000 price gain + $10,000 in paid principal). You can perform a cash-out transaction by refinancing into a $240,000, 6 percent, 30-year mortgage loan. In this transaction, you could "take out" up to $50,000 in cash. (Notice that the home owner needs to maintain 20 percent equity—$60,000 in the case of a $300,000 home—so that he doesn't have to pay private mortgage insurance. Home owners are required to pay private mortgage insurance when the equity they have in the home falls below 20 percent of the home's value.)

Cash-outs are usually limited to times when mortgage rates are falling, since that is what triggers a refinancing. In addition, there are closing costs associated with a refinancing loan that are usually higher than a traditional home equity loan or taking out an equity line of credit. There are also tax implications of a cash-out refi that you should be aware of. In the example above, if the $50,000 cash-out is spent on home improvements/renovations, then all of the interest on the new $240,000 mortgage is deductible. However, if the $50,000

CASH-OUT REFINANCING

1999

Home price	$250,000
Down payment (20%)	$50,000
8%, 30-year mortgage	$200,000

2004

Home price (20% appreciation)	$300,000
Original down payment	$50,000
Paid-off principal	$10,000
Stored value in home	$110,000

Cash-Out Refinance Loan

Home price	$300,000
Maintain 20% equity	$60,000
6%, 30-year mortgage	$240,000
Cash-out	$50,000
($110,000–$60,000)	

was spent on non–real estate expenditure, such as a vacation or a boat, only the first $190,000 of the $240,000 mortgage qualifies for interest rate deductions. The interest on the remaining $50,000 is not deductible (i.e., the $50,000 is treated as a regular consumer loan).

Home Equity Loans

The closing process involved in a home equity loan is simple and low cost and can be processed in a relatively short period of time versus a refinancing loan. The interest payments on an equity loan are tax-deductible up to $100,000. The benefits of a home equity loan are that you need not refinance the entire loan. Again, there will be a limit on the amount of the loan, constrained by maintaining at least a 20 percent equity position in your real estate. The interest you pay on a home equity loan is usually priced off the prime lending rate (this is the rate that banks charge their best corporate borrowers). When the prime lending rate is below the 30-year mortgage rate, a home equity loan may be preferable to a cash-out refinancing. Home equity loans are also popular for short-term borrowing and relatively small expenditures. These loans have a term of 5 to 15 years.

Home Equity Lines of Credit (HELOC)

Establishing a home equity line of credit is a bit different from taking out a home equity loan. The line of credit is in effect like having a checkbook on your home's equity. With a line of credit, home owners have cash available when they need it. You are given a checkbook with writing privileges on your stored equity. The interest rates on lines of credit are typically priced off the prime lending rate that banks offer commercial companies and are usually variable. You cannot lock into a fixed-rate loan with a credit line.

Tax and Government Housing Subsidies

America made a value judgment more than seventy-five years ago— real estate is special, and everyone in the United States should be given the opportunity of achieving the dream of home ownership. Anyone contemplating purchasing real estate should be aware of the many tax and government subsidies bestowed on property and should take advantage of them.

Tax Benefits

Over the past decade, while many individual and corporate tax deductions have been wiped off the U.S. tax code, most of the important real estate tax breaks still remain. The greatest deduction on an individual tax return still remains the mortgage interest deduction. Let me review some of the more important tax breaks for owning and purchasing real estate. (I discuss tax strategies for rental property acquisitions in Chapter 9.) For a more thorough review of tax benefits and liabilities in real estate, I strongly suggest that you consult a tax guide, a tax expert, or a certified public accountant, preferably one specializing in real estate.

Mortgage Interest and Property Taxes

The interest you pay on a mortgage loan of up to $1 million for your primary residence is tax-deductible on your tax return. You may also deduct the interest paid up to $100,000 on a second home and/or home equity loan. However, the total loan amount on a primary and second home cannot exceed $1 million. Property taxes, too, are completely deductible on all real estate owned.

Let me demonstrate the tax benefits of property ownership in the chart below. I am assuming a $200,000, 6 percent mortgage and a 1.4 percent property tax rate. By deducting $14,244 in interest paid and $3,360 in property taxes, this home owner had a $17,604 deduction on his gross income. At a 30 percent tax rate, he would have saved $5,281 in taxes.

Home Purchase Deductions

A home buyer may deduct items associated with a real estate purchase on his or her personal income tax in the year of the purchase only. These items include points (origination fees and loan discounts) and items such as transfer taxes, recording fees, and title insurance that serve to increase the basis (the original cost of the property), which lowers future capital gains.

Capital Gains Exemption from Home Sale

There is a very generous tax exemption on the capital gains from a sale of a home. The current exclusion is $250,000 for individuals and $500,000 for married couples filing jointly. The only requirement for capital gains exclusion is that a seller live in the home for at least two

TAX BENEFITS ON A $240,000 HOME
Assuming a 6%, 30-Year, $200,000 Mortgage

Mortgage Interest Paid (year 1)	$14,244
Property Taxes (at 1.4% on $240,000)	$3,360
Total Deduction	$17,604
Reduced Federal Income Tax (at 30% tax rate)	$5,281

of the previous five years. If you move before satisfying the requirement due to a change in place of employment or a change in health, your exclusion will be prorated based on the time spent in the home. The exclusion or reduced exclusion can be taken an unlimited number of times by a seller of any age if all requirements are satisfied. Losses on the sale of your home are not deductible.

The capital gains exemption provides a distinct advantage for the purchasing and selling of real estate over other assets. With a $500,000 ceiling, most home owners will never have to pay taxes on their home price gains.

Government-Subsidized Housing Institutions and Programs

No other sector of the economy receives more of the attention, and generosity, of the federal, state, and local governments than real estate. On a national level, the Department of Housing and Urban Development (HUD), the Federal Housing Administration (FHA), the Veterans Administration (VA), Fannie Mae, Freddie Mac, and the Federal Home Loan Bank system (among others) are dedicated to promoting housing. And the list goes on and on. . . . This is true on the state and local levels, as well.

Each government housing institution has a particular focus in assisting households in purchasing homes. Here are some of the major federal agencies and organizations that directly or indirectly subsidize home buying.

Housing and Urban Development (HUD)

The mission of the Housing and Urban Development Department, or HUD, is to increase home ownership, support community development, and increase access to affordable housing free from discrimination. To fulfill this mission, HUD forges new partnerships—particularly with faith-based and community organizations—that leverage resources and improve HUD's ability to be effective on the community level. The federal government has committed billions of dollars to permit HUD to accomplish its mission.

Federal Housing Administration (FHA)

The Federal Housing Administration, or FHA, is an agency within the U.S. Department of Housing and Urban Development. Its main activity is the insuring of residential mortgage loans made by private lenders. The FHA sets standards for construction and underwriting but does not lend money or plan or construct housing. Its primary focus is to insure loans directed to low- and moderate-income households.

With FHA insurance, you can purchase a home with a down payment of as low as 3 percent to 5 percent of the FHA appraised value or the purchase price, whichever is lower. FHA mortgages have a maximum loan limit that varies depending on the average cost of housing in a given region. In general, the loan limit is less than what is available with a conventional mortgage through a lender.

Veterans Administration (VA)

The Veterans Administration is a federal government agency authorized to guarantee loans made to eligible veterans under certain conditions. The VA guarantee allows qualified veterans to buy a house costing up to $240,000 with no down payment. Moreover, the qualification guidelines for VA loans are more flexible than those for either the Federal Housing Administration (FHA) or conventional loans.

Fannie Mae/Freddie Mac

Fannie Mae is a New York Stock Exchange company and the largest nonbank financial services company in the world. It operates pursuant to a federal charter and is the nation's largest source of financing for home mortgages. Since 1968, Fannie Mae has provided nearly $4.5 trillion of mortgage financing for over 49 million families. Freddie Mac, the Federal Home Loan Mortgage Corporation, is smaller than Fannie Mae but is still one of the largest corporations in the United States. Both of these organizations were conceived by the federal government but are publicly traded on the stock exchanges and have private boards of directors. Fannie Mae's and Freddie Mac's primary mission is to purchase mortgage loans originated by mortgage lending companies and then securitize these loans by selling mortgage-backed securities in the financial marketplace.

Both Fannie Mae and Freddie Mac represent large government subsidies for the nation's housing sector. There is an implicit government guarantee, as well as a $3.5 billion government guarantee from the Department of the U.S. Treasury, that the government will not permit these institutions to fail. This guarantee has encouraged the investment community to treat Fannie Mae and Freddie Mac as quasigovernment agencies, reducing the risks associated with investing in them. As a result, Fannie's and Freddie's borrowing costs (debt issuance) are lower than private company borrowing costs in the domestic and global financial markets. This translates into lower mortgage rates—$\frac{1}{4}$ to $\frac{1}{2}$ percentage point lower on Fannie Mae– and Freddie Mac–purchased mortgage loans than private mortgages (i.e., jumbo loans: loans greater than the Fannie/Freddie conforming limits). This is an important subsidy for households seeking Fannie and Freddie mortgage loans.

Federal Home Loan Bank System

The Federal Home Loan Bank System consists of the Federal Housing Finance Board and twelve Federal Home Loan Banks across the nation. The Federal Housing Finance Board regulates the twelve Federal Home Loan Banks. These banks were created in 1932 to improve the supply of funds to local lenders (e.g., savings-and-loan institutions) that, in turn, finance loans for home mortgages. Today, the Federal Home Loan Banks and their 8,104 member-owners, which constitute the Federal Home Loan Bank System, form a cooperative partnership that continues to help finance the country's urban and rural housing and community development needs. This partnership supports community-based financial institutions and facilitates their access to credit.

Real Estate Versus Stocks, Bonds, and Other Income-Generating Assets

If real estate is so special as an investment, it should compare favorably with stocks, bonds, and other income-generating assets, shouldn't it? Yet most home owners choose to invest in stocks and bonds rather than real estate. I would argue they are missing great opportunities. Most home owners mistakenly assign, say, $200,000 to real estate in their asset portfolio because they are living in a $200,000 home. Yet, in most cases, the home owner has only 20 percent equity in his home. In other words, he has invested only $40,000 in real estate ownership.

Because real estate is a highly leveraged asset and experiences steady price increases, home ownership, as an investment, outperforms equities and bonds over the long haul. Most stocks and bonds have to be purchased outright and are subject to greater price fluctuation over time. The advantages of real estate are even greater in the case of a primary residence, once the tax deductions are taken into account. Let's say from 1992 to 2000 you chose to invest $20,000 in the stock market rather than real estate. I chose this period because it includes some of the best and worst years of the stock market. Throughout those years, real estate returns held steady. If you had put $20,000 into the S&P 500 Index during those years, your $20,000 would have grown to $52,694 by the end of the ten years. The $20,000 in real estate, however, would have grown to almost $75,133. You would have earned an additional $22,439!

Real estate is a unique asset. Its downswings are much less pronounced than those of other assets/investments, and its upswings (the leveraged return on equity) are as great as or greater than returns of stocks and bonds. In addition, the variation (which reflects riskiness) of home prices is substantially less than the variations in stock price returns—just compare the value of your house over the past five years versus the price of IBM or General Electric stocks. Also, the perfor-

HOUSING BUILDS MORE WEALTH THAN STOCKS
(A $20,000 Investment)

	1992	2002
S&P 500 Index	$20,000	$52,694
Real Estate Property	$20,000 (down payment)	$75,439
Additional Wealth Gain from RE		$22,439

mance of residential real estate (i.e., price appreciation) marches to a different drummer than the performance of the stock and bond markets. Just look at our most recent recession in 2001. Real estate performed well while the stock market plummeted. In other words, adding real estate property to an existing investment portfolio composed of stocks and bonds improves diversification, lowering the risk of your overall portfolio.

The table on the following page compares the returns of real estate (as represented by the actual annual home price appreciation for a 20 percent down payment on a $250,000 property) to the returns of stocks (as represented by the S&P 500 index) over the 1988–2003 period. For the sixteen-year period, home price appreciation averages 4.4 percent, generating an average annual wealth gain on real estate of 22.1 percent, compared to an annual return of 13.9 percent on the S&P 500 index.

Overcoming Intimidation

So why doesn't real estate play a larger role in your asset portfolio? The problem with real estate is that most people still believe that purchasing property is complicated, expensive, and downright intimidating. That might have been true ten years ago, but nothing could be further from the truth today. Buying and selling real estate has gotten simpler and faster. Just consider the huge number of refinancing transactions during the past several years to take advantage of falling mortgage rates. During the 2002 to 2003 period, individuals collectively initiated over $4 trillion in refinancings. In many instances, an individual refinanced his or her home twice, and sometimes three times. Clearly, the financing process of purchasing and/or refinancing property is no longer an intimidating process. If a household is going to go through the process of refinancing multiple times just to save a few dollars, why not go through the same processes to purchase additional real estate and earn a significant return?

Whether you buy property to live in or as an investment, the buying and closing processes are virtually the same. Taking advantage of

HOME OWNERSHIP RETURNS VERSUS S&P 500,
Assuming 20 Percent Down Payment on a $250,000 Home

	Home Appreciation	Capital Gain	Leveraged Return (%)	S&P (%)
1988	4.2	$10,500	21	16.6
1989	0.2	500	1	31.7
1990	2.7	6,750	14	−3.1
1991	5.4	13,500	27	30.5
1992	3.0	7,500	15	7.6
1993	3.0	7,500	15	10.1
1994	4.1	10,250	21	1.3
1995	2.7	6,750	14	37.6
1996	5.2	13,000	26	23.0
1997	5.1	12,750	26	33.4
1998	5.4	13,500	27	28.6
1999	3.9	9,750	20	21.0
2000	4.1	10,250	21	−9.1
2001	5.8	14,500	29	−11.9
2002	7.5	18,750	38	−22.1
2003	7.6	19,000	38	28.7
Annual Avg.	4.4	$10,922	22.1	13.9

Source: National Association of Realtors®, Standard & Poor's

the real estate boom is all about attitude—overcoming the belief that buying real estate is awkward, costly, and a hassle. You need to take emotion out of the equation. For most individuals and households, real estate is the largest financial purchase you'll ever make. It needs to be treated more as an investment like stocks and bonds. By the time you finish reading this book, you will have a deeper appreciation of real estate as an investment—and as an opportunity.

HOW TO DEAL WITH REAL ESTATE AGENTS AND BROKERS

I n this chapter, I want to give you the inside scoop on how the real estate business really works. Most people who are buying a home understandably see the transaction as complex and intimidating, because it involves thousands of dollars and a battery of real estate agents, lenders, attorneys, and so on. Perhaps you feel vulnerable because you don't really understand what all of these people are supposed to do for you. The most important thing to bear in mind is that there are laws and regulations that protect buyers' rights. By knowing what those rights are, you'll know what to expect from everyone else at each stage and avoid unpleasant surprises.

Whether you are a first-time buyer or a buyer who is trading up (or down), whether you are buying a rental property, a vacation home, or a fixer-upper property, you need to know how to deal effectively with a real estate professional. Understanding a real estate agent's role and responsibilities, as well as how he operates, and how you should negotiate with him could save you thousands of dollars. Moreover, by understanding your agent's objectives in the transaction, and making him work for you, you will become a more successful real estate investor.

I have represented both lenders and real estate agents in my professional life—and have a tremendous appreciation for their expertise and professionalism. The real estate agent you select to work with will be your most valuable resource in purchasing real estate. Building a strong relationship with him will help you to create a more successful buying (or selling) strategy. Similarly, finding the right lender (see Chapter 5) can save you thousands of dollars over the course of a loan. In the pages that follow, I will provide you with some important insights and tips on how to deal effectively with real estate agents and brokers. I urge you to read this chapter and the following chapter, on working with a lender, in their entirety before taking the next step in expanding your real estate investments.

Realtors® and Real Estate Agents

Some people think "Realtors®" and "real estate agents" are one and the same. But there is a significant difference between the two. A real estate agent qualifies as a Realtor® when he or she becomes a member of the National Association of Realtors®, or NAR—the world's largest professional trade association, with more than 1 million members. The term Realtor® is a membership mark, registered and protected by law. Only members of the NAR can identify themselves as a Realtor®. What does that mean? A licensed real estate agent who is a member of NAR is required to conform to the association's strict code of ethics, which requires them to treat all parties in a real estate transaction honestly. Real estate agents acquire their license only after passing a state examination to demonstrate that they know the basics of the laws that regulate real estate transactions and the proper way to handle these transactions. A Realtor®, however, usually knows more about the real estate business and works to maintain a higher level of knowledge via continuing education courses and conferences.

Since I represent the National Association of Realtors®, of course I'm biased in favor of Realtors®. But I also know how effective they are. There are some 1.5 million real estate agents in this country, and the overwhelming majority—over 1 million of them—are Realtors®, people who have pledged to conduct their business in a professional and ethical way. Why take a chance on someone who has not made this pledge?

Establishing a good working relationship between you and your real estate agent can make a huge difference in your effort to obtain the right property for you. First, your agent, after thoroughly discussing your needs and price range, will preview properties and locate homes that meet your criteria in terms of cost, size, number of bedrooms, the neighborhood, and so on. He or she can search for low-down-payment programs and arrange for home buying counseling for first-time buyers, search the multiple listing service, or MLS, to identify properties that satisfy your home buying needs, and help you decide what sort of vacation home or investment property you should look for. Here is a brief checklist of what a real estate agent offers. An agent can:

- Help determine how much house you can afford.
- Recommend a lender(s) and other settlement service providers to work with.
- Help establish what you want in a home, and the trade-offs you might have to make to find a home in your price range.
- Actively search the multiple listing services and other sources for properties that match your purchase needs.
- Show you those homes best suited to your needs—size, style features, location, proximity to schools (and the quality of those schools), transportation, shopping, and other preferences.
- Provide valuable information on communities.
- Provide guidance on local property values, utility costs, municipal services, and local zoning changes that could affect your decision to buy.
- Suggest simple, imaginative changes that make a home more suitable for you and increase its value.
- Help formulate an offer on the home you wish to purchase.
- Facilitate negotiation of an agreement that will satisfy both you and the seller.

Real Estate Agents Are Independent Contractors

Here are some facts you may not know. Most real estate agents are self-employed, independent contractors. They are not employees of their real estate companies. Large national companies like Long & Foster and John L. Scott Company employ real estate agents as independent contractors. Although some licensees are salaried, the majority of agents are not salaried employees of the real estate companies they are affiliated with. And only a small proportion of agents receive health benefits from their real estate company.

As a result, most real estate agents are not obligated to refer ancillary business to the company with which they are affiliated. Their independence works to your advantage. An agent's goal is to make sure a transaction is successful and goes smoothly for you. They will be your independent advisor throughout the entire process (although, as I'll discuss shortly, they have obligations to both sellers and buyers). If requested, they can recommend mortgage lenders and title insurance companies to you. They will recommend their own company's lending subsidiary if that company can offer you quality services and price. But most real estate agents are not obligated to represent their company's interests. Agents are as close to being objective advisors as you will find in a real estate transaction. Yes, they make their commission from the sale, but they also work diligently to make sure the purchase of a property goes smoothly for the buyer and seller. Their strength lies in knowing your community and the real estate business. They can be of enormous help in guiding you through the often intimidating process of buying a home. They will refer you to other real estate service providers when they cannot provide the service themselves. Their only motivation is to keep you happy and complete the sale so that you will come back to them in the future when you decide to trade up or buy additional property.

Different Types of Real Estate Brokerage Companies

Three types of real estate brokerage companies dominate the real estate industry: traditional brokerage, real estate services companies, and agent service bureaus (e.g., RE/MAX). There are also franchise organizations, like Century 21, that offer their brand name and services to independent real estate brokerage companies, including advertising, supplies, and so on. (The arrangement is similar to a McDonald's franchise.) All three types of companies have grown significantly during the past decade, largely because they can use the Internet to gather information for buyers and sellers. Some companies, known as "unbundled service providers," let you limit the functions of the real estate agent to some degree, reducing your costs in the transaction, and if you are selling a property and want costs kept to the absolute minimum, you can list and sell your property as a FSBO—For Sale by Owner—and avoid using the services (and incurring the expenses) of a real estate agent.

Traditional Brokerage Companies

Most of the real estate firms (over 30,000 of them) in the United States are traditional brokerage companies. As many as twenty independent real estate agents work in a typical traditional firm; the company receives a share of the agent's commission. These are the mom-and-pop real estate companies in your local communities.

Traditional brokerage companies are sometimes affiliated with a franchise organization like Century 21. These traditional firms handle just one thing—real estate brokerage. Their agents tend to be well known locally and have a very good "feel" for local housing market conditions. They have developed good relationships with the local lenders, home inspectors, title insurance companies, and others who have helped them close real estate deals before. As they help guide you through the buying process, they are able to recommend these companies to you with confidence.

If you are not looking for one-stop shopping—a realty service company that handles every aspect of the transaction, from mortgages to title insurance—this type of real estate agent can be very effective.

Real Estate Services Companies

These companies are at the core of the real estate industry. Most of the independent real estate agents work for these types of companies. The firm receives a share of the agent's commission.

A typical real estate services company has more than 200 agents in multiple offices in your state, and sometimes regionally or nationally. Some of the largest companies have more than 4,000 affiliated agents.

Real estate services companies offer more services than a traditional brokerage company. They can provide you with "one-stop shopping."

What do I mean by that? Typically, they offer real estate brokerage services (agents), mortgage lending services (through a subsidiary), and title insurance (through a subsidiary). Again, your agent is not obligated to refer your lending and title insurance business to their company or one of its subsidiaries. In fact, most of these agents have developed close working relationships with outside local lenders and title insurance companies in your town, just like the agents working for the smaller traditional brokerage companies. The difference is that these larger companies may be able to offer you more research services on local market conditions, professional property management services if you are buying a rental property, and greater access to and knowledge of special lending programs available to certain households (e.g., minorities, low income).

Real estate services companies continue to add services to attract new customers and retain those with whom they have done business. The most popular (and profitable) services aside from buying and selling real estate are mortgage services, home warranties, and title insurance. Here is a list of some of the additional services offered by many real estate services firms:

- Home owner's insurance
- Settlement attorney
- Home inspector
- Radon inspection
- Termite/insect inspector

Some real estate services companies also offer what we in the industry call "concierge" services, to assist you after you own your home:

- Home security
- Home improvement contracts
- Moving services
- Landscaping
- Home repair services (e.g., appliances)

Real estate services companies tend to have strong market presence and name recognition. They often affiliate with a franchise such as Century 21 to get even stronger name recognition, building off the reputation that a franchise offers. Almost two-thirds of the real estate services companies across the nation affiliate with a national franchise.

Working with a real estate agent affiliated with a real estate services company gives you access to all the services that the firm offers. Nonetheless, your agent might recommend that you go to an unaffiliated company because it offers better financing or can deliver services more efficiently and at a lower cost.

Agent Service Bureau Companies

Agent service bureaus provide office and marketing support to independent sales agents who pay the company a fee rather than a share of their commissions. This payment usually includes a management fee and covers all other costs, including a pro-rata share of office expenses, individual property advertising, and personal promotion. RE/MAX is the largest agent service bureau franchise in the nation. You can find RE/MAX agents in almost every community. The company has more than 4,400 independently owned offices with 80,000-plus member associates.

This type of real estate agent depends on a high dollar volume of transactions in order to cover his or her payments to the agent service bureau. They are usually top-selling agents from the traditional and real estate services companies who are looking for a greater share of the profits from the commissions they generate. They tend to be highly motivated people who will work very hard for you, particularly if you are selling or looking for property in the higher price ranges.

Sellers Only

Unbundled Service Providers and FSBOs (For Sale by Owner)

If you want to reduce the costs that come with selling your home, an unbundled service provider can handle certain parts of the real estate transaction, such as negotiating the contract and conducting the closing. Some sellers use the service provider to market their home but handle the contract and transaction themselves. You can pick and choose from a menu of real estate services. But you will have to take on some of the work that would normally be done by a real estate agent.

If you want to reduce the costs of selling your property to the bare minimum, you can use a for-sale-by-owner strategy. In such cases, you will have to do most, if not all, of the work yourself.

Using unbundled service providers sounds appealing. But proceed with caution. Selling or buying a property is one of the most significant financial transactions you will ever be involved in. Full-service agents guide you through the process, using their years of experience and expertise to ensure that you avoid pitfalls and unnecessary problems. Going the unbundled or FSBO route can be a major commitment. It inevitably becomes a drain on your time and energy. Be sure you are up to it.

For Whom Is the Real Estate Agent Working?

Today, most property buyers are represented by their own real estate agent, who looks after the buyer's interests. In most locales, buyers are advised of their choices for representation at the beginning of a transaction, typically in writing.

As a seller, you sign a listing agreement with a licensee (real estate agent), and the licensee and his company become your agent and you are their client.

If you are a buyer working with a real estate agent who is acting as an agent of the listing company, and a subagent of the seller, be careful. This agent is required to seek a transaction that is acceptable to the seller, because the agent is working on behalf of the listing company, which represents the seller. In this transaction, you are the agent's customer—not his client. This is an important distinction, because in such cases the agent is ultimately working for the seller, not the buyer.

As a buyer, you need to clarify up front that you are represented by your own real estate agent, who represents your interests, not the seller's. This can be easily accomplished by forming your own brokerage relationship by written agreement with a licensee who becomes your agent and is responsible to only you.

How to Select a Real Estate Agent

There are many ways of selecting a real estate agent, but the best way is through word of mouth. Brokering the buying and selling of property is a local phenomenon, and what better way to select an agent than by word of mouth in the community in which you are targeting a property for purchase. According to home buyer surveys conducted by the National Association of Realtors® during the past several years, people select their real estate professional based on representation, word of mouth, experience, or signage, not the type of firm they are associated with.

If you are relocating into a community that you have never been to, there are other ways of selecting a real estate agent. First, I would look at the property listings in that community and see what agents have the most listings. These agents are usually the most active in the area and would have a reliable network working for you. You can view these listings in the local newspaper and/or a listing site such as REALTOR. com. Second, I would visit two or three local real estate brokerage offices and ask to speak to an agent. Select one of the larger real estate companies and contrast their services against those of a smaller local company. Third, if you are meeting for the first time with a real estate agent whom you don't know, ask for references of past and current clients. There is nothing wrong with calling these clients to see if they were satisfied with the agent's services. And finally, I would see what other services the agent can offer you, such as title insurance, mortgage brokerage, and home inspection. But the bottom line is this: Selecting a real estate agent is a personal decision that only you can make. With whom are you most comfortable? Whom do you feel you can trust to be an objective real estate advisor?

If you are looking to purchase a property but are undecided about which community to buy in, you may have to retain more than one real estate agent, if the first agent doesn't cover or is weak in one of the communities you're interested in. Be up front with the agent about your situation. He may not want to represent you in a community half an hour from the town his company specializes in. In such cases, it is okay to have more than one agent represent your interests.

How to Work with Your Real Estate Agent

It is important to know what to expect from your real estate agent so that you can get the most out of his or her services. Your agent should earn his or her commission with good hard work. I recommend that they perform the following services for you. If for any reason your agent is not willing to perform these services in full, select another agent who is willing to participate more fully in the process of real estate investing. Your agent should:

- Provide guidance in real estate–related financial matters.
- Conduct a property search.
- Evaluate market conditions and home values.
- Assist in contract negotiations.
- Participate in due-diligence activities.
- Guide you through the closing process.

Let me explain what I mean more fully.

Provide Guidance in Real Estate–Related Financial Matters

Real estate agents are not qualified to give financial advice—their expertise is real estate, not real estate financing. But you should expect your agent to provide guidance in two financial areas: (1) helping you estimate how much you can afford to spend on a home, which is very different from advising you on how much to spend for a specific house; and (2) helping you learn the basic financing options so that you can be more informed when dealing with the mortgage offerings from a lending institution.

Making a realistic decision about how much you can spend on a home should be your first step in working with a real estate agent. Your agent needs to know what your price range is in order to find suitable properties. Some households are understandably reluctant to disclose personal financial information, and some agents do not want to get involved in personal financial affairs of the people living in their communities. I suggest that you disclose only as much financial information as you think is necessary to help your agent to work with you to determine the maximum amount you can pay for a property. There is no point looking at properties that are simply beyond your price range. An experienced real estate agent can also help you estimate how much money you can afford to borrow and give you an idea of what financing solutions are available from appropriate lenders.

Even if you have already selected a lender and are preapproved for a mortgage amount, ask your real estate agent to recommend alternatives, lenders with whom she has worked in the past. Selecting a reliable lender that can deliver on time and will offer fair, competitive pricing is a crucial step in buying a property. In most communities, real estate agents and lenders have a strong relationship. Many lenders depend on real estate agents for referrals. A real estate agent acts almost like a wholesaler—she brings a large number of customers to one or two or maybe three lenders every year. In return, the lender offers quality service on a timely basis, competitive interest rates, and other financing terms. You may not be able to obtain as favorable financing on your own. If you have not yet developed a solid relationship with a lender, take advantage of your agent's lender relationships. You may be glad you did.

Conduct a Property Search

Here, you should expect your real estate agent to do an outstanding job. A successful search takes hard work, access to a wide range of information, and good relationships. You can contribute to the success of your agent's search by conducting a "presearch" for properties by using the Internet. Go online to one of the Web-based listing services to begin your search. Your agent's company will likely have listings on the Internet for you to review, as well. Better yet, go to www.REALTOR. com, which offers the largest number of advertised home listings in the nation. Identify some homes with the characteristics you desire. Print them out for you and your agent to review. Think through in advance the features in a house or property or community that you want. You may need to compromise to get a house you want at a price you can afford. What elements are essential? What can you give way on? Do you need four bedrooms, or will three suffice? Can you live without two bathrooms? Are you set on a Colonial, or will a modified ranch or Cape Cod do? Do you want a big backyard? A quiet street? Is the quality of the school system important? Is it important to be near mass transportation? Do you need to be relatively close to work, or are you willing to commute quite a ways to get the property you really want? All of these trade-offs will affect the price. The more you've thought through your needs, the better your real estate agent will be able to help you.

Your real estate agent will initially focus on searching the multiple listings, as well as using existing relationships with other agents and applying his knowledge of the targeted local communities, in order to identify prospective properties. Today, real estate agents can e-mail you many property listings for your review, if you prefer. Sometimes, however, properties that meet your criteria are for sale but not actively advertised in the market, so it will take some investigation by your agent to put together a comprehensive list of available and suitable properties.

Evaluate Market Conditions and Home Values

Successful real estate purchasing is based on estimating home values and studying market conditions. Some real estate companies offer what is called comparative market analysis, or CMA, which will help you determine what a fair price for the property is. Ask your real estate agent about real estate values in the town you are looking in so that you can make an informed decision about a prospective property.

The ultimate goal of searching for a home to purchase is to identify properties that will appreciate in value, generating healthy capital gains over time. There are so many factors that influence the future price of a home—local economic conditions (including future employment opportunities), population-growth projections, and the local inventory of homes, to name a few. Gather as much information as you can about the general direction of real estate values both nationally and locally so that your decision to buy will be an informed one.

Of course, if you are just buying a house down the block you live on, you don't need to do this sort of extensive research. It may be that you already have an excellent feel for the local housing market. But more likely, you are purchasing a new home that is some distance from your present residence. If your company transfers you to a job in a different city, or you are looking for a vacation property, or you are planning to purchase a retirement home in another part of the country, you will have to research and evaluate factors in the area that will affect your purchasing decision. Most real estate agents are more than willing to provide you with pertinent housing market information in their area. They have access to a great deal of data about the housing market in their community. Ask a prospective real estate agent to provide you with reports covering the following information:

- National housing outlook
  - Mortgage rates
  - Housing construction (starts)
  - Home sales
  - Housing inventory
  - Home price appreciation
  - Demographic population trends
- Local housing conditions
  - Population/employment growth
  - Housing starts
  - Home price appreciation
  - Local home inventory
  - Rent growth (for rental properties)
- Community report
  - Local school system
  - Transportation
  - Zoning issues
  - Utilities—cost and quality of services

- Home report
  - Comparables—houses that have sold in the community or neighborhood that are of comparable value
  - Neighborhood traffic
  - Days on market

These reports will help you get a good idea of the direction of real estate values nationally and locally. It is useful to compare local housing data with national housing data. For example, knowing that the Washington, D.C., metropolitan area experienced a 12 percent price appreciation in 2003 (compared to a 7 percent appreciation for the nation as a whole) will help you to evaluate the prices of comparable homes in the D.C. metro area.

I discuss these information reports in more detail in Chapter 12, "How to Navigate the Real Estate Boom." The important thing to keep in mind is this: Although I believe that the U.S. real estate boom will continue into the next decade, I cannot guarantee that every community in America will experience a boom. Some communities will do better than the national trend, and some communities will not do as well. Real estate is a local business, dependent upon local supply and demand. That is why you have to obtain and study the relevant information in your prospective area.

Assist in Contract Negotiations

When you are ready to make a bid on a property, your real estate agent is invaluable. Let your agent assist you in negotiating with the seller and the seller's agent. Most people forget that price is just one of many factors included in a negotiation. You can also negotiate financing terms, such as seller financing, "date of possession," and repairs and furnishings (an agreement by the seller that he will make necessary repairs, or include in the purchase price certain furniture or furnishings). You should also negotiate how long you have to complete inspections of the property before you are bound to the contractual purchase agreement.

Before submitting a bid on a property, meet with your real estate agent and review the following checklist of things that should be part of your negotiations:

- **Price.** Use your real estate agent as a sounding board on what price to bid. Remember, *you* decide what you're going to bid. You may want to underbid the seller's asking price. Listen to your agent's input. Are multiple bids expected? Are there any current bids on the table? How long has the house been on the market? Are the sellers desperate to close by a certain date? Ask anything and everything you can. Is the seller going through a divorce? Your real estate agent may not be able to answer questions about the seller's motivation or price flexibility, but it doesn't hurt to ask. Remember, the agent is anxious to get the sale so he or she can collect his or her commission. You are first looking for a win for *you*—the buyer. If you can't get that, settle for a split decision.

- **Financing.** Depending on the seller and market conditions, seller financing may be a possibility. This form of financing is usually more attractive to buyers than the traditional route of obtaining a mortgage loan from a lender. Upfront costs are much lower in a seller-financed deal. Talk with your real estate agent about this.

- **Date of Possession.** Other than price, date of possession is often the most important factor in a negotiation. For many home owners, it is difficult to coordinate the sale of their present house and the purchase of their new home. The date set for the closing becomes an important negotiating item. Setting a favorable closing date could save you thousands of dollars in bridge loans, or having to float two mortgages if you can't time it with the sale of your original home.

- **Repairs/Furnishings.** Use your real estate agent to tell the seller or the seller's agent that they need to repair the hot-water heater or replace the torn carpet in the family room before you close on the home. Similarly, you can get your agent to request that your offer be contingent on the seller's agreement that, as part of the purchase price, he will transfer ownership to you of items like the pool table in the basement or the piano in the living room or the draperies on the first floor. Making an offer contingent on repairs or furnishings can save you a significant amount when you first move into a home.

Other factors that can come up during a negotiation are the length of the period during which an inspection of the home can be carried out prior to the closing, requesting an allowance for landscaping, requesting that the seller pay some of the loan origination points, and so on. An experienced and knowledgeable real estate agent may suggest additional points in negotiating on your behalf.

Participate in Due-Diligence Activities

There is a great deal of due diligence involved in the purchase of property. Ask your real estate agent for guidance on how to evaluate the property, as well as for a recommendation in inspecting the property. Some of the due diligence depends on where the property is located. For instance, you may want to check for mold if the house is located in a wet area (even Texas has experienced mold problems) as well as dry rot. Other problems may include termites, asbestos, faulty structure, radon levels, roof leaks, and septic tank or drain field malfunctions. Ask your agent to refer a qualified professional to conduct such due-diligence investigations. You also should request written reports of the investigations.

You should get a preliminary report on the title of the property. Title indicates ownership of property. The title to most properties will have some limitations: for example, easements (access rights) for utilities. Your real estate agent, title company, or attorney can help you resolve issues that might cause problems later.

Guide You Through the Closing Process

It is in your real estate agent's best interest to make sure the closing goes smoothly and that you are satisfied with the transaction. Part of the closing process is to make sure that you have everything in order to complete the sale. This includes:

- Obtaining financing
- Obtaining title insurance (after completion of a title search)
- Obtaining mortgage insurance if necessary
- Conducting a home inspection
- Obtaining an appraisal
- Other closing tasks when applicable and required

Once you have reached an agreement with a lender, either your real estate agent or lender or both will recommend a title company and an appraisal company to take care of these "due-diligence" requirements for the closing. Your agent will probably recommend a few home inspection companies and pest/termite inspectors.

The closing involves the actual transfer of funds from you to the seller. There are many other papers to read and sign. Most of these documents are required for the financing portion of the transaction; others verify due diligence—a title search has been conducted and title insurance obtained, the property has been properly inspected, and so on. Your lender is usually not at the closing; a real estate attorney or the title attorney usually facilitates the signing and exchange of documents at the closing meeting. But your real estate agent sits by your side throughout the entire closing, reassuring you and making sure that the transaction is done properly. Of course, you may wish to have a real estate attorney present at the meeting, as well. That is your call.

The Selling Side

Because the focus of this book is on expanding your real estate investments, most of the information I cover concerns the buyer's side of the transaction. But most buyers eventually become sellers. The strategies of selling property successfully and profitably can be a book in itself. There are countless books, articles, and presentations on this subject. Just type "real estate sale" or "selling property" or "property sales" on Google.com to assist your search.

If you do sell a property, here are some of the important seller's tasks that you can expect your real estate agent to undertake:

- **Pricing and Terms of Agreement.** Your real estate agent will help you assess the value of your home. What price should you set when you list your home? Your agent may also recommend sales terms that might quickly attract buyers. For example, you may want to offer a seller credit to the buyer at closing. Some buyers do not have much money at closing and would be more motivated to purchase a home if the seller provided some money up front (if the lender permits) at the closing rather than just lowering the price of the home by the same amount.

- **Marketing Your Home.** This is where your real estate agent really earns his or her commission. Your agent will expend a good deal of time and energy advising you on how to enhance the value of your home so that it "shows" well and is clearly worth the price you are asking. To get the home in "show" condition, your agent may recommend repairs, upgrades, and cosmetic changes, such as stripping the wallpaper and painting the room a neutral color. Your agent will then place the listing with the local multiple listing service and advertise it on larger sites like REALTOR.com. He or she will also spend some time and resources on other advertising (e.g., home guides or newspapers) and networking the property with other agents.

- **Negotiating Sale of Property.** Your real estate agent will help you determine an acceptable offer on your property. He or she will help you evaluate the bid price and the financing capacity of a potential buyer. Often, real estate agents will recommend that you get a preapproved letter of financing from the buyer's lender, so that you are confident the buyer will be able to obtain the financing they need. One important contribution of the real estate agent in this process is to help you determine if you can negotiate from a position of strength, depending on market conditions. Your agent will also advise you on making a counteroffer to the buyer. Real estate agents are also useful in helping you decide which offer to accept if you receive multiple offers on your property, as has frequently been the case as the real estate boom has continued. Is

Bidder A willing to waive the mortgage contingency? That could be important in assuring you he'll be able to close as promised.

- **Closing the Sale.** Your real estate agent will guide you through the entire closing process. He or she will help you with the timing of the closing and confirm that the due-diligence actions required for a successful closing have been taken. And, of course, your agent will be sitting at your side during the actual closing meeting, looking out for your interests.

Real Estate Agent Pricing/Commissions

Real estate agents typically earn a commission based on the sales price of a property (commissions could range anywhere between 4 to 7 percent). Again, there are usually two (or more) agents involved in the transaction, so they split the commission. Each agent probably has to share part of that net commission with the company with which he or she is affiliated. So real estate agents end up earning a good deal less than most people think on an individual sale.

In addition, it is the seller who actually pays the real estate agent's commission, not the buyer. But in actuality, the buyer is really paying for part of the commission, because sellers "price" or factor the selling costs (including commissions) into the asking price of the property to some degree.

According to a recent 2003 National Association of Realtors® survey, the average income for a typical real estate agent is about $67,000 per year, not an extraordinary amount of money. A typical agent completes eleven "sides" of a transaction per year. A "side" is one side of the transaction—the buy side or the sell side. In many cases, real estate agents work with the same household for three to six months before closing a deal. So while commissions seem high, there are many upfront costs that get factored into that.

Some agents and their real estate companies offer discounted commissions—you can find many of them on the Internet. Just as there are discount stockbrokers, there are discount real estate brokers. But remember, you usually get what you pay for—discount brokers usually do not offer the full range of real estate services. In addition, there are companies like Zip Realty that are beginning to pay agents salaries rather than have them work for commission. This business model is still a negligible part of the overall market. Most of the 1.5 million real estate agents across the nation stick to traditional commissions on the sale and purchase of a property.

Nonetheless, there's no reason why you can't, in special circumstances, negotiate a reduction in commission with a real estate agent. You just need to know when it *is* possible. Here are some situations in which you might be able to negotiate a lower commission:

- **Identify a real estate agent up front who is willing to negotiate commission**. As a seller, you can always interview real estate agents until you find one who is willing to lower the commission. But be careful here that you are not actually reducing the amount of marketing or advertising that the real estate company does for your home as a result of the reduced commission. Make sure, first and foremost, that you are getting a top-notch agent who will market your house aggressively and enthusiastically. Is it worth saving 1 percent—$1,000 to $3,000 in most cases—when with a more experienced real estate agent you may be able to get a much higher offer, worth tens of thousands of dollars?

- **Using the real estate agent's commission to improve your bid**. Sometimes, as a buyer, your bid price is as high as you can afford, but not high enough for the seller to agree. If the agent wants to get this deal done as much as you, you may ask that he or she reduce the commission rate to seal the deal.

- **A lower commission for double the business**. When your real estate agent is representing you on the buy and sell side—you are selling one house and buying another—you are giving your real estate agent double the business. You may wish to request that he or she discount the commission percentage on one or both properties.

- **For sellers—an extremely hot market.** When inventory is low and demand for houses is high, it might be worthwhile to interview more than one agent to obtain the lowest commission percentage possible. For example, if commission percentages, nationally, range from 5 to 7 percent, it is possible to identify an agent whose commission is on the lower end of the range. But again, be careful not to sacrifice quality for a few thousand dollars.

CHAPTER

5

EVERYTHING YOU NEED
TO KNOW ABOUT FINANCING
REAL ESTATE

I f you are going to take advantage of the real estate boom by buying real estate property, it helps to know about the wide variety of financing options available for real estate buyers, ranging from special mortgage loans and programs for first-time home buyers, to traditional financing for trade-up buyers, to nontraditional financing for real estate investors. It also helps to know how lending and settlement services businesses work, and the best way to deal with them on a real estate transaction, as I explore in the following pages. Use this chapter as a resource to help you match your real estate purchasing strategy to a financing solution.

Mortgage Bankers, Mortgage Brokers, and the Lending Markets

Mortgage Banker Versus Mortgage Broker

A mortgage banker is the actual lender providing the funds for financing a property purchase. A mortgage broker simply acts as an intermediary between you and the mortgage banking company. All too often, home buyers looking for financing make the costly mistake of thinking they are dealing with a mortgage banker when they are actually dealing with a mortgage broker.

Most mortgage banking companies are subsidiaries of larger financial services companies. For example, two of the nation's largest commercial banks, Bank of America and Wells Fargo, own mortgage banking company subsidiaries, as does Washington Mutual, the nation's largest savings-and-loan association. There are also a number of independent mortgage banking companies that are not owned by a financial services company. The nation's largest is Countrywide Credit Industries. And there are also thousands of small mortgage brokerage companies (companies with fewer than ten brokers) located in virtually every community across the nation.

Though bankers and brokers offer similar lending services, a mortgage banker offers a variety of lending services—a selection of different types of mortgage loans, market research (e.g., analysis of housing markets, mortgage rates, and so on), loan approval, and, in many cases, loan servicing (they receive and process your mortgage payments). A mortgage broker, on the other hand, deals with a number of mortgage bankers and shops around to see which of them offer the kind of loan and interest rate you're looking for. But they can't provide you with a full complement of services the way a mortgage banker can.

So whom do you go with? It depends on a number of factors. If you are purchasing a property and are looking for what I call plain vanilla financing (e.g., a 30-year, fixed-rate mortgage loan), you can go with either a mortgage broker or mortgage banker, depending on the terms of the loans they offer you. If you need some advice and market research, you may want to consider a mortgage banker. If you have already used a mortgage banker for other financial services (e.g., checking and savings accounts), you should look into what kind of loans they have to offer you. As an established customer, you may be offered a discount on some related services (e.g., appraisal) and/or mortgage rate or points.

Price competition between mortgage brokers and mortgage bankers is usually fierce, because most mortgage banking companies divide their lending business into two segments: retail lending and wholesale lending. The retail-lending division houses the mortgage loan officers who make mortgage loans. They compete head-on with the local mortgage brokers. The wholesale lending division purchases mortgage loans from its retail-lending network, as well as from mortgage brokers. As a result, the price competition between mortgage brokers and retail mortgage bankers can get quite competitive, depending on how much profit brokers and bankers expect to make from the transaction. Shop for the best possible terms, as well as for a lender who knows the community in which you are purchasing property and can provide you with personal attention and timely service. Both mortgage brokers and retail mortgage bankers provide these services to varying degrees.

Unfortunately, some mortgage brokers take advantage of unsuspecting, desperate, or poorly informed borrowers, charging overages, which result in significantly higher-than-market mortgage rates. The lending industry calls this predatory lending. HUD and other regulators constantly monitor brokers and lenders and will take appropriate action against predators. If you suspect that your lender is engaged in such practices, contact your local HUD office.

How the Lending Market Works

Today's lending markets are composed of a primary lending market, a secondary lending market, and the capital markets. The primary lending market is composed of mortgage brokerage companies, independent mortgage banking companies, and commercial bank- and thrift-owned (savings banks) mortgage banking companies. The secondary mortgage market is composed of Fannie Mae, Freddie Mac, Ginnie Mae, and the Federal Home Loan Banks (discussed in Chapter 3). The capital market is composed of Fannie Mae, Freddie Mac, insurance companies, mutual funds, pension funds, state governments, and foreign investors. By following the path that a mortgage loan takes through the housing finance process, we can see how these financial markets work. Let's assume that a home buyer obtains a 7 percent, 30-year, fixed-rate $250,000 mortgage loan to purchase a home. The following will occur:

The Housing Finance Process

- A home buyer enters the primary lending market by obtaining a $250,000, 7 percent, 30-year, fixed-rate mortgage loan from Lender A to purchase a home.
- Lender A will usually pool this $250,000 loan with other 7 percent, 30-year, fixed-rate mortgage loans it has recently funded. Lender A will then sell this pool of loans (say, a $1 million pool) to the secondary mortgage market. Let us assume that Fannie Mae was the secondary mortgage market purchaser.
- To purchase the pool of loans from Lender A, the secondary market investor (e.g., Fannie Mae) borrows funds from the capital market investors.
- The secondary market investor (Fannie Mae) can keep the loans in its portfolio or issue its own mortgage-backed securities based on pools of loans in its portfolio (e.g., pools from Lender A plus pools from Lender B, and so on).
- Capital market investors such as insurance companies, pension funds, mutual funds, and foreign investors will purchase the mortgage-backed securities, thereby replenishing the supply of funds for the secondary market investor, who in turn has replenished the supply of funds for the primary market mortgage lenders.
- The cycle repeats as the mortgage lenders originate additional mortgages.

A Step-by-Step Guide for Obtaining Real Estate Financing

The world of real estate finance is somewhat complex and not so easily understood. For the uninitiated, obtaining a mortgage loan can be an intimidating experience. For the first-time buyer, qualifying for a loan can be like climbing a steep mountain. To most home buyers, selecting a lender can be stressful. And how many of us who have been through the financing process are comfortable with signing the endless series of papers and contracts involved in the loan-closing meeting? Let me help demystify that process. Here are the nine steps for obtaining real estate financing:

Step 1: *Qualifying for a Mortgage Loan*
Step 2: *Selecting a Lender*
Step 3: *Determining How Much Home You Can Afford*
Step 4: *Reviewing Mortgage Loan Options (menu of products)*
Step 5: *Determining What Type of Government Assistance Is Available*
Step 6: *Completing the Loan Application Process*
Step 7: *Negotiating with Your Lender*
Step 8: *Dealing with Settlement Service Providers*
Step 9: *The Loan Closing*

Step 1: *Qualifying for a Mortgage Loan*

Qualifying for a mortgage loan is like filling up your gasoline tank before going on a long trip. You might as well cancel your trip if your automobile has no gas. Similarly, if you don't qualify for financing, you simply won't be able to purchase a home. So qualifying for a mortgage loan has to be your first order of business.

Lenders have a split personality with regard to loan approval. On one hand, they want very much to grant you a loan since it means more business and profits for them. On the other hand, every time they lend money they are assuming some risk that the borrower may not be able to repay them. They need to be very careful assessing your ability to meet your debt obligations in a timely manner. The better qualified you are for a mortgage loan, the lower the cost of obtaining financing. Lenders charge borrowers who are bad credit risks more money for the use of their funds. So it is in your best interest to work toward showing you are a low-risk borrower.

There is a general rule of thumb that lenders use when qualifying borrowers for financing. Assuming that you can afford the required down payment on the mortgage loan in question, they look at your debt-to-income ratio, which compares the sum of monthly debt oblig-ations (including the prospective mortgage) to monthly gross income. Conservatively, they are looking for debt payments to be 36 percent or less of gross income. However, most of the low-down-payment mortgage loans and other flexible mortgage products involve somewhat less stringent credit guidelines.

Lenders also measure a household's ability to meet its mortgage payments by looking at the housing expense-to-income ratio. This ratio compares the sum of monthly housing expenses to monthly gross income. Generally, lenders are looking for this ratio to be 28 percent or less. Monthly housing expenses include mortgage payment, property taxes, private mortgage insurance, hazard insurance, and home owner's fees.

Lenders also factor in the sources of your annual income. For example, sales commissions and overtime can vary widely from year to year, and a lender may not consider that source of your income reliable. Any long-term debts such as car payments will also be taken into account. The bottom line is that you need to demonstrate that you have steady employment and that your financial situation is reasonably stable according to the above ratio tests.

Your lender will request your credit score from one of three credit bureaus (Equifax, Experian, and TransUnion). A credit score is a number that indicates how likely a borrower is to repay future debts. These credit bureaus generate credit scores based on consumer credit data, including debt and payment history on credit cards, student loans, consumer loans, auto loans, and so on; tax liens, judgments, and bankruptcies; and previous collections and inquiries for new credit. The most common credit scoring system, called FICO, assigns scores that range from 300 to 950. The greater your credit score, the lower the risk that you will fail to repay a loan. The FICO score is based on a mathematical formula, developed by Fair Isaac Company, that uses all of the above consumer credit data to measure the probability of timely repayment.

Take an objective look at your employment situation—is it steady? Then calculate your income, assets, and debts over the past couple of years. What is your debt-to-income ratio? Include your projected mortgage payments in this calculation (see Step 3). Is the total of your debt to income less than 36 percent? Next, gather information about your expected housing expenses for the home you wish to buy;

include your mortgage payment, property taxes, private mortgage insurance (required by lenders if your down payment is less than 20 percent), hazard insurance, and home owner's fees. Calculate your housing expense/income ratio. Is it under 28 percent?

You can request your credit score at any time from the three credit bureaus to see if you make the grade. Visit the following sites: www.experian.com, www.equifax.com, www.transunion.com. A single credit report and score will probably cost you $9.95. Each of the credit agencies also offers a 3-in-1 credit report, providing you credit information and credit scores from all three agencies for about $29.95.

If you have a low credit rating, here is what you can do to improve it:

- Establish steady employment with a stable annual income.
- Pay your bills (e.g., credit card, utilities, etc.) on time, at least the minimum amount due.
- Work to reduce your credit card and consumer loan balances. Your credit rating should improve as your debt balances decline.
- If you are serious about buying a home in the near future, avoid applying for any new lines of credit. I would also suggest that you close as many credit card accounts as possible. Fewer open accounts mean a higher credit rating.
- Review your credit records for accuracy. Your credit report could have gross errors; correcting them could make the difference between credit approval and credit denial.

Step 2: *Selecting a Lender*

There are numerous ways to shop for a lender. Again, I would first ask your real estate agent for a referral to one or two lenders that he or she has worked with in the past. Experienced agents work with lenders every day and know who are the ones that offer competitive pricing and timely delivery of services. Get referrals from friends and family in your community, or by looking in the real estate section of your Sunday newspaper. Show this list to your real estate agent to see if he or she has worked with any of them. Compare their pricing— both mortgage rate and points (origination fees, etc.).

Remember, there is more to a lender than just price. If you intend to invest in real estate on a regular basis, through rental properties, I would make sure that you are comfortable with your lender. Is he or she someone you can trust? Is the lender capable of guiding you through many different types of real estate financing options for different property types (first-time purchase, trade-up, rental, vacation)?

Step 3: *Determining How Much Home You Can Afford*
You need to know how much home you can afford. The actual calculation is straightforward, but there are many factors that you first need to consider. Ask yourself the following questions:

- What is my budget for buying and maintaining a home (property)?
- What type of assistance is available to reduce my purchase costs (e.g., government-assistance down payment programs)?
- What is my credit score? Will this number impact the loan amount I can obtain?
- How great a loan can I afford?
- How much down payment can I raise?
- How big a mortgage will I qualify for?
- How large of a monthly mortgage payment am I willing to assume?

Only you can answer these questions. Keep in mind what lenders are looking for—a debt-to-income level below 36 percent and a housing expense-to-income ratio of 28 percent or less. Now you are ready to calculate how much house you can afford. An easy way to do this is to go to REALTOR.com and use its Home Affordability Calculator. You will find the following:

HOME AFFORDABILITY CALCULATOR
Required Information

Gross Income. Your household's total income before taxes.
Minimum Monthly Debt Payments. The sum of all of your monthly debt obligations (credit-card debt, auto loans, etc.) minus mortgage payments.

Funds Available for Home Purchase. Funds available that you can use to pay your down payment and closing costs.

Mortgage Rate. Rate charged by the lender.

Optional Information

Closing Costs. The one-time fees paid at closing for the loan and expressed as a percentage of the mortgage amount. This includes points (an origination fee, which reflects some of the costs of processing the loan; and discount points, which are used to lower the interest rate on your loan) paid to the lender and transfer fees required to make the transaction (e.g., title insurance and appraisals). These costs vary by loan type and local jurisdiction. We use 3 percent as the average rate. A more detailed description of closing costs is provided in Step 7: Negotiating with Your Lender.

Minimum Down Payment. The minimum amount of cash you want to put down on your home purchase, as a percentage of the property value.

Property Tax Rate. Assume that the annual local property tax is 1.25 percent of the property's value.

Hazard Insurance Rate. Insurance used to compensate home owners for property losses due to fire, wind, and so on. Assume an annual premium of 0.5 percent of the property's value.

Private Mortgage Insurance (PMI). This is required by banks if the home buyer puts down less than a 20 percent down payment.

Housing Expense-to-Income Ratio. Compares the sum of monthly housing expenses (mortgage payment, property taxes, hazard insurance, etc.) to monthly gross income. Again, most lenders look for housing expenses to account for 28 percent or less of income.

Long-Term Debt-to-Income Ratio. Compares sum of monthly debt obligations (prospective mortgage payments, credit cards, consumer loans, etc.) to monthly gross income. Most lenders look for debt payments to total 36 percent or less of income.

The Affordability Calculator relies on the general credit guidelines of lenders—the housing expense/income ratio and the debt/income ratio. To complete these calculations, you must provide some of your financial data and some estimates for the other items, such as property tax, hazard insurance, and private mortgage insurance. REALTOR.com recommends that you run three tests to calculate affordability: (1) housing expense/income ratio, (2) debt/income ratio, and (3) minimum-down-payment requirement. The results of any one of these tests may constrain your ability to buy a more expensive house. Here's an example:

Required Information

Gross income	$75,000
Minimum monthly debt payments	$600
Funds available for home purchase	$40,000
Mortgage rate	6.5%

Optional Information

Closing costs	3%
Minimum down payment	5%
Property tax rate	1.25%
Hazard insurance rate	0.5%
Private mortgage insurance	0.5%
Housing expense-to-income ratio	28%
Debt-to-income ratio	36%

As you can see, the above example assumes that you have a gross (before tax) income of $75,000 and your minimum monthly debt payments total $600. You have saved $40,000 for this home purchase, and the mortgage rate your lender has quoted you is 6.5 percent (30-year fixed-rate). I will use the default percentages for optional information such as closing costs, property taxes, and so on.

After running the calculations, an estimate of the home price you can afford is $229,393. This home price generates a loan amount of $195,250 and a down payment of $34,142 (14.9 percent). The closing costs are estimated to be $5,858 (thereby consuming all of the $40,000 you have saved up). Your monthly mortgage payment is $1,234, property taxes are $239, hazard insurance is $96, and private mortgage insurance costs are $81 (required because your down payment is less than 20 percent).

Notice that a home price of $229,393 takes your debt/income ratio up against the 36 percent ratio limit:

$1,234 + $239 + $96 + $81 = $1,650 x 12 months = $19,800

$600 in other debt payments x 12 months = $7,200

Total debt obligations = $27,000

Debt/income ratio ($27,000/$75,000) =   36%

Step 4: *Reviewing Mortgage Loan Options (menu of products)*

Just a couple of decades back, obtaining a mortgage loan was simple: You selected a 30-year, fixed-rate mortgage. There were no other types of mortgages readily available to home buyers. While a 30-year, fixed-rate mortgage is still the most common loan, there is now a long and varied menu of mortgage loans available to most home buyers.

Do not expect every lender to offer the entire menu of mortgages available in today's marketplace. Lenders tend to specialize in a limited number of mortgages. Some offer the traditional fixed-rate and adjustable-rate mortgages, while others specialize in convertible and hybrid loans and still others focus on government and low-down-payment loans.

The three most common types of financing in real estate today are fixed-rate, adjustable-rate, and balloon financing. The type of financing you select will determine the interest rate, amortization, speed of paying off the principal balance, and monthly payment of the loan. Some of these financing types also offer a convertible feature (explained later).

Fixed-Rate Financing

The 30-year, fixed-rate mortgage loan remains the most popular fixed-rate mortgage, because it results in the lowest monthly payment for a fixed-rate loan, but most lenders also offer mortgage loans with 10-, 15-, and 20-year terms as well. Generally, longer-term mortgages (e.g., 30-year) result in higher mortgage rates and lower monthly payments than do short-term mortgages. For example, a 15-year mortgage rate is about ½ percentage point less than a 30-year mortgage rate. Because of the amortization schedule (which I discuss in Chapter 3), you will end up paying significantly more in interest on a 30-year mortgage than on a 15-year mortgage over the life of the loan. What should be particularly important to you is that the shorter the term of the mortgage, the faster you build equity. The offsetting problem is that the monthly payment increases as the term of the mortgage shortens. So there is a trade-off between building equity and keeping the size of your monthly mortgage payments down.

Some lenders also give you the option of making biweekly payments on your fixed-rate mortgage loan. By making essentially two smaller payments a month (which, combined, equals the original monthly payment), the loan is paid off sooner (23 years), providing you with significant interest savings. You can usually arrange to get the biweekly payments automatically deducted from your banking account.

Adjustable-Rate Financing

Adjustable-rate mortgages, or ARMs, became popular in the 1980s when mortgage rates began to rise. The reason? These variable-rate loans have lower interest rates than their fixed-rate brethren. ARMs keep your monthly payments lower during periods in which interest rates are rising and let you qualify for a larger mortgage than you could get with a fixed-rate loan.

ARMs have four basic components: (1) an initial interest rate that is about 2 percentage points lower than rates for fixed-rate mortgages; (2) an adjustment interval (the amount of time that elapses before the mortgage holder can adjust the interest rate); (3) an index and margin (e.g., the Treasury Bill yield plus 2 percent), which is what the adjustable rate is priced off (usually a 1-year Treasury Bill); and (4) an interest rate cap, which limits the amount that the interest rate can be raised during an adjustment period (e.g., 2 percentage points) and/or the life of the loan (e.g., 5 percentage points). There are several types of ARM mortgages available: 10/1, 7/1, 5/1, 3/1, and 1/1 products. The first number is the length of the initial period before an interest rate adjustment. For example, a 3/1 ARM is one of the most popular adjustable-rate products with borrowers; it locks the ARM interest rate for 3 years and then is adjusting to a market rate based on an interest rate index at the end of the third year. Thereafter, the rate will adjust every year (the second term). Of course, adjustable-rate financing has its risks. If interest rates rise, so will your costs of financing. Many home owners who obtain ARMs are younger borrowers who expect their incomes to grow over time, providing them with the extra funds to absorb payment increases. In addition, some households obtain ARMs with the expectation that they will hold their property for a relatively short period of time and avoid any meaningful increase in their monthly payments. And if you buy rental property using an ARM, you are hoping that the growth in rental income over time will offset any increase in mortgage expenses due to rising interest rates. As long as you understand the risks, adjustable-rate financing can be an effective way to go.

Balloon Financing

Balloon mortgages are popular among households that are planning to live (stay) in their homes for only a short period of time—say, five or seven years. Balloon mortgages are based on a 30-year amortization schedule, but the entire loan balance becomes due at the end of the 5- or 7-year term. However, there is usually a reset option where a borrower may be able to reset the mortgage rate (at the market rate) for the remainder of the amortization period if the borrower satisfies certain creditworthiness tests. Most households secure balloon mortgages because of their short-term expectations of owning a home, but some households take out balloons because the credit requirements are somewhat less stringent than those for fixed-rate and adjustable-rate mortgages.

The most popular balloon loans are 5- and 7-year terms. Balloon mortgages charge a lower interest rate than do their longer-term counterparts—for example, 30-year and 15-year loans. The catch is that the borrower is required to refinance at the end of that period, or pay off the loan, or convert it to a fixed payment schedule. If you are a property investor with a short-term investment horizon, balloon financing may be an option.

Convertible Financing

Increasingly, lenders are offering mortgage loans with convertible features. It is common for both ARMs and balloon mortgages to have a convertible feature. Convertible ARM loans give the borrower the ability to convert to a fixed-rate mortgage after a certain number of years. There are also interest-only loans, where you pay only interest for a fixed period (usually one or two years) and then convert to a fully amortized loan (in which you pay both interest and principal). Balloon loans are convertible by definition, since at the end of 5 or

MORTGAGE FINANCE OPTIONS
Fixed-Rate

Term:	30, 20, 15, and 10
Mortgage Rate:	Higher than ARMs and balloons. Rate falls as term decreases.
Benefits:	Ability to lock in to a fixed interest rate for the life of the loan; monthly payments stay the same. Can always refinance if market rates fall.
Wealth Building:	A good equity builder, particularly 10- and 15-year terms.
Risks:	Low risk compared with ARMs and balloons.
Borrower Type:	A household that is planning on owning home for the long term; a household seeking to avoid interest rate risk.

Adjustable-Rate

Term:	10, 7, 5, 3, and 1
Mortgage Rate:	Lower than fixed-rate but higher than balloons. Rate falls as term falls.
Benefits:	Helps you qualify for a more expensive home compared with a fixed-rate loan. Lower monthly mortgage payments.
Wealth Building:	Based on a 30-year amortization schedule. Wealth building is fair, but not as fast as a shorter-term amortization schedule (e.g., 15-year).
Risks:	Monthly mortgage payments may increase in a rising-rate environment when the adjustment is due. However, there are usually annual and term caps on rate adjustments. Common caps are 5 percent for the term of the loan and 2 percent for an annual rate change.
Borrower Type:	Popular in a high-rate or rising-rate environment. More suited to "young households" who are suited to absorb interest rate risk due to their income growth potential.

Balloon

Term:	7 and 5
Mortgage Rate:	Lower than fixed-rate and adjustable-rates.
Benefits:	Lower monthly payments for households willing to pay entire balance in 5 or 7 years. Helps households qualify for a home that they would otherwise not qualify for using fixed-rate mortgages.
Wealth Building:	Fair, based on 30-year amortization schedule.
Risks:	Relatively high because of rate risk when entire balance is due to re-price.
Borrower Type:	A household that is planning on owning home for the short term.

7 years you owe the entire balance and are forced to convert via refinancing. Again, sometimes you can get a special conversion feature that automatically converts a balloon into a fixed-rate loan at a specified interest rate after a specified period of time.

Types of Mortgage Loans

FHA mortgage loans. As I mentioned in Chapter 3, the Federal Housing Administration insures mortgage loans taken out by low- and moderate-income households. Because of government insurance, these loans usually require lower down payments than do conventional loans. If you qualify for a FHA loan, you can purchase a home with a down payment of as low as 3 to 5 percent of the FHA appraised value or the purchase price, whichever is lower. FHA mortgages have a maximum loan limit that varies depending on the average cost of housing in a given region. In general, the loan limit is lower than what is available with a conventional mortgage through a lender. For example, the FHA loan limit for a single-family residence in Fairfax County, Virginia, is $290,319, compared to the $359,650 conventional loan limit.

Most lenders offer FHA mortgages, and lenders usually have less demanding credit-qualifying criteria because the government is assuming most of the risk. FHA mortgages are usually fixed-rate loans, but some adjustable-rate financing is now available. If you qualify for a FHA mortgage, you will be required to pay an insurance premium as part of your mortgage payment. The premium is usually around 0.5 percent of the loan balance per month. However, the FHA requires an upfront premium of 1.5 percent of the mortgage loan. In general, the closing costs associated with a FHA loan are a bit higher than those of a conventional loan. Similarly, the interest rate on a FHA loan may be a bit higher, as well.

I strongly recommend that those qualified for a FHA loan take advantage of it. The government is essentially subsidizing the risk of default to the lender, which permits you to put less equity into your home purchase because of the lower down payment requirement. The lower the down payment, the greater your leverage in the property purchase, and thus the greater the potential return on your invested equity.

VA mortgage loans. The Veterans Administration is a federal government agency authorized to guarantee loans made to eligible veterans. The VA guarantee allows qualified veterans to buy a house costing up to $240,000 (but it appears Congress may soon raise the limit to the conforming $359,650 limit) with no down payment. Moreover, the qualification guidelines for VA loans are more flexible than those for either the Federal Housing Administration (FHA) or conventional loans. If you are a qualified veteran, this can be an attractive program. Most lenders offer VA mortgages.

Conventional mortgage loans. Conventional mortgages are the largest segment of the U.S. mortgage market. Loans that satisfy the lending criteria and standards of Fannie Mae and Freddie Mac are labeled "conventional" loans. Fannie Mae's and Freddie Mac's mission is to purchase mortgage loans originated by mortgage lending companies in the conventional marketplace and then securitize these loans by selling mortgage-backed securities to the capital markets. Similar to FHA loans, Fannie and Freddie loans are limited in size. For mortgage lenders to obtain Fannie Mae– and Freddie Mac–backed financing, your mortgage loan can be no higher than $359,650 in the mainland United States and up to $539,475 in Hawaii, Alaska, Guam, and the U.S. Virgin Islands. Essentially, Fannie Mae and Freddie Mac, for a guarantee fee charged to lenders, cover risk of loan default for the mortgage lending companies.

Both Fannie and Freddie have a large number of Fannie Mae/Freddie Mac–approved mortgages for lenders to offer home buyers. I recommend that you visit their Web sites to see the long menu of mortgage loan products that are offered in the marketplace today. For a complete list and description of their loan offerings, visit Fanniemae.com and Freddiemac.com. Here is a brief list of some of their loan offerings:

Fannie Mae Mortgage Products
- Standard ARMs, including 6-month, 1/1, and fixed-period ARMs
- Flex 97 and Flex 100 ARMs
- 7-year balloon mortgage
- Biweekly fixed-rate mortgage

- Expanded Approval with timely payment rewards mortgage
- Fannie 3/2 mortgage
- Fannie 97 mortgage
- InterestFirst mortgage
- Pledged-Asset mortgage
- Energy Efficient mortgage

Freddie Mac Mortgage Products
- A-minus ARMs
- Cost of funds Rate-Capped ARM
- Initial Interest-ARM
- Alt 97 fixed mortgage
- Freddie Mac 100 mortgage
- Initial Interest-Fixed rate mortgage
- Streamlined purchase mortgage
- 30-, 20-, and 15-year fixed-rate mortgages
- 5- and 7-year Balloon/Reset mortgages

Jumbo mortgage loans. Sometimes called nonconforming loans, jumbo mortgage loans are not insured or guaranteed by a government agency. These loans are called jumbo because they are the large-balance loans—balances that exceed the Fannie Mae/Freddie Mac limits (over $359,650 for most of the nation as of this writing). Jumbo mortgage loans are funded by mortgage banking companies (the lenders) and then sold into the marketplace to individual and/or institutional investors willing to assume the cash flows from these mortgages. But a large portion of these loans are pooled and packaged and securitized into mortgage-backed securities by private institutions (e.g., Morgan Stanley, Merrill Lynch) that, in turn, sell the securities to capital market investors (pension funds, foreign investors, Wall Street companies, etc.). If you need to obtain a loan that is too large for Fannie Mae/Freddie Mac financing, you will be requesting a jumbo mortgage from your lender. You will typically pay ¼ to ½ percentage point more on the mortgage rate than you will with a conventional (non-jumbo) loan.

Special mortgage loans. There are a number of what I call special mortgage loans currently offered by most lenders. These include:

- Rural Housing and Community Development Service (RHCDS) Mortgage Loans. These provide financing to qualified borrowers who are unable to obtain financing via the conventional marketplace. To qualify, you must be a farmer and/or live in a rural area. Your lender can tell you if you qualify.
- Low/No-Document Loans. Such loans cater to those households having difficulty verifying all of its income (e.g., self-employed individuals like waitresses and hairstylists). The lender offering these loans will not require proof of income. The trade-off is that you will pay a higher interest rate because you pose a higher risk to the lender. Lenders also require a larger down payment for issuing these loans.
- Buy-down mortgages. These are loans that are subsidized (bought down) by a builder or seller who pays an additional discount point to the primary mortgage lender so that the loan has an initial below-market interest rate.
- Reverse mortgages. Typically called a reverse annuity mortgage, or RAM, this loan uses the current equity in a home to fund monthly payments from the lender to the borrower, who would receive a lump sum from the lender to pay for the property purchase under a conventional mortgage. These loans are becoming increasingly popular, and their share of the mortgage market will grow substantially as the boomer population ages into retirement. The loan is designed to help seniors cash out the equity in their home without selling or moving.

Fannie Mae Affordable/Special Mortgage Products

Fannie Mae offers a host of affordable/special mortgage loans that are typically targeted to first-time home buyers and low- and moderate-income households. You can view their complete list of mortgage products at www.fanniemae.com.

- **MyCommunitymortgage**. Flexible mortgage loans for low- and moderate-income borrowers.

- **Community renovation mortgage**. Loans designed to make renovation more affordable.

- **Fannie 3/2 mortgage**. A loan that requires a 3 percent down payment from borrower's funds and another 2 percent from outside funds and one month's cash reserves at closing.

- **SmartCommute Initiative mortgage**. A loan designed to promote home ownership in neighborhoods near public transit.

- **Native American Conventional lending initiative**. Conventional loans on unrestricted fee simple land, federally restricted trust land, and tribally restricted fee simple land.

- **Guaranteed Rural Housing/Section 502 mortgage**. Loans for low- and moderate-income rural residents.

- **Community Living mortgage**. Loans for small, community-based group homes for home owners who are unable to live independently.

- **Community HomeChoice mortgage**. Loans designed for low- and moderate-income borrowers who have disabilities, or who have family members with disabilities living with them.

- **Community Home Buyers Program**. Loans for low- and moderate-income borrowers that require 5 percent down payment and no cash reserves at closing.

- **Flexible 100 and Flexible 97**. Loans that require no down payment and a low (3 percent) option for borrowers who have limited funds available for a down payment.

Freddie Mac Affordable/Special Mortgage Products

Freddie Mac also offers a host of affordable/special mortgage loans that are typically targeted to first-time home buyers and low- and moderate-income households. You can view their complete list of mortgage products at www.freddiemac.com.

Freddie Mac 100. Designed for a borrower with excellent credit history, the 100 is a 100 percent loan-to-value, LTV, mortgage. This means that if the price of the home is $100,000, a Freddie Mac 100 will provide a $100,000 loan, which covers the entire value of the property.

Streamlined Purchase 400 mortgage. A mortgage for borrowers with excellent credit who are willing to pay a nominal fee or high interest rate for the convenience of a preapproved loan, with less documentation and a faster processing time.

Streamlined Purchase 401 mortgage. A mortgage for borrowers with good credit who want the convenience of a streamlined purchase loan with minimal documentation requirement and no fee.

Freddie Mac Alt 97 mortgage. A mortgage for borrowers with good credit but limited savings. The mortgage offers more down payment options to those borrowers who have worked hard to establish and maintain a strong credit history. An Alt 97 mortgage may require less cash to close than an FHA mortgage, particularly in higher-cost areas where the average house price exceeds $132,000. This makes it ideal for first-time home buyers and move-up borrowers interested in obtaining maximum financing.

A-Minus. A mortgage for borrowers with a less-than-perfect credit history or limited funds for a down payment. Typically, these borrowers are consigned to a limited choice of higher-cost financing options. With A-minus, borrowers get competitive rates and may qualify for a down payment of as little as 5 percent.

Affordable Gold Mortgages 5. This loan requires only a 5 percent down payment from borrower funds—made up of a variety of borrower's assets, including Individual Development Accounts. Borrowers may combine a variety of sources to fund their down payment, closing costs, financing costs, etc.

Affordable 3/2. This mortgage requires a 95 percent loan-to-value (LTV) ratio, but with just 3 percent of the down payment coming from borrower funds. The other 2 percent of the down payment can come from an expanded source of funds, including grants and unsecured loans from government agencies, nonprofit organizations, and other eligible sources as defined by Freddie Mac.

Affordable 97. This mortgage opens doors for more low- and moderate-income borrowers by lowering the down payment barrier and increasing the number of acceptable sources of funds that borrowers can use for their down payment and closing costs.

Step 5: *Determining What Type of Government Assistance Is Available*
There are many types of loan assistance programs available in your community. HUD, FHA, and VA administer national loan assistance programs, and there are many other programs administered by housing finance administrations, state and local government agencies, housing-related associations, and private organizations. The Appendix "National Assistance Housing Programs" offers some of the national assistance programs that, if you qualify, could be well worth considering.

Step 6: *Completing the Loan Application Process*
Once you decide on a lender and the type of mortgage you want, the next step is to make a formal application for preapproved financing. Or, if you have waited to approach a lender until after you have bid on a house, this is what to expect in applying for financing of the home you wish to buy. The loan application process may seem intimidating and stressful, but it doesn't need to be. If you know what to expect from your lender, you are 90 percent there. Here is what to expect during the application process:

- You apply for a mortgage loan by filling out an application and providing information about your employment situation, income, assets (auto, investments, etc.), and liabilities (credit-card debt, auto loans, etc.). You will be asked to provide paycheck stubs, bank account statements, tax returns, proof of insurance, and other documents that verify the information you submit.
- The lender will check all the information you have provided. This process could take a few days to one to four weeks, depending on

the type of mortgage you choose, whether or not you are buying a home outside your local community, and other factors, such as job stability.

- Within three days of receiving your application, the lender must give you an estimate of your closing costs—called a Good Faith Estimate, or GFE. The closing is the actual settlement of the loan.
- You will also receive a statement that shows your estimated monthly payment, the cost of finance charges, and other information about your mortgage.
- If everything has checked out, the lender will issue a loan commitment.

Step 7: *Negotiating with Your Lender*

Find out whether the lender is a mortgage broker or mortgage banker so you know the type of firm you are dealing with. The typical pricing that you can expect from a lender includes: mortgage rates, origination fees, discount points, application fees, credit fees, loan-processing fees, and underwriting fees. The Good Faith Estimate provided by the lender covers all of the closing costs of the loan transaction, including the items mentioned above plus all other settlement service provider costs. Below, I will take you through each item with a brief description, explaining how the lender prices the service and whether there is any negotiating room on the lender's stated price.

- **Mortgage rate**. This is the rate that the lender will charge the borrower. Rates change on a daily basis and are determined largely by the movement in U.S. Treasury rates. For example, the 30-year mortgage rate usually follows movements in the 10-year Treasury bond rate. The spread between the 10-year Treasury bond and 30-year mortgage (remember, a 30-year mortgage typically has a life of only 5 to 7 years because people sell or refinance) is usually in the 1.5–2.0 percent range. As this book went to press, 30-year mortgage rates were about 1.75 percentage points above the 10-year Treasury bond yield. You can check rates at any time on any online real estate or lending site. I recommend that you get a sense of whether rates are trending up or down by looking at longer-term forecasts, as well.

To get the best loan rate possible, compare rates among lenders. Look at the real estate section of your local Sunday newspaper and compare your local lender loan offerings. You should also understand the difference between the mortgage rate you are quoted on your loan and the annual percentage rate, or APR. The APR, always presented in the lender's truth-in-lending disclosure, is higher than the quoted mortgage rate because it also includes the origination fee, loan discount points, prepaid interest, and mortgage insurance. The APR permits you to compare the total cost of your mortgage loan among competing lenders. Because of these other costs, the lowest rate may not always be your best choice. As you will see, there is a trade-off between rates and points.

- **Origination fees**. These are paid by the borrower to the lender at closing. The fee reflects some of the costs of processing the loan. Part of the compensation for the person at the lending institution handling your loan is based on the size of the origination fee. Depending on the lender, you may be able to negotiate part or all of the origination fee.

  Sometimes the larger the down payment, the lower the origination fees. For example, a borrower who qualifies for a mortgage loan at 28 percent of gross monthly income should be able to negotiate a lower origination fee than a customer who needs to allocate 35 percent or 40 percent of gross monthly income to qualify. If you are able to put more than 20 percent down, try to get your lender to reduce the origination fee.

- **Discount points.** Such points are used in a trade-off to lower the interest rate on your loan. You pay a discount point, and the lender will permanently lower the mortgage rate. The rule of thumb is that one discount point (i.e., one percent of the loan balance) will lower your mortgage rate by a quarter (0.25) of a percent. Similarly, one discount point would lower the adjustable rate by 0.375 percent. How does this trade-off work? Ask your lender to quote you the mortgage loan in mortgage rate and discount point pairings. For example, you may be given the choice of taking a 6 percent, 30-year mortgage loan with 1 discount point or a 6.25 percent, 30-year mortgage loan with zero points. Of course, the more points you are willing to pay, the lower the mortgage rate. You can also pay points in fractions. For example, you could pay 1.25 points. The discount point is tax-deductible if you itemize your deductions.

- **Lock-in versus float.** As a borrower, you have the right to "lock in" your mortgage rate or "float" the rate. A lock-in is when a lender commits to loan you funds at a particular mortgage rate within a specific closing period. A fee is charged by some lenders at the time of the lock-in. The lock-in period is usually 30 or 60 days. This is the number of days that a lender will guarantee you a specific interest rate and terms on a mortgage loan. When interest rates are rising, it makes sense to utilize the lock-in feature offered by lenders. If you choose to "float," the lender-quoted mortgage rate will fluctuate with the market and could be up or down when you are ready to close.

- **Application fee.** When you complete your mortgage application you are assessed a small fee, which usually covers the lender's initial costs to process your application.

- **Credit report fees.** During the application process, the lender will use a credit bureau to gather your credit information, calculate your credit score, and compile other personal financial information. There is a small fee for this service.

- **Processing or underwriting fees.** The lender will usually charge you either a processing fee or an underwriting fee to cover part of these costs. For mortgage lending, underwriting refers to the fact that the lender will be "funding" the loan.

- **Prepaid interest.** This is the interest that accrues on the loan from the date of the closing to the beginning of the period covered by the first monthly payment. For example, if your closing is scheduled for March 15, the first mortgage payment is due May 1. The lender will calculate the prepaid interest amount to be collected at the time of closing, covering the interest accrued from March 15 to May 1.

- **Good Faith Estimate (GFE).** As I noted above, this is an estimate of all closing fees, including prepaid and escrow items as well as lender charges; it must be given to the borrower within three days after submission of a loan application. The items in the GFE will include the funds required for origination and discount points, taxes, title insurance, appraisal, home inspection, financing costs, and other items that must be prepaid or placed in escrow.

Remember, when you receive a Good Faith Estimate from a lender, the costs are only estimates. Actual costs may vary. I strongly recommend (as does HUD) that you keep your Good Faith Estimate so you can compare it with the final settlement costs that are presented on what is called a HUD 1 statement by the lender at closing. The lender is required to provide you with this HUD 1 form one day prior to closing. Do not hesitate to ask the lender and settlement attorney about any discrepancies between the cost estimates on the original Good Faith Estimate and the actual costs numbers itemized on the HUD 1 statement.

Negotiating from a Position of Strength

There are some things that you can do as a borrower to negotiate with your lender from a position of strength. A common theme should have emerged throughout the seven steps above in obtaining financing: The lending institution wants to reduce its risk! That is the secret to dealing with lenders. Lenders have good reason to minimize the risk of your defaulting on the loan, and they are willing to pay for it (by reducing your costs). Lenders will charge more for riskier properties, riskier financing, less down payment, poor credit record, and so on. If you do everything possible to demonstrate that you pose the lowest possible risk, you'll be negotiating from a position of strength:

- **Raise your credit score.** First and foremost, increase your credit score. The lower the credit score, the higher the mortgage rate and costs. Look at your own credit report and correct any inaccurate items. Pay off any debt you can to lower your debt/income ratio. Another way to improve your credit rating to the lender is to find a cosigner (e.g., a family member) with additional income to support the loan.
- **Know the risk associated with your property.** Using history as a guide, lenders will charge more for condos, apartments, and investment properties because they know that they are riskier than single-family primary residences. When you select a property to purchase, you are also making choices about risk to the lender.
- **More down payment reduces risk.** The more equity you put into a property purchase, the less risk you pose to the lender, since you have more money at stake in case of default. Lenders look at loan-to-value, or LTV, ratios; and the higher the ratio, the higher the mortgage rate and other costs to the borrower. Any LTV over 80 percent usually requires private mortgage insurance, another cost of financing. You lower the lender's risk by putting more money down in the transaction, thereby reducing the LTV ratio.
- **Avoid bankruptcies, foreclosures, etc.** It goes without saying that if you have a history of bankruptcy and foreclosure, you pose a greater risk to the lender.
- **Type of loan.** Lenders will also look at the loan type you choose and assess the risk it might pose for a borrower. In some situations, adjustable-rate mortgages pose greater risk than fixed-rate mortgages, since a rise in rates could jeopardize the borrower's ability to make monthly payments. Interest-only loans are also deemed riskier than loans following traditional amortization schedules.

Negotiating the Mortgage Rate and Terms

Your success in negotiating price and terms with your lender depends largely on business conditions. If business is slow, you may be able to convince the loan officer to drop the rate by ⅛ to ¼ of a point. If you are dealing with a mortgage broker, the rate you are quoted may be marked up, giving the broker maneuvering room to reduce the rate in a negotiation. The difference between the broker rate and the market rate is called the yield-spread premium. Sometimes, brokers/lenders charge higher-than-market rates so that borrowers can put their upfront settlement costs (i.e., many of the closing expenses, such as processing fees, origination fees, and appraisals) in the loan balance. By paying a higher rate, the lender is compensated for this service. In other words, the broker/lender charges higher rates in return for the borrower not paying some costs at the closing because they are built into the total principal of the loan. Some less-scrupulous brokers and lenders have taken advantage of their ability to charge higher-than-market rates by doing so without putting the upfront expenses in the loan balance. In effect, these brokers and lenders are using the yield-spread premium to increase the borrower's interest rate, while increasing the overall compensation (profit) to the broker/lender.

I bring these issues to your attention to help you deal candidly with a broker or a lender. Make sure the broker or retail lender you are dealing with is not "adding on" the mortgage rate without reason. Ask two questions of your prospective broker/lender: (1) Can I put my out-of-pocket expenses in the loan balance and pay for it with a slightly higher mortgage rate, thereby reducing my upfront costs (if this is what you want to do)? and (2) Can you assure me that the mortgage rate you are offering is competitive with other market rates?

Step 8: Dealing with Settlement Service Providers

You might regard all the charges and paperwork that come with the services provided by settlement services companies as the most annoying (and expensive) part of the closing. But these services are necessary; they assure the lender that the property transfer is in order so that the lender can use the property as collateral in case of your default. Most of the time, your real estate agent and/or lender will recommend the settlement service providers, so that you will not have to spend time lining them up. Here are the ways these providers facilitate the purchase and transfer of property:

- Title insurance
- Private mortgage insurance
- Appraisal
- Home inspection
- Home owner's insurance
- Credit report
- Escrow fee
- Closing costs

Title Insurance

Title insurance protects you from any claims (e.g., from previous owners or their heirs or creditors holding liens against previous owners) against your ownership of the property. Your lender usually requires you to purchase a title policy that will protect their interests in the property and ensure its proper transfer. Your real estate agent or lender will usually recommend a title company that they have successfully worked with in the past. Title insurance is issued after a careful title search—an examination of copies of the public records.

Why do you need title insurance if the previous owner already has title insurance? Or why do you need title insurance to refinance a loan, when you already paid for title insurance when you purchased the home? These are fair questions, and there is really not an adequate answer. But the standard answer is that a separate policy is needed by the lender to guarantee the validity of your mortgage. Each time you take out a new mortgage loan, you will have to pay for title insurance. However, to save some money, I recommend that you ask the title company to cut their search expenses when you are refinancing. For example, if you paid $1,500 for title insurance when you purchased your home and you are refinancing a year later, you should only pay between $250 and $750 for a reissued title search. Based on the value of your home, title insurance should cost between $500 to $2,000 on the initial mortgage and half of that amount for a refinance.

Private Mortgage Insurance

Private mortgage insurance (PMI) is required when your down payment is less than 20 percent. Essentially, lenders are willing to finance a home with 20 percent down because they believe that if a borrower defaults, they can foreclose and sell the property and completely recover the 80 percent loan balance (it is very rare for the value of a home to drop 20 percent). If you cannot afford 20 percent or more in down payment, the lender will require you to take out private mortgage insurance to reduce the lender's risk in making a loan. The PMI premium varies with the size of your down payment. For example, a 5 percent down payment would require a .78 percent PMI premium, while a 10 percent down payment would require a .52 percent premium.

There are ways you can save money on private mortgage insurance. The more you put down, the less coverage you will have to pay for. If you can't afford a 20 percent down payment, put down as much as possible. In addition, insurance costs may drop a bit for a fixed-rate loan versus an adjustable-rate loan. You can get your private mortgage insurance canceled once your equity in your home has grown to 20 percent of the loan balance. The Home Owners Protection Act of 1998 covers mortgages that fall into this category. It states that if a borrower has maintained a good payment history, the lender must notify him or her about cancellation rights.

Appraisal

A lender will require an appraised value for your property. In most circumstances, an appraiser comes to your house and performs a careful inspection of its condition and features. The appraiser will also compare your home with other similar homes that have sold recently in your neighborhood or community. The actual appraisal is an estimate of how much your home may sell for. Your lender will most likely select a quality appraiser who has a good track record of being reliable and fair. An appraisal is essentially just one person's opinion. An unjustifiably low estimate of your home's worth could limit the size of the loan you can obtain from your lender. But a high appraisal could force you to pay higher property taxes. There are also times when you may not need to spend money on a new appraisal of your home, particularly if you had your home appraised within the past one or two years. You should discuss the need for a new appraisal with your lender before you commit to funding a new one. Appraisal fees can range from $200 to $500.

An appraisal can also help you determine if your investment in a property is a good one or not. If the appraisal comes in considerably lower than the amount you have agreed to pay, it may suggest that you are overpaying—something neither you nor your lender wants. So even though lenders require an appraisal on your property, an objective valuation, which is what an appraisal is supposed to be, may serve you as well.

Home Inspection

A professional home inspection is strongly recommended for every buyer. Make sure your home inspector is licensed as a professional if your state requires licensing. In some cases, your lender may require a home inspection. The inspection should cover all the home's major systems and structural components. You may also want to get a pest inspection to check for termite damage or mold infestations. You should make every effort to be present during the inspection so you can see any problems firsthand. Do not inspect the property on your own. You need the report of an objective third party whom you can trust and who has only your best interests in mind. Home inspection fees range from $150 to $400.

Home Owner's Insurance

Most lenders require proof of purchased home owner's insurance at closing. Home owner's insurance pays for damages to the property in the event of a loss such as a fire, tornado, or burglary. Home owner's insurance can also protect you from loss if someone is injured or their personal belongings are damaged while on your property.

Credit Report

As I noted earlier, lenders, as part of their due diligence, will obtain credit reports from one of the three major credit bureaus—Equifax, Experian, and TransUnion—and run the charges through to you. If a credit report costs $100 at one company and $25 at another, but the second lender's deal is better overall, point out this discrepancy and ask the preferred company to lower its charge. Credit report fees range from $25 to $100.

Escrow Fee

Escrow services refer to a neutral third party who carries out the instructions of both the buyer and seller to handle all the paperwork of settlement, or "closing." Escrow may also refer to an account held by the lender into which the home buyer pays money for tax or insurance payments. To help ease the burden on home owners who have to come up with large, lump-sum payments at tax time, lenders take on the responsibility by collecting smaller monthly sums from home owners along with their mortgage payment. These are fees paid to a disinterested third party who processes all of the paperwork and keeps the funds and legal documents on behalf of a buyer and seller in a safe place and distributes them according to the buyer's and seller's instructions. Usually, the escrow company that you pay will be associated with a financial institution or an independent escrow company. The escrow holder also responds to the lender's requirements in the transaction and prorates and adjusts insurance, taxes, rents, and so on. Escrow fees can range from $150 to $800, depending on the complexity of your transaction, the purchase price of the property, and the location of the property. Escrow fees are not generally regulated by law or by state statute.

Your title company and/or lender will most likely recommend an escrow company to handle your transaction. If you would like to search for an escrow company on your own, go to the American Land Title Association site, www.alta.org, which will give you a list of the member title companies in your area, or visit the American Escrow

Association site at www.a-e-a.org. Shop around for three good choices and ask for references.

Closing Costs

If you take all the items that the lender charges you, as itemized on the Good Faith Estimate form, and combine it with all of the above settlement costs, including taxes, document preparation fees, legal fees, recording and survey fees, home owner's association fees, wire-transfer fees, and escrow fees, you'll arrive at a fairly accurate estimate of your closing costs. You should have a clear idea of what these costs are so that you know what to expect at closing. These costs typically range from 2 percent to 4 percent of the purchase price of the property, depending on where you live. But they could get as high as 6 percent. That's why a Good Faith Estimate (GFE) of the closing costs is essential. Again, your lender is required to give you a Good Faith Estimate within three days of receiving your loan application. You can compare GFEs among different lenders. Sometimes lenders offer low mortgage rates to attract customers, only to charge them higher closing costs (e.g., loan origination fees) on the back end. In actuality, it is difficult to negotiate each item on the closing costs form—the GFE that eventually becomes the HUD 1 statement at closing. I have given you a few suggestions on how you can keep your costs down. But your best strategy is to compare the Good Faith Estimate of one lender with one or two other lenders' GFEs. This will give you the leverage to negotiate the closing costs. You may save a small amount of money on items like a credit report or application fee, or you may save a great deal of money on an item like title search/insurance.

Step 9: The Loan Closing

Assuming you have a house to buy and have gone through the previous steps to getting financing, you are now at the last step to purchasing a home—the loan closing. The closing is the settlement of the property transfer. At the closing, the property is formally sold and transferred from the seller to the buyer. The closing involves the delivery of a deed, the signing of legal documents, and the disbursement of funds necessary to consummate a sale of the property.

The actual closing meeting usually takes place at the settlement attorney's (sometimes the title company) office. Your real estate agent will accompany you to the closing. Your settlement attorney will also be present and will probably run the meeting. Sometimes your lender will appear, but that is highly unlikely. On the other side of the table will be the seller, the seller's real estate agent, and, possibly an attorney representing the seller.

During the meeting, you will spend most of your time signing legal documents. There are two papers that you will need to bring to the meeting: a copy of your home owner's insurance policy (showing that you have insured the home) and a cashier's check to pay for the purchase and the settlement charges. The most important document at the table will be the settlement sheet, listing all of the closing costs and the details of your loan.

Although it may take an hour or two, there really isn't much to a closing. All the hard work has been done by you, your real estate agent, your lender, and the settlement attorney before the meeting takes place. You are there just to sign documents.

Congratulations to you first-time buyers: You are now property owners.

Traditional Financing Strategies

The financing option you eventually choose is influenced by a number of factors including:

- Length of period you intend to hold the property.
- How fast you want to build equity in your property.
- The amount you can afford in monthly payments and down payment.
- The amount of risk you are willing to assume (e.g., the risk of rising interest rates with an adjustable-rate mortgage).

Financing strategies can be divided into three types: interest-rate strategies, down-payment strategies, and payment strategies. Together these strategies cover almost all possible traditional financing solutions for all property types.

Reasons to Obtain Fixed-Rate Financing

- When mortgage rates are low.
- When you have the income (i.e., cash flow) to be able to afford a higher fixed-rate monthly mortgage payment, rather than an adjustable rate.
- When you are planning to hold on to the property for more than 5 to 7 years.
- For rental property on which you wish to increase cash flow over time with fixed interest costs and rising rents.

Reasons to Obtain Variable-Rate Financing

- You do not have the necessary income level to qualify for the mortgage loan balance you desire. An adjustable-rate mortgage will increase your qualifying balance, since the monthly payments are lower.
- When fixed rates are at historically high levels. Why lock in to these high rates long-term?
- If you are planning to hold your property for less than 5 years, ARMs will keep your monthly payments lower.
- If you are planning to hold your property between 5 and 7 years, 5- and 7-year balloon mortgages may be a financing option to consider.
- If you have reasonable expectations of a considerable growth of income so that you could afford higher monthly payments if the rate adjustment rises over time.
- On rental property, if the asking price makes the carrying costs (negative cash flow) too high, rather than walk away from the deal, you might consider obtaining an adjustable-rate mortgage, which will have lower monthly payments.
- If you intend to hold a rental property for 5 years or less.

- When rent growth projections are favorable, the rise in rental income can cover any increase in future mortgage payments due to interest-rate increases.

Reasons to Pay More Than the Minimum Down Payment
- If you have more upfront money and know that your future income growth has limited potential.
- On vacation property purchases where you will be receiving no or little rental income.
- In order to keep monthly mortgage payments low on a higher-priced rental property.
- In order to keep your investment mortgage rate as low as possible on a rental property. To be eligible for a low rate, you typically need a down payment of at least 20 to 25 percent. If you put more money toward the down payment, you may be able to lower the interest rate even further.

Payment Strategies
- If you are over 40 and you have the income to afford the higher monthly payments, consider shortening your financing terms (e.g., to 15 years from 30 years) so that you can build equity faster for retirement and/or college tuition.
- If wealth building is a priority for retirement, arrange to make more frequent and larger payments each year.
- If you need to keep monthly payments low, take out a longer-term mortgage, such as a 30-year loan or an ARM.
- If you are a young household with income growth potential, you may want to begin with a longer-term mortgage loan (e.g., a 30-year loan), knowing that you will be able to refinance to a shorter term (e.g., to a 15-year) when your income grows.

Nontraditional Financing

Aside from the traditional financing products and sources of lending, there are a number of nontraditional financing options available to property purchasers. Below are some of the most common.

Buy-downs

For investors sitting on some cash, you have the option of buying down your mortgage rate from a lender. The way to buy down is to pay the lender some upfront money with the understanding that the lender will lower the borrowing rate commensurately. Buy-downs can be temporary or they can last the life of the loan. The investors can negotiate the buy-down with the lender. Buy-downs come in many different shapes and sizes. The most popular are the 2-1 and 3-2-1 buy-downs. The 2-1 buy-down requires a borrower sometimes to pay 3 points (a point is 1 percent of the loan balance) up front in order to receive a below-market interest rate for the first two years of the loan. For the remaining term of the loan, the borrower pays the original rate offered on the loan. A 3-2-1 buy-down is the same as the 2-1 buy-down, but the initial below-market rate drops by 3 percentage points during the first two years.

Buy-downs improve the cash flows for the early years of a rental property investment. By the time the rate adjusts to the market rate, the investor is banking on rents rising to offset the higher mortgage payment costs.

A seller of a property may arrange a buy-down to the purchaser as an incentive to attract buyers. We see this in the new home marketplace when builders buy down the mortgage rates in the first and second year to induce potential buyers to come to the table. If you are in a favorable negotiating position with the seller, don't be bashful about bringing up the notion of buy-downs.

Seller Financing

When purchasing a rental property, give the seller the option of financing your purchase. Seller financing can be a very attractive financing option for small rental investors. With seller financing, the seller usually doesn't charge upfront points, and you do not have to pay private mortgage insurance or loan origination fees. You can also better leverage your investment by negotiating a lower down payment. More important, if a traditional lender is uncomfortable with your credit experience and hesitates to provide you with traditional financing, seller financing may give you another option.

A seller-financed transaction is as simple as it sounds. The seller deeds the property to the buyer, and the buyer signs a promissory note back to the seller. The promissory note is secured with the property on a mortgage or trust deed (depending on the state where the property is located). The terms of the seller-finance sale are basically identical to a traditional mortgage: sales price, interest rate, term of maturity, and down payment. To facilitate the process, always make sure that you use a third party who has extensive experience in seller-financed deals. Depending on what part of the country you are from, seller-financed sales are assisted by real estate agents, real estate attorneys, or escrow agents of title companies.

Sellers who find seller financing attractive are usually attracted to high-yielding investments that offer a steady flow of income. The investment mortgage rate is usually higher than government and most corporate bond yields, providing the seller with a healthy flow of income throughout the life of the loan. If the seller is flexible, you can get adventuresome with seller financing. For example, the seller may permit you to make interest-only payments and prepay the principal anytime. Another popular option of seller financing is working out a balloon note with the seller so that in, say, five years, you will pay the seller off by refinancing the loan through traditional lending channels. Usually, you are more able to do this after five years, because you have built up a meaningful amount of equity in the property through price appreciation.

Piggyback Loans

Piggyback loans, also called 80-10-10 loans, are a relatively new low- (less than 20 percent)-down-payment loan product that circumvents paying private mortgage insurance. Lenders call it a piggyback mortgage because a second mortgage is piggybacked onto the original mortgage loan.

Basically, a piggyback mortgage loan is a second mortgage that closes simultaneously with the first mortgage. The typical piggyback loan offers a first mortgage for 80 percent of the value of the home (thus, you don't have to pay private mortgage insurance), and a second mortgage for 10 percent of the value of the home. The buyer pays the remaining 10 percent as a down payment. The mortgage rate on the second loan is typically 1 to 2 percentage points higher than that on the first mortgage, because second mortgages are riskier than first mortgages (in case of default, the first mortgage gets paid before the second).

What makes a piggyback loan more favorable on a low-down-payment loan than private mortgage insurance is the fact that the mortgage interest on both the first and second mortgages of the piggyback are tax-deductible, while the monthly private mortgage insurance payments are not.

Piggyback loans are also used by home buyers to take out a first mortgage that qualifies for Fannie Mae and Freddie Mac financing (i.e., the loan amount is below their loan limits of $359,650), so that they pay a lower mortgage rate than they would if they had to obtain a jumbo mortgage loan.

But piggyback loans are not always a less expensive financing option. Qualifying for a piggyback loan is somewhat more difficult than qualifying for a traditional mortgage. Also, if you expect the property to rise in value in a relatively short period of time, you would no longer need private mortgage insurance. In such cases, a piggyback loan is not the best option. In addition, the second mortgage is usually limited to $100,000, and the property usually has to be a primary residence. I recommend that you discuss these issues with your lender if you think a piggyback loan may make sense for you.

Private Lenders

You can also go to private lenders for a loan—they are looking for a good return on their investment, and the borrowing rate is usually higher than traditional financing rates. There are private investors on both ends of the spectrum: the low-priced end, looking for borrowers with a blemished credit history and willing to pay an interest rate above market, and high-end borrowers seeking jumbo loan financing.

Interest-Only Loans

Interest-only financing has become increasingly popular among rental buyers. Interest-only loans permit you to pay below-market rates in the early years, because you are paying only interest and not principal, thus lowering your monthly mortgage payments compared to conventional mortgage loans. The interest-only period lasts for about 2 to 7 years, then converts to a 28- to 23-year amortizing loan, which carries much higher mortgage payments.

The cash savings that you experience in the early years of the loan improves cash flow for an investment property, making the property a more viable investment to an investor. For example, you can save about $200 per month in mortgage payments for a $200,000 loan balance.

Rental investors who obtain such a loan tend to have one of two strategies: (1) hold the property for the long term, hoping that rental income growth will match or exceed the higher mortgage payments after the interest-only term expires; or (2) plan to sell the property before the interest-only period expires, profiting from the property's price appreciation.

Both strategies make sense from an investment perspective. If used carefully, interest-only mortgages can be an effective tool. But there is one obvious risk: If rental income for your property does not grow over time, you may have a difficult time meeting the higher mortgage payments as the interest-only period expires.

Builder Incentives

Investors intending to purchase a new home or condominium for rental investing may be able to take advantage of builder incentives. Builders will sometimes offer several thousands of dollars to buyers to put toward their mortgages as incentive to purchase. These buy-downs can reduce the mortgage rate (payment) for the first and/or second year. For example, a builder may give you two points (2 percentage points of the loan balance) to buy down the mortgage loan for the first two years. In the present real estate boom, these deals are becoming more difficult to find, but they are still out there.

Builders usually permit 20 to 30 percent of the properties in their development or condominium building to be allocated as investment property. Sometimes, in order to receive a builder incentive, you have to live in the property. If so, you may want to consider living in the property for the first year before renting it out.

IF YOU ARE A FIRST-TIME HOME BUYER . . .

For those of you who have made the decision to buy your first home, congratulations—you're positioning yourselves to take advantage of one of the greatest real estate booms of recent generations. For those of you who are undecided about becoming a home owner, I urge you to consider how much money you have *already lost* by not purchasing a home during the past several years as prices have continued to rise. The simple reality, I believe, is that you really can't afford *not* to buy a home. Let me show you what I mean.

A first-time buyer living in Anaheim, California, who purchased a $300,000 home at the end of 2001 experienced 16.1 percent price appreciation in 2002 and an 18 percent appreciation in 2003, generating $110,994 of increased equity in just two years. A first-time buyer in the Nassau-Suffolk, Long Island, New York, area purchasing a $300,000 home experienced 26 percent appreciation in 2002 and 16.5 percent appreciation in 2003—$140,370 of increased equity in two years! There are tens of thousands of examples of first-time home buying families that enjoyed enormous wealth gains across America during the past several years. Now, I can't promise that homes will experience the same outsized returns in the years ahead, but what I can tell you is that over the past ten years, real estate has far outstripped all other investment vehicles. In fact, in the third quarter of 2004 alone, forty-five major metropolitan areas have experienced double-digit price appreciation already.

Even without a real estate boom, the decision to postpone buying a home can be costly. As I'll show you, taking that first step to home ownership will reap significant rewards. And with the real estate expansion continuing into the next decade, the rewards will be that much greater.

The Rent-Versus-Buy Decision

If you don't own a home, you are likely paying rent on an apartment or rental home. What you may not realize is that over the past several decades, rent payments have increased an average of 3 percent per year in the United States. Rent payments are a one-way street—you pay money to the landlord (property owner) and the landlord makes a profit on it, after paying his or her mortgage and maintenance costs. You never see that money again. The table below shows how much money a typical household today will spend on rent over the next ten years. With an initial rent of $1,000 per month, a renter would hand over $12,000 to the property owner by the end of the first year alone. In five years, a renter will have paid, with standard increases, $63,720. Over ten years he or she will have paid $137,640. Even after subtract-

RENTER
(3% Annual Growth)

	Monthly Rent	Annual
Year 1	$1,000	$12,000
Year 2	1,030	12,360
Year 3	1,061	12,732
Year 4	1,093	13,116
Year 5	1,126	13,512
5-Year Total		63,720
10-Year Total		137,640

ing for mortgage costs, your landlord will have received a substantial profit on his or her investment, as well as benefiting from the increased value of the house. And you will have received nothing.

Renters also are unable to take advantage of the enormous tax benefits that one receives for owning his or her home. The table on page 106 makes a compelling case for owning over renting. In the example, I show a household purchasing a home that costs $167,000, with a 10 percent down payment ($17,000) and financing the balance with a $150,000, 30-year, fixed-rate mortgage at 6 percent. By the end of the first year, the mortgage payments ($899 per month) plus typical property tax payments total $12,875, compared to $12,000 of rent payments for the renter. So where's the benefit in that, you ask? Well, unlike paying rent, part of the mortgage and property tax payment comes back to the home owner in the form of tax savings. The tax code permits property owners to deduct mortgage interest—usually 90 percent or more of your mortgage payments in the early years of a mortgage—as well as property taxes. Of course, not every household can take advantage of the tax benefits of home ownership. Low-income households that are unable to itemize their income tax returns fall into this category. For everyone else, tax benefits are an inducement to owning over renting. In addition, renters do not have to pay directly for insurance and home maintenance. These expenses can be large at times and somewhat unpredictable. Assuming the purchaser is in the 30 percent income-tax bracket, he or she would be able to deduct $8,950 on mortgage interest and $2,087 in property taxes, resulting in a savings of $3,311 in taxes. (The family's after-tax payment in year one would be only $9,564.)

But the benefits of ownership only begin with tax savings. Owning property *generates* wealth through gains in price appreciation and principal accumulation. Assuming a 4.5 percent annual growth in home prices (that is a bit below the average for the past several decades), the purchaser of a $167,000 home would experience a $7,515 unrealized gain (although it's only a paper gain until the owner actually sells the house) in the value of his or her home after the first year. In addition, because the home owner is making mortgage payments according to a 30-year amortization schedule, the principal paid just in that first year yields an increase of an additional $1,842 in home equity. The wealth gain in owning the property that first year is $9,357 by the end of the year ($7,515 plus $1,842). If you subtract the $9,564 after-tax payment from your (unrealized) gain, the result is that you have incurred an overall yearly cost of only $207 for the privilege of living in a $167,000 home! Compare that against the cost of renting—$12,000. The renter paid $11,793 more than the home owner in the first year alone! And that, of course, is assuming a gain in home values of only 4.5 percent—a fraction of the actual increase in home values in recent years. If we used the historical price gain average of 6 percent, the home owner would have actually earned $2,298 while the renter paid $12,000—a $14,298 difference in just the first year!

Moreover, the longer you own a home, the greater the financial benefits of home ownership. After five years, the wealth gains from home ownership more than offset the after-tax mortgage and property tax payments; in fact, the home owner actually *earns* $3,345. After ten years, the wealth gains are greater yet, generating a $19,356 net payment to the home owner after all the mortgage costs have been deducted. Assuming 6 percent price appreciation, the home owner earned $18,718 after five years and $59,087 after ten years. To give you a sense of magnitude, if the home price were $334,000 instead of $167,000, the wealth gains would have been $20,040 for the first year, $112,967 for the first five years, and $264,143 after ten years!

I've summarized the renter and home owner outcomes in the table on page 107. The comparison should leave no doubt that home ownership is far superior to renting in terms of providing shelter. Unlike renting, ownership not only provides a roof over one's head but also generates significant long-term wealth. In fact, for most people it is the primary vehicle for wealth creation in America today.

How to Find Your First Home

When you are ready to purchase your first home, you will not be the first person who feels confused and intimidated about the home buying process. Nearly all home buyers, whether this is their first time or

HOME OWNER
($150,000, 30-Year Loan at 6%)
$167,000 Home Price; 10% Down Payment

	Year 1	5-Year Total	10-Year Total
Mortgage payment	$10,788	$53,940	$107,880
Property tax (1.25%)	$2,087	$10,435	$20,870
Total payment—before tax	$12,875	$64,375	$128,750
Mortgage interest paid	$8,950	$43,541	$83,448
Interest deduction (30% bracket)	$2,685	$13,062	$25,034
Property tax deduction (30%)	$626	$3,130	$6,260
Total after-tax savings	$3,311	$16,192	$31,294
Total payment—after tax	$9,564	$48,183	$97,456
Home value (4.5% appreciation)	$174,515	$208,110	$259,340
Price gain	$7,515	$41,110	$92,340
Principal accumulation	$1,842	$10,418	$24,472
Total wealth gain	$9,357	$51,528	$116,812
Net payment	$207	($3,345)	($19,356)
Home value (6% appreciation)	$177,020	$223,483	$299,071
Price gain	$10,020	$56,483	$132,071
Principal accumulation	$1,842	$10,418	$24,472
Total wealth gain	$11,862	$66,901	$156,543
Net payment	($2,298)	($18,718)	($59,087)

not, feel a bit uneasy and seek help and advice. I recommend that you follow the steps below to help guide you through what will be one of the greatest adventures of your life.

Step 1: *Select a Real Estate Agent*

You need to get educated about how to find and purchase a home. I strongly recommend talking to a real estate agent about the housing market in your local area, the process of how to find a home, and the process of how to purchase a home. See Chapter 4 to learn how to work with real estate agents.

RENT-VERSUS-BUY COMPARISONS

	Renter	Home owner
1 Year		
Rent/mortgage payments	$12,000	$10,788
Property taxes	0	2,087
After-tax payments	12,000	9,564
Wealth gain (price/principal)	0	9,357
Total cost	$12,000	$207
5-Year Total		
Rent/mortgage payments	$63,720	$53,940
Property taxes	0	10,435
After-tax payments	0	48,183
Wealth gain (price/principal)	0	51,528
Total cost	$63,720	($3,345)
10-Year Total		
Rent/mortgage payments	$137,640	$128,750
Property taxes	0	20,870
After-tax payments	0	97,456
Wealth gain (price/principal)	0	116,812
Total cost	$137,640	($19,356)

Step 2: *Determine How Much Home You Can Afford*

Working with your real estate agent, you will be able to determine how much home you can afford. Chapter 5 presents a worksheet that you can use to determine how much you can afford to pay. Once you determine your spending limits, you may proceed to the next step.

Step 3: *Determine the Type of Home and Location You Desire*

Write down on a piece of paper what features you desire in a house as well as what features you desire in your community or neighborhood. Your real estate agent may provide you with a simple survey on desired home and community features to gain a better understanding of where your agent should begin a home search. A sample survey,

called a home buying wish list, provided by the Housing and Urban
Development Department (HUD) at http://www.hud.gov/utilities/
intercept.cfm?/buying/wishlist.pdf, appears on pages 110–111.

HUD also offers a checklist for shopping for a home that may be
useful particularly when seeking the type of neighborhood and location that you desire. Here is what I believe to be the most important
checklist items that you need to consider for each location:

Neighborhood
   Appearance/condition of nearby homes/businesses
   Traffic
   Noise level
   Safety/security
   Age mix of inhabitants
   Number of children
   Pet restrictions
   Parking
   Zoning regulations
   Neighborhood restrictions/covenants
   Fire protection/police
   Snow removal
   Garbage service

Schools
   Age/condition
   Reputation
   Quality of teachers
   Achievement test scores
   Play areas
   Curriculum
   Class size
   Busing distance

Convenience to
   Supermarket

Schools
Work
Shopping
Child care
Hospitals
Doctor/dentist
Recreation/parks
Restaurants/entertainment
Church/synagogue
Airport
Highways
Public transportation

Step 4: *Get Preapproved for a Mortgage Loan*

If you do not know a lender to use for the financing of the home purchase, ask your real estate agent to recommend two or more lenders. Visit with each lender and select the one you are most comfortable with. It is important for a first-time buyer to get preapproved for a mortgage loan. Work with your lender by providing the necessary personal financial and employment information so that you can be accepted for preapproval.

Step 5: *Shop for a Home*

You are now ready to find a home. At this stage, you should be able to provide your real estate agent with the necessary search criteria for your future home: location, type of home, home features, and price range. There are two steps involved in shopping: First, do some preliminary search on your own via the Internet or by driving around neighborhoods, and second, have your real estate agent select a limited number of homes for you to visit. The first step is made easy by visiting REALTOR.com or any major real estate brokerage site in your area. You can simply type in your zip code, enter your search criteria (home type, home features, and price range), and view the listings. This process will enable you to narrow the "field" a bit so that your time with the real estate agent will be used efficiently.

HOME BUYING WISH LIST
The Basics

1. What part of town (or country) do you want to live in? _____

2. What price range would you consider? No less than _____, but no more than _____.

3. Are schools a factor, and if so, what do you need to take into consideration (e.g., want specific school system, want kids to be able to walk to school?

   _____

4. Do you want an older home or a newer home (less than five years old)?

   _____

5. What kind of houses would you be willing to see?
   □ one-story   □ two-story   □ split foyer   □ Colonial   □ no preference

6. What style house appeals to you most?
   □ contemporary   □ traditional   □ southwestern   □ Colonial   □ no preference

7. How much renovation would you be willing to do?   □ A lot   □ A little
   □ None

8. Do you have to be close to public transportation?   □ yes   □ no

9. Do you have any physical needs that must be met, such as wheelchair access?
   □ yes   □ no

10. Do you have any animals that will require special facilities?   □ yes   □ no

11. The lot:

	Must have	Would like to have
Large yard (1 acre or more)	_____	_____
Small yard (less than 1 acre)	_____	_____
Fenced yard	_____	_____
Garage	_____	_____
Carport	_____	_____
Patio/deck	_____	_____
Pool	_____	_____
Outdoor spa	_____	_____
Extra parking	_____	_____
Other buildings (barn, shed, etc.)	_____	_____
Special view	_____	_____

The Interior

---

12. How many bedrooms must you have? ____ would you like to have? ____
13. How many bathrooms do you want? ____
14. How big would you like your house to be (sq. ft.)? no less than ____ more than ____
15. What features do you want to have in your house?

	Must have	Would like to have
Air-conditioning	____	____
Wall-to-wall carpet	____	____
Ceramic tile	____	____
Hardwood floors	____	____
Eat-in kitchen	____	____
Separate dining room	____	____
Formal dining room	____	____
Family room	____	____
Greatroom	____	____
Separate den/library	____	____
Fireplace	____	____
Workshop	____	____
No interior steps	____	____
In-law apartment	____	____
Spa in bathroom	____	____
Lots of windows (light)	____	____

Community Features

---

16. Do you want to live in an area with a community association? ☐ yes ☐ no
17. What else do you want in your community?

	Must have	Would like to have
Community pool	____	____
Golf course	____	____
Basketball court	____	____
Tennis courts	____	____
Gated community/doorman	____	____
Clubhouse/activities	____	____

18. Are there any other special features or needs that you must consider when you are looking for a home?

The second step is for your real estate agent to take you to physically visit the targeted homes. Listen to your agent and treat him or her as a trusted advisor. They will make money whether you purchase house A, B, or C. Let them help you find the "right" home that satisfies your needs.

Step 6: *Identify Resources That Are Available for First-Time Buyers*
You need to talk with both the real estate agent and lender on what resources are available for first-time home buyers. In every city or town, there are a number of local first-time-buying programs and products offered. On a national level, there are a wide variety of first-time home buyer mortgage loan products and programs, as well.

Most of these resources focus on assisting first-time buyers into a home with some type of financial assistance. The two major hurdles to buying a first home are the down payment and credit history. For many households, it is difficult to accumulate savings for a down payment. And some first-time-buying households have poor credit records and are unable to qualify for a mortgage to finance a home. The earners in some households just don't have enough annual income to qualify for financing. Others may have a blemished history of meeting their debt obligations or holding on to a steady job.

The good news is that there are many down-payment-assistance mortgage loans and programs available to help first-time buyers. There are also products and programs that have flexible underwriting guidelines for first-time buyers with credit problems. FHA, Fannie Mae, and Freddie Mac offer a wide variety of mortgage loan products that assist first-time buyers. Ask your real estate agent and/or lender for information about these products. Also ask them to identify all of the local and national first-time-buying assistance programs that may be available to you. The programs range from assistance for firefighters to Native Americans to low-income households. A more complete discussion and listing of first-time-buying products and programs for both national and local levels are presented in Chapter 5.

And finally, there are many types of educational and counseling programs designed to help first-time home buyers. The two most popular are credit counseling and home buyer education. Credit counselors help people understand credit reports and deal with credit problems, and show how to keep a family on a budget. Educational programs for home buyers help prepare households for home ownership, assisting them with shopping for a home, obtaining financing, and preparing for the closing and postpurchase responsibilities.

Counseling is particularly important for potential home buyers with language or cultural differences that could interfere with home buying. Many brochures, counseling sessions, and home buyer courses are given in different languages. If you are an immigrant or if English is your second language, these programs are extremely valuable.

There are HUD-approved housing counseling agencies all across America. HUD funds housing counseling agencies throughout the nation that can give a first-time buyer advice on purchasing a home. They also give advice on all of the aspects of home buying, such as credit issues, defaults, foreclosures, and a variety of mortgage products available for different financing needs. The HUD Web site (www.hud.gov), Fannie Mae (www.fanniemae.com), Freddie Mac (www.freddiemac.com), and the National Association of Realtors® (www.REALTOR.org/hop) all can provide you with the resources to choose the right counseling program for you.

First-Time Buying and the U.S. Tax Code

First-time home buyers or, for that matter, any home buyer can take advantage of the tax incentives on savings that are built into programs designed to assist people with down payments. Tax rules have been relaxed in recent years on retirement accounts to allow cash-poor first-time buyers to tap into funds without paying the 10 percent penalty on early withdrawals. Both IRA accounts and 401(k) plans are available for first-time buyers to use for this purpose.

Individual Retirement Accounts (IRAs)

There are two types of individual retirement accounts (IRA): a traditional IRA and a Roth IRA. A traditional IRA permits you to contribute up to $2,000 annually. If you have no other employer-sponsored pension plan, your traditional IRA contribution is fully deductible and begins earning tax-free income. Roth IRAs, which became available in 1998, offer more advantages than traditional IRAs, particularly if you aren't planning to retire soon. The contributions are not deductible, but the earnings on your contributions are tax-free and you can withdraw funds without paying any taxes (including earnings) if you meet the time and age requirements. Individuals can contribute up to $2,000 ($4,000 for couples), subject to income requirements (see your accountant for specifics).

The great thing about IRAs and Roths is that you can draw up to $10,000 penalty-free from both the IRA and Roth IRA accounts to purchase your first home as long as you buy your home within 120 days of withdrawing the funds. Previous home owners who have not owned a home for the past two years also qualify. (Note: Participants still pay state and federal income tax on the withdrawn funds. If you were, for example, in the 30 percent tax bracket, you would net $7,000 on a $10,000 withdrawal to apply toward a home purchase.) Such funds can be used for a down payment and/or to pay for closing costs. For a Roth IRA, a withdrawal cannot be made until five taxable years after the first contribution to the account, and the withdrawal can only be used to buy a first home.

401(k) Plans

A 401(k) plan borrows its name from Section 401(k) of the Internal Revenue Code of 1981, which spelled out the rules for this retirement plan. Contributions are made pretax, and any earned interest, dividends, and/or capital gains are also recognized as tax-free earnings. An employee may make an annual pretax contribution up to a maximum of $13,500 to a 401(k) plan, and the employer can match any percentage of the employee's contribution.

You can borrow up to a specified limit from your 401(k) account penalty-free to purchase a house for yourself or for a relative. A relative who participates in such a plan also can draw from his or her account to give you a gift or a loan to buy a home. Withdrawing funds from your 401(k) is a bit complicated. You are really borrowing the funds from yourself, so you have to pay the money back to your account. Thus, when you withdraw from a 401(k) plan, you are incurring a debt and must include that obligation in your credit calculations when you apply for a mortgage loan. This will have a significant impact on your income-to-debt ratio when loan officers are evaluating your creditworthiness.

First-Time Buying Strategies

So you have made the decision to buy a home and invest in real estate. Congratulations! You have somehow managed to save enough for a down payment—on your own or through a government-assistance program. You were also rated creditworthy by a mortgage lender. What strategy should you follow to purchase property in today's expanding real estate market? Do you buy a single-family residence or a condominium? Do you finance a house by obtaining a fixed-rate mortgage with a 30-year term or a 15-year term, or do you finance it with an adjustable-rate mortgage?

For many the primary objective in buying a house is to achieve the dream of home ownership. But I urge you to think of buying a house as an *investment* in your real estate portfolio, rather than as just a house that provides shelter. Your timing could not be better to take advantage of what our expanding housing market has to offer—rising home values, healthy home sales, and relatively favorable financing terms (mortgage interest rates are expected to remain in single-digits for the remainder of this decade).

I have identified two types of first-time buyers: (1) young households and (2) established households. Young households are those in their twenties or thirties who can look forward to steady increases in their incomes. They are in the early- to mid-stages of their careers. During the next two decades, they are likely to accumulate significant financial resources through job promotions, investments, and business initiatives. Established households tend to be those with steady but low/moderate incomes. They usually do not have the potential for substantial salary advancement and wealth accumulation. Usually, such households' expenses (children, car payments, etc.) are high relative to their income levels. Young householders can usually take on more risk in their property purchases—they can afford to buy a more expensive home—than can their established counterparts.

Determining a First-Time Price

Purchasing a home is very different from purchasing an automobile or refrigerator, where buying decisions are based primarily on price because each product is the same (e.g., a Ford Explorer with package A is the same product whether it's sold by a dealer in New York or Houston). But no home for sale anywhere in America is quite like another one, despite real estate ads that tend to use common descriptive categories such as "ranch" or "center-hall Colonial" or "Cape Cod style." Every home has its own unique history. A home's value is influenced by many factors that can add to or subtract from its price. The size of the home (square footage), its location (e.g., near a school or near a commuter rail line or on the water), the age of the home, physical condition and characteristics (brick or aluminum siding, wood floors or wall-to-wall carpet, etc.), and local market conditions are just a few of the things that help to determine the value of a home.

Although there are many factors influencing value, the most direct and simple way to select a house to buy is to make a decision based on price. A first-time buyer should rely heavily on the information provided by a licensed real estate agent who is able to show you the price range of comparable homes in your neighborhood and make recommendations on price based on current local market conditions (i.e., demand and supply).

However, there may be something you like about the house that is unique to you. You may be willing to pay a bit more for the home because of that "good feeling" you have about it. My advice to you is that when it comes to negotiating price, keep emotion out of the process as much as possible. Use your real estate agent as an objective advisor. But remember, only you can make the ultimate decision on what the home is worth to you.

Purchase Strategies

Better High Than Low

If you can afford a higher-priced home, I believe it makes sense to buy it. Why? Buying a home is first and foremost an investment, and higher-priced homes usually generate a greater accumulation of wealth (equity) than lower-priced homes. A 10 percent price appreciation creates $10,000 of wealth for a $100,000 priced home, but $20,000 of wealth for a $200,000 home. In addition, if you can afford to buy the higher-priced home, payment of principal throughout the term of the loan is greater because the loan is larger. In other words, a higher-priced home creates a greater amount of *forced savings* for first-time home buyers. And because the loan is tax-deductible, you get a portion of these extra payments back, depending on your tax bracket. That is why stretching a bit and buying a higher-priced home is often an effective financial strategy, particularly for the young household group, who can expect to see their income rise over the years ahead.

If you are not able to afford the higher-priced home, don't stretch as much. Fortunately, more modestly priced homes are projected to rise in value over the next decade, too. I expect strong and steady demand as a result of the millions of echo boomers coming into the market during the next decade, as well as from the sizable numbers of immigrants that entered America during the 1990s and 2000s who will become first-time buyers.

Take Advantage of the Hot Condo Market

I believe condominiums also offer a great real estate opportunity for first-time buyers. During the past several years, half of all condominiums sold were purchased by first-time buyers. And the market is sure to grow as empty nesters buy condominiums to accommodate lives without children and need less room. More than 40 percent of all condominiums in recent years were purchased by buyers who were forty-five or older. In other words, condos are good investments for both ends of the housing market, having enjoyed double-digit appreciation during each of the last three years. With the empty nester population group projected to grow at an increasing rate during the next decade as boomers age and retirees live longer, the demand for condos is expected to remain strong, pushing up both sales and prices.

Location Strategies

Location, location, location. You've heard it before. If it isn't necessary for you to live in a particular neighborhood, location becomes an important factor when purchasing property. Location has a major influence on the future value of real estate property. With the real estate boom expected to continue into the next decade, most regions of the country should yield healthy price increases. But some home locations will experience greater increases than others (see Chapter 12). What are some of the factors that enhance value? Two obvious ones are proximity to good transportation (highways, trains, buses, airport, etc.) and a high-quality school system. For parents with school-aged children, a strong school system is often a foremost concern. Your real estate agent should provide you with the necessary local information to compare school systems within a metro area.

Avoid locations that are highly dependent on one or two industries. If the industries suffer a setback, it could undermine the local economy. Nothing depresses housing prices more than local job losses. I suggest you look for a home located in an economically diversified area that is not dependent on one or two large companies and/or industries.

Avoid purchasing a home located on a busy street or highway; it will not rise in value as much as other homes, even if it is physically more attractive. On the other hand, homes located on a golf course, on the waterfront, or with a special view may enjoy a substantially higher increase in value.

One popular rule of thumb for buying by location: "You will make more money purchasing a lesser house in an above-average neighborhood than purchasing an above-average house in an average neighborhood." Generally speaking, this is true. It is usually better to play follow the leader in the real estate markets. If you are the highest-priced home in the neighborhood, the other homes may keep your home's value from rising too quickly. But if you are one of the lowest-priced homes in the neighborhood, a healthy price increase to the more expensive homes lifts all homes in the neighborhood to some extent.

If you have the freedom to consider different towns in your region, I suggest that you follow the echo boomers, the generation in their twenties. What towns or suburbs are they moving to? There are 76 million echo boomers in the United States. As they become first-time buyers, they'll create enormous demand for reasonably priced homes, exerting upward pressure on home prices over the years ahead. Net migration numbers are usually a good indicator of where the echo boomers and their parent generation—the boomers—are moving. Arizona, Colorado, and Oregon are some of the "hot" net migration states today.

Financing Strategies

For most first-time buyers, the financing terms of the property purchase are as important as the purchase itself. As I pointed out before, there is a wide range of mortgage products designed for first-time buyers today. Reread the preceding chapter (Chapter 5) to identify the types of financing options available. It should provide you with a road map for obtaining financing for a first home.

Making the Right Financing Decision

Selecting the right mortgage—the term of the loan, the interest rate, and the down payment—is the most important choice you'll make after the purchase of the home itself. Whatever decision you make will likely lock you in to a lender for a long time. In general, young buyers and households can afford to take on more risk, because their income is likely to go up over time. As a result, they have more flexibility in choosing among mortgages. If rates are high, an adjustable-rate mortgage would help them to qualify for a higher-priced home than they could afford at a 30-year fixed rate. The upside? Again, higher-priced homes are likely to appreciate more in value than lower-priced homes. A 5 percent rise in the value of a $200,000 house results in an increase of $10,000. A 5 percent rise in the value of a $400,000 house results in an increase of $20,000—twice as much. Moreover, because young households are statistically more likely to trade up to a larger home within five years, as their family and their income grows, it may make sense for them to go with a lower-rate adjustable loan.

Established households do not have as much flexibility as young households, because their income is unlikely to grow as much. Moreover, they are likely already saddled with the high costs of raising a family. Such households are also less likely to trade up in the near future. Such first-time buyers should take advantage of the subsidized mortgages offered by the government and housing agencies. If you are such a prospective buyer and you are having a difficult time getting the necessary down payment saved to buy a house, take a look at a low-down-payment mortgage. It can get you, or such families, into a home with little upfront funds. Locking into a fixed-rate mortgage makes more sense than assuming the interest-rate risk of an adjustable-rate mortgage. You should focus on obtaining a 30-year mortgage with the lowest possible monthly payments, because you are relying more on price appreciation, and less on the accumulation of home equity, to build wealth.

Whenever You Are in Doubt, Build Wealth First

The *primary* goal for first-time buyers is to build wealth through property acquisition—not simply to own a home. In other words, this is all about attitude. Do not be satisfied with just owning your home in the midst of a real estate boom. The American dream is not just about home ownership—it is about accumulating wealth and financial security. This is just as important for low-income households as it is for middle- and high-income families. For most Americans, property ownership is their primary opportunity to create wealth!

Real estate wealth is built through price appreciation—through the increasing value of your home—and accumulation of equity in your home, as your monthly payments reduce the outstanding amount due on your loan and increase your principal. By taking advantage of the boom now, first-time buyers can accomplish both. The real estate markets have been growing for thirteen years—and I expect them to grow into the next decade. Home appreciation is expected to average at least 5 to 6 percent per year. Because of the power of leveraging via a low down payment, as well as the tax benefits the government provides, your returns and ability to build wealth have never been better.

If you are a young prospective household, I urge you to purchase your first home as soon as you are financially able. Each year you postpone purchasing a house, the greater the lost opportunity. Take advantage of your *future* income stream by leveraging your income and savings today. There will be substantial demand for starter homes and relatively low-priced homes across the United States in the years ahead.

Once you have become a home owner, don't stop there. Especially with young households, work to build up your home equity as your income increases. Funnel a percentage of any "extra" funds into your house—or accumulate them toward a down payment on a second home or rental property. It may take a bit longer for an established household to build some extra funds from home equity appreciation. But when you have done so, you should follow the same road map as the young household.

In the chapters ahead, I'll discuss how to expand your real estate investment in your home through remodeling/renovating, as well as through trading up to a larger home, purchasing rental property or vacation property, and investing in real estate indirectly through real estate investment trusts, or REITs, and real estate mutual funds. In the meantime, congratulations on taking the first step toward accumulating wealth through real estate.

CHAPTER

7

PROFITING THROUGH
HOME IMPROVEMENTS

I f you've owned a home for a while and currently do not have the interest in or resources to move up to a larger home, consider home improvements as a way to further participate in the real estate boom. According to the National Association of the Remodeling Industry, NARI, the remodeling market (i.e., home improvements) was a $214 billion industry in the United States in 2003 and is projected to total $225 billion in 2004 (the data is not yet compiled as of this writing). NARI estimates that more than one million homes per year undergo major renovation or remodeling!

According to a 2004 NARI survey, home owners tend to remodel for three reasons (in descending order): (1) to update their homes to their taste or the latest trends; (2) to address the changing needs of their family; and (3) to increase a home's market value. Half of all remodeling jobs cost less than $5,000; another 23 percent cost $5,000 to $10,000. Only 9 percent cost more than $30,000. For renovations that cost more than $30,000, the most common remodeling job was a new addition, followed by a major kitchen renovation.

Clearly, most Americans spend a great deal of time and money improving their homes—fixing up, renovating, adding on, landscaping, and anything else that will make their homes more attractive and comfortable. And with good reason. Next to buying a house, improving it can be your best real estate investment.

Because your home is probably the largest asset you will ever own, it makes sense to increase the market value of your residence through home improvements. Unfortunately, most home owners improve their homes for other reasons, according to the NARI survey. Remember, on the list of reasons for renovating a home, increasing a home's value came in number three.

Not everyone sees the logic (and emotional rewards) of home improvements. They think paying for additions and/or renovations is money wasted, because they believe the improvements won't add all that much to the value of their house. Sometimes, of course, that's true. Not every improvement is going to increase the value of your house in proportion to the cost of the improvement. Some "improvements" can even reduce the value of your home. It used to be that bathroom Jacuzzis were the order of the day. But gradually home owners realized they rarely used them and they were not worth the cost. Today, luxury showers with multiple showerheads are much more in fashion—and likely to add to the value of your home. In addition, there is the cost of your time in making improvements, and the sheer aggravation factor. Despite Americans' fascination with home improvement shows like *This Old House*, most home owners are better off leaving major renovations to the professionals. Even minor improvements like hanging new wallpaper can take up far more of your day than you expect. Is this really how you want to spend your time? In general, if you are not absolutely sure you can do it right, don't do it yourself.

Remember, home improvements that *don't* add value to your home aren't really home *improvements*. Keep in mind that you are investing in your home. Rather than purchasing additional property, you are improving your current property and changing the cost basis for accounting purposes. Of course, you can leave the accounting to your accountant. Your job is to understand how to make investments in home remodeling and renovation that will pay off and find the best form of financing to pay for improvements. It's yet another way of taking advantage of today's real estate boom.

Investing Wisely in Home Improvements

There are a lot of valuable home improvements home owners can make to their homes. What improvements will add the most value to your home in the long term? Home improvements fall into three categories:

- Major renovations/remodeling (additions, significant upgrading)
- Repair work: energy-efficiency improvements, roof repairs, plumbing, electrical work, etc.
- Cosmetic changes: painting, carpeting, and so on.

Renovations and remodeling are the kinds of home improvements that can significantly add to the value of your home. Renovating your kitchen, for example, should not only add value, it should also make life easier and make your house more attractive to live in. But how do you decide what to do—and when?

First, take a look around your neighborhood. Talk to your local real estate agent to see what different houses are selling for. What are the features people most seem to want? Is it worth putting money into renovating/remodeling your present home? Or does it make more financial sense to trade up to a larger, possibly newer, house that already has the features you had planned to add through renovation? Adding on a fourth bedroom and family room is far more expensive per foot than buying a house that was built as a four-bedroom house. There are times when trading up to a larger home (see Chapter 8) is a more financially sound way to go. But there are also times when it makes more financial (and emotional) sense to stay where you are and invest in remodeling. Making that decision requires, first and foremost, an accurate picture of what property values are in your area, and the future direction of real estate in your state, region, or community.

Certainly, if your neighborhood is on the upswing and property values are rising, it may be an ideal time to remodel/renovate. How does your house compare with other homes in your neighborhood? Do you have the smallest home? The largest? Generally, if other homes are slightly larger and in better condition than your home, home improvements can significantly enhance your home's value. But if you already have one of the largest and most expensive homes in the neighborhood, home improvements may not increase the value of your property very much and may not be the best use of your funds. Moving to a better neighborhood may be a better way to go.

Next, ask yourself how long you plan to stay in your home. Home improvements usually don't generate a dollar-for-dollar return on your investment. As a rule of thumb, home owners need to stay in their homes for at least three years before they see the money invested in improvements reflected in the rise of their homes' market value.

How to Add Value to Your Home by Renovating/Remodeling

Your family and friends thought it was just great that you installed a $10,000 hot tub on your deck. While you can count on seeing a lot more of them, you can't count on this improvement adding much, if anything, to the value of your home. That's not a reason why you shouldn't have the hot tub if you want it and can afford it. But you should think of it for what it is: a plus for entertainment or health, but not an investment that will add value to your house. If you are intent on building equity and value in your home, you need to be very hardheaded about what improvements *will* do that.

In planning to renovate/remodel, always think about the resale value of the house—even if you're not planning to move anytime soon. First, consult with a real estate professional to find out what improvements buyers in your neighborhood tend to be looking for. Are buyers in your neighborhood looking for four bedrooms? Kitchens with islands, breakfast nooks, and high-quality cabinets and granite countertops? A third bathroom? A deck or built-in outdoor grill?

Many home improvement–type magazines publish tables presenting the returns on home improvements across the nation every year. There have also been some serious studies attempting to empirically estimate the return on home improvements across different regions of the country. Unfortunately, the returns on home improvements vary widely among these studies and tables, which means there is no definitive source for this information. Let me share some of the results from these studies and/or annual tables with you, as well as offer some general comments about returns on home improvements that may help guide your decision-making process.

Home Improvement Studies/Estimates

Sirmans/Macpherson Study

According to a study conducted by B. Stacy Sirmans and David A. Macpherson,* there are a number of home improvements that meaningfully increase the value of a home. The study also identifies other home improvements that can actually detract from a home's value. Some of these findings should not be taken literally. For example, do not expect your home's value to rise by a whopping 24 percent if you add a bathroom. This study is useful in that it gives you a sense of which home improvement adds value or detracts value. It also suggests which home improvement contributes more to a home's value than others. Adding a bathroom may not increase your home's value by 24 percent, but it certainly contributes more to the value of a home than adding nine-foot ceilings. The kitchen features that buyers consider most valuable are a built-in refrigerator, a kitchen island, and a double oven; exterior features that affect selling price the most include a patio, a deck, a sprinkler system, and a tennis court; any location on the water, or having a water view, adds value to a house.

Here are their findings on items that tend to increase the selling price of a home:

*"The Value of Housing Characteristics" by B. Stacy Sirmans and David A. Macpherson, Florida State University, December 2003.

Home Improvement Project	Price Effect (%)
Additional 1,000 sq. ft. of living space	3.3
Additional full bathroom	24
Additional partial bathroom	4
Central air-conditioning	12
Inground pool	7.9
Nine-foot ceilings	6
Sitting area in master bedroom	8
Finished basement	9
Security system	5.6
Den/study	7.3
Fireplace	12
Garage	13
Attic	2
Close proximity to golf course	8

Items that may actually detract from the value of the home:

Home Improvement Project	Price Effect (%)
Vinyl/aluminum exteriors	−4
Basement laundry	−2
Without laundry facilities	−15
Flat roof rather than pitched roof	−10
Fixer-upper vs. house in good condition	−24

This study's conclusions are obvious: Some improvements add more value to your home than others.

Cost Versus Value Annual Study (Remodeling *Magazine)*

Remodeling magazine (published by Hanley-Wood, LLC, Washington, DC) conducts an annual study on home improvement costs versus the value added to the home. Its 2002 annual study suggests that kitchen and bathroom remodels add the most value to a home but are also the most costly. The study presents the following improvements as those that offer the greatest return on investment and the least return on investment:

GREATEST RETURN ON INVESTMENT

Remodeling Project	Project Cost	Cost Recouped (%)
Bathroom remodel	$9,786	80
Bathroom addition	$14,216	81
Minor kitchen remodel	$14,773	87
Major kitchen remodel	$38,769	80
Second-story addition	$67,744	83

LEAST RETURN ON INVESTMENT

Remodeling Project	Project Cost	Cost Recouped (%)
Home office	$10,526	54
Reroofing	$10,111	60
Sunroom	$27,081	60
Window replacement	$9,026	68
Basement refinish	$39,658	69

And for households with smaller home improvement budgets, here is what you can get for under $10,000:

RETURN ON SMALL HOME IMPROVEMENT PROJECTS

Remodeling Project	Project Cost	Cost Recouped (%)
Window replacement	$9,026	68
Siding replacement	$6,286	73
Exterior paint	$8,336	74
Deck addition	$5,865	75
Bathroom remodel	$9,786	80

Real Living *Survey (2003)*

For comparison to the *Remodeling* magazine study, a *Real Living* survey (see www.realliving.com/selling/resource/roi.sap) also tracks the return on investment for home improvements. The study's numbers are close to, but also somewhat different from, *Remodeling*'s numbers.

Remodeling Project	Return on Investment (%)
Major kitchen remodeling	150
Revitalized lawn and garden	100
Fireplace	100
Second bath	90
Room addition (family or bedroom)	80
Remodeled bath	60–80
Deck	70
Exterior paint	50
Finished basement	40
Heating system	40
New windows and doors	35

Although there is no definitive source for estimates on the returns on home improvements—there are significant differences among the above studies and surveys—it is very clear which improvements add great value and which improvements do not. Use the above estimates as a guide for determining which home improvements to focus on.

Remodeling with a Contractor

Once you've identified what improvements you want to tackle in your home, you are faced with the task of establishing a remodeling strategy for the project. Most people do not have the time or expertise to handle a major renovation themselves. Putting in a new ceramic or tile floor might be one thing; a major renovation of the kitchen is something else. If you are like me and struggle with hanging pictures and repairing leaky faucets, the choice is straightforward—you need to hire a reputable contractor. If your addition is complicated, you may need to hire an architect as well. He will hire whatever subcontractor you need and help you get any necessary variances and approvals from your local government.

How do you hire a contractor? I would suggest you talk to at least three neighbors who have undertaken successful and significant renovations. You can also check your local Better Business Bureau to see if any of the contractors on your list have outstanding complaints against them. Ask your real estate agent for recommendations. Always check references, focusing on the quality, cost overruns, and timeliness (ability to stay on schedule) of their work. Get at least two or three written bids from contractors you are interested in. The bids should include a breakdown of their work, the cost of materials, and a time schedule. After selecting a contractor with whom you are comfortable, it is important that you and the contractor sign a written contract statement of work, including a detailed outline of the responsibilities of the contractor and home owner; a description of the home improvement project; a payment clause stating when payments are due; a breakdown of the materials, labor costs, and so on; a time line from the start to the projected completion date; and all of the relevant warranties, insurance, and permits that are necessary to complete the project. There should be a final inspection clause in the contract before final payment. It is important that you go through a checklist on final inspection. Do not—I repeat, do not—make the final payment until you are satisfied with the completion of the project. Unfortunately, once you submit a final payment to the contractor, you have no more leverage over him. He is off to another job, and it is difficult to get him to focus on completing yours.

Financing Solutions

There is a wide variety of financing options available to most households when it comes to home improvements. Whether you are financing a $10,000 project or a $125,000 renovation, selecting the right financing solution is critical to the overall success of your investment. A number of financing options follow, ranging from borrowing against the equity in your home to special home-renovation loans. Some of these options have already been presented in some detail in Chapter 5. Rather than repeat that discussion, I will offer some brief descriptions and refer you to Chapter 5 when necessary.

Home Equity Loans, Equity Lines of Credit, and Cash-Out Refis

Because you are already a home owner, you can tap into your stored wealth (i.e., the equity in your property) by borrowing against it. Home equity loans, equity lines of credit, and cash-out refinancings all provide this opportunity. Review Chapter 5 for more detail.

Borrowing Against Other Assets

If you have tapped out your ability to borrow against your home equity and you need additional funds to complete your home improvement project, you might be able to borrow against other assets, such as your stock (equities) portfolio. With a margin loan, some brokers will permit you to borrow up to 50 percent of the value of your stocks and up to 90 percent of the value of U.S. Treasury securities. You can deduct the interest against investment income for tax purposes, but not against ordinary earned income. I frankly don't recommend this type of borrowing, as it is risky. If the value of your stock holdings falls, you are subject to a margin call and will be asked to deposit more money into your account and sell your securities when the market is low.

Special Types of Home Improvement Loans

You can get a special renovation mortgage from a lender. There are several things the lender will require: First, that your contractor meets all required licensing, bonding, and certification standards. Second, an appraisal of the property to determine its current value and whether the cost of the renovation will be recouped in the form of a higher property value after the renovation. Your lender may also review the construction contract before you sign it. Most lenders will also require you to set aside 10 to 15 percent of the renovation costs in a contingency reserve fund to cover cost overruns and unexpected project changes.

FHA Loans

The Federal Housing Administration, or FHA, offers financing for property improvements to households that qualify for FHA funding.

These loans permit home owners to borrow up to $25,000 without any equity in the home. See your lender to inquire about these loans.

Fannie Mae HomeStyle Mortgages

Fannie Mae offers a suite of home improvement loans for property improvements and repairs. The loan amount for renovation may be as much as 75 percent of the "as-completed" appraised value of the home. There are also loans for home buyers who would like to reno-vate a new home before moving in. Basically, Fannie's Renovation Mortgage permits you to buy a home and improve it with just one loan. Theses mortgages typically have lower interest rates than stan-dard renovation loans, and repairs and other costs can be financed as part of the mortgage loan. See your lender to inquire about them.

Home Improvements and the Housing Boom

The beauty of investing in home improvements is that you can partici-pate in the continuing real estate expansion by putting your money into your own home, rather than spending time and money to purchase a second property or trade up. You can also take advantage of the lever-aging power of real estate by borrowing against your home equity to fund your improvement project. In today's real estate expansion, home improvements usually lead to a higher value for your home, greater price appreciation potential, a tax deduction, greater forced savings via principal accumulation, and an opportunity to invest in real estate that you know all about—your own home. It would be hard to find a better investment than the one you already live in.

8

TRADING UP AND TRADING DOWN IN A BOOM PERIOD

A real estate expansion gives you many opportunities for trading up to a larger home. Trading up is another way of expanding your real estate investments in a boom period. Selling your home for $300,000, for example, while purchasing a $500,000 home, increases your total real estate reach by $200,000. With home sales growing and home prices rising, trading up can be a very successful investment strategy.

Surprisingly, however, trading down to a smaller home, in the right situations, can create even greater opportunities to expand your real estate investments. The key to trading down is to reinvest the funds that are left over from trading down into other real estate that will grow in value. Of course, you have to be willing to get by with less space or less property or a less prestigious neighborhood. But for empty nesters, it can be the perfect solution to having too much space and smaller needs.

Trade-Up Buying

Trade-up buying gets you the best of all worlds. You are expanding your investments in real estate. If you need more living space, trading up allows you to get more without living through the chaos or in-convenience of a home renovation or addition. And in thinking of real estate as an investment, buying up allows you to expand your real estate portfolio without the hassle of purchasing an investment property—thereby avoiding the additional costs of time, money, and dealing with tenants or developers if you are purchasing rental or commercial real estate.

Consider trade-up buying when one or more of the following are true:

- You can sell your current home for a lot more than you paid for it, and you have plenty of cash available for the down payment on your new home.
- You have accumulated enough principal on your current home to provide the necessary cash for the down payment (this is usually the case when you have been paying off your mortgage for at least 5 years, thereby reducing the original loan balance).
- Your household income has increased significantly, allowing you to afford more house (i.e., larger mortgage and tax payments on a larger home).
- Your assets and overall wealth increases from other sources, such as stock options or an inheritance, providing additional cash for a down payment or purchase.
- Current interest rates are significantly lower than the fixed-rate mortgage you are paying on your current home. At the lower interest rates, you could service a larger loan or bigger mortgage without significantly increasing your monthly payments. (You could, of course, simply refinance your existing mortgage and thereby reduce your monthly payments, but this will not allow you to increase your investment in the real estate boom.)

To Trade Up or Renovate

In the previous chapter, I spelled out how you can decide whether it is better to trade up to a larger home or undertake a home improve-ment. Evaluate your neighborhood. If your home is already high-priced in relation to other homes in your neighborhood or town, it may be time to move. The highest-priced home in the neighborhood is usually held down a bit by the lower-priced homes with regard to future value. Other typical reasons home owners trade up include a desire for a better school system, improved access to transportation, more property, moving closer to work or to a less urban neighborhood, and so on. The point is, trading up is a very simple and practical way to increase your investment in real estate.

Understanding the Market

Trading up to a larger home usually involves having to sell your current home. Is it better to buy your new home first, or sell your existing home? The safest course to take is to get the seller's agreement that the closing for your new house will take place only after you sell your current home. (Of course, you would have to sell your home within a limited period of time.) But during a real estate boom, this is unrealistic. There are too many buyers and not enough sellers. Houses often receive multiple bids, allowing sellers to dictate the terms. Sellers are in the driver's seat and will find an offer contingent upon selling your existing home unacceptable. On the other hand, you can take advantage of being a seller by selling your current home first, and get the buyer of your new home to agree that you can, if necessary, delay the closing for a limited period after going to contract. You can also ask for an arrangement with the buyer that you will be allowed to rent your existing home for a period of time, giving you room to find and close on a new home. And finally, the simultaneous buying and selling of two homes requires preapproval with your lender to finance the purchase side if there is a timing problem with the selling side.

Your decision on whether or not to trade up may depend on how many homes are on the market. A "tight" or "lean" housing inventory makes it a seller's market—there are a lot of buyers looking for homes and not enough homes up for sale. This makes it difficult for trade-up buyers to time the selling of their current home with the purchase of the trade-up home. With a lean supply of homes available for sale, you will find it hard to compete against a buyer making a cash offer. But if you sell your current home first, it may take a while before you are successful bidding on a trade-up home. Arranging to delay the closing on the sale of *your* home for a set period is a way to allow you to keep a roof over your family's head until you can find and buy your new home. In today's healthy buying market, you could probably extend the deal by one to three months.

But don't allow a tight inventory of homes in your neighborhood or region to deter you from trading up. Remember, you are playing both sides of the market—what weakens you on the buying side will strengthen your position on the selling side.

Trading up is a successful strategy in markets experiencing both healthy home price appreciation and a softening in home prices. In investment terms, high price appreciation is the very reason for trading up (because higher-priced homes provide larger equity gains than lower-priced homes appreciating at the same pace). It is a solid strategy to build wealth. On the other hand, even if home prices are softening a bit, you will benefit in the short term, because you will *save* more from the price softening on a higher-priced trade-up home, compared with the softening of price on the current, lower-priced house that you are selling. Of course, you need to carefully monitor both ends of the market before knowing if a trade-up strategy is a financially viable one. At the extreme, you would probably not want to trade up to a high-priced home that has experienced significant appreciation during the past several years, while the value of the home you are selling dropped in value during the same period. But this scenario is unlikely in a healthy real estate expansion.

When you are buying one home and selling another, I suggest that you try to use the same real estate agent, as you may be able to negotiate a lower commission rate on the sell side. Also, remember to factor in the cost of your broker's commission (on the sell side) when determining how much cash you'll need for the down payment and closing costs of your new home.

Position Yourself to Trade Up

What if you bought your house recently and it hasn't yet appreciated much in value? Aside from taking advantage of the equity buildup from price appreciation on your current home, how can you position yourself to trade up in the future? The key is to find ways to build your existing home equity and/or lower your monthly mortgage payments so that you can eventually afford a higher-priced home.

Make Extra Mortgage Payments

Making extra payments that are applied against the principal on your existing mortgage loan is a great way to build up equity faster. By just making one extra monthly payment per year, you can shorten the payoff period of a 30-year term down to 24 years. Making an extra monthly payment annually on a $250,000 mortgage loan will save you $69,981 in interest payments during the life of the loan. The shorter the mortgage term, the faster equity accumulates. Similarly, if you paid your $250,000 mortgage biweekly rather than once a month, you would reduce a 30-year mortgage to about 23 years and save $69,987 in interest (assuming a 6.5 percent rate).

Refinancing into a Shorter-Term Mortgage

Refinancing into a shorter-term mortgage loan (if you can afford the higher monthly payments) will also build up your equity faster. For example, refinancing a 30-year loan into a 15-year loan builds equity at a significantly faster pace. A 30-year, $200,000 mortgage loan would have paid off only $7,831 in principal after 3 years, and only $13,890 in principal after 5 years, not enough to add toward a down payment on a higher-priced home when you factor in sales commissions on your current home. But with a 15-year amortization schedule, you would have $27,651 paid in principal after 3 years, and $48,579 after 5 years. The household holding a 15-year mortgage loan is far better positioned to trade up than the household holding a 30-year mortgage loan.

Using Adjustable-Rate Mortgages

If at first glance it appears that you might have a difficult time qualifying for a higher-priced home, or you need to hold down the monthly mortgage payments, adjustable-rate mortgages might be the answer. Adjustable-rate mortgages (ARMs) are usually two percentage points lower than the current 30-year, fixed-rate mortgages, enabling a trade-up buyer to purchase a lot more home without increasing his monthly payments. For example, a home buyer purchasing a $250,000 home with a 20 percent down payment would pay $1,467 per month on a $200,000 30-year, 8 percent mortgage loan. If the home buyer took out a $200,000, 6 percent, adjustable-rate loan instead—for the same $1,467 monthly mortgage payment—he could now purchase a $323,000 home. By going to an adjustable-rate mortgage, the home owner is now able to trade up to a house worth 30 percent more in value. Of course, any time you take on an adjustable-rate mortgage loan, you are incurring greater interest-rate risk. If rates should rise over the next several years, so too will your monthly mortgage payments. When interest rates are historically low, a fixed rate may be the better option. On the other hand, when rates are higher, or if you plan on selling your home in the next five to seven years, an ARM may make sense. Households that expect to see their future income rise are better equipped to absorb higher mortgage payments should rates rise on ARMs.

The Financial Consequences of Trading Up

Let me run through an actual "trade-up" home transaction, to show you the financial benefits of trade-up buying in a healthy real estate expansion. Let's say you have lived in your current home for five years; its original purchase price was $250,000, and your down payment was $50,000. Using the national home price appreciation rates during 1999 to 2003 (3.9, 4.1, 5.8, 7.5, and 7.5 percent), your home would now be worth $330,603, for a price gain of $80,603. Similarly, during this five-year period, the principal paid on a 30-year, fixed-rate mortgage totals $13,890. The equity in your home equals the down payment, price gains, and principal paid, or $144,499. The trade-up transaction would look something like this:

	Current Home	Trade-Up Home
Market Price	$330,603	$550,000
Selling Costs (6%)	$19,836	
Est. Closing Costs (3%)		$16,500
All-In Price	$310,767	$566,500
Funds Available	$124,657	
Down Payment		$108,157

You would net $310,767 from the sale of your current home, assuming you pay 6 percent commission to the real estate agent. After paying off your remaining loan balance of $186,110 ($200,000 – $13,890), you would have $124,657 available for a down payment on the trade-up home. Assuming you put 20 percent down on your new home and pay $16,500 in closing costs, you would be able to purchase a $550,000 home, assuming you could afford the monthly payment on the higher mortgage. Thus, in just a five-year period, trading up allowed you to more than double your investment in real estate to $550,000 from $250,000! This is the beauty and essence of trade-up buying.

There are some other additional costs to trading up that need to be accounted for in some circumstances. If you are trading up to a home above the conventional (Fannie Mae and Freddie Mac) loan limits from a loan that was below the conventional loan limits, there will be an additional cost for obtaining a jumbo mortgage loan compared to the lower-cost (i.e., lower-mortgage-rate) conventional mortgage. In our example above, the new loan balance was $441,843, which is now a jumbo loan. Depending on market rates, jumbo loan mortgage rates might be ¼ to ½ percentage points greater than conventional loan rates. Assuming a 6.5 percent conventional rate, the jumbo rate could fall within the range of 6.75 to 7.0 percent, which could increase the monthly mortgage payments by $73 to $147 per month. The larger home would also have higher property taxes, maintenance costs, insurance premiums, and so on. These added expenses need to be factored in to your final decision on trading up.

Trading Down

Can trading down be seen as an opportunity to expand your real estate investments? Yes, in what I call "multiple trade-downs." A multiple trade-down is when a home owner sells his or her high-priced home and uses the funds to invest in multiple real estate investments. The home owner usually trades down to a smaller, lower-priced primary residence and uses the remaining funds from the sale of the original home to make other real estate investments.

Multiple trading downs became popular in 1997, after the IRS granted a generous tax exemption on the capital gains from a sale of a home. The current exclusion is $250,000 for individuals and $500,000 for married couples filing jointly. To qualify for the exemption, a seller must have lived in the home for at least two of the last five years before the sale. (More details on this exemption in Chapter 3.)

Making the Exemption Work for You

Before the capital gains exemption, the tax code didn't give you any real options for real estate investment. If you made a $500,000 profit, or gain, when you sold your home, you would have to pay taxes on all of it—unless you reinvested all of your gain by purchasing another primary residence (at a price equivalent to or greater than the gain) within a two-year period of time. You were effectively limited to only one type of real estate investment. If you were an empty nester and wanted to trade down to a smaller house once the kids had moved out, you couldn't simply buy a smaller house for less money unless you were sixty-five and used your one-time exemption. Otherwise, you had to purchase a new home at a price comparable to the price you got when you sold your former home.

But with today's $500,000 exemption for married couples, you can make that $500,000 gain on the sale of your home and then trade down to a $250,000 home, using the remaining $250,000 for investments of your choice with no tax consequences. Of course, you can decide to use the remaining funds to invest in other things—stocks, bonds, and so forth. But if you do so, you will be underinvested in real estate. I believe it is important to take advantage of the real estate boom and reinvest a significant percentage of such funds in real estate.

There are several options available, depending on your social and financial situation. There are two types of households that tend to be interested in trading down: (1) empty-nester households consisting of forty-five- to sixty-five-year-olds still in their peak earning years but with children who have left home, and (2) households consisting of sixty-five-year-olds or older who have retired or are close to retirement and are beginning to live off their savings rather than income.

Empty-Nester Households

If you are an empty-nester home owner who is still working, earning income, and striving to build wealth for eventual retirement, I would argue that you are an ideal candidate to trade down. Let's say you make a $500,000 capital gain by selling your home for $700,000 after buying it for $200,000 fifteen years ago. Because you no longer need the same space that you did while you were raising children, you can trade down to a smaller house—purchase a home for, let's say, $450,000, which leaves you with $250,000 (minus your broker's commission, which we will ignore for the sake of simplicity). What should you do with the $250,000? I would argue that most of these funds should go *back* into real estate. One option would be to purchase property that you can rent out. This can be a very effective way to leverage your funds in real estate while covering your mortgage costs and taxes, allowing you to build wealth and enjoy additional income. However, there are risks and management responsibilities associated with rental property that you need to be willing to assume. Rental property investing is not for everyone. (See Chapter 9 for more details.) Another option would be to purchase vacation property (see Chapter 10) or invest indirectly via real estate investment trusts (REITs), for example (see Chapter 11), thereby avoiding the responsibilities of maintaining and managing rental property. Alternatively, you could invest the money in stocks and bonds. But in doing so, you would miss out on the next decade of the real estate boom.

Empty nesters are in the enviable position of having the option of purchasing a rental property with all cash or some combination of financing and cash (down payment). If you do buy a property with all cash, however, you lose the advantage of leveraging your investment (being able to buy one or more properties by using your capital gains as the down payment). Your purchase at this point is really a pure investment play. Compare the returns of an all-cash investment in real estate with the current returns in both equity and bond investments. As you can see from the following table, because of price appreciation, the return from an all-cash transaction in real estate is a quite impressive 12 percent, comparable to the historical returns of stocks, which range between 10 and 14 percent, depending on the company type (bond returns are much lower). But the real beauty of real estate is that you can leverage a down payment to buy a far more expensive property, taking full advantage of the price appreciation and the accumulation of principal (which I've calculated from an amortization table, on the next page) by purchasing properties through financing. With a 50 percent cash/50 percent financing, the return on investment increases to 14 percent. A 20 percent cash/80 percent financing generates a 23 percent return per year. This is one of the reasons so many wealthy individuals use real estate as one of the central pillars in their investment portfolio. While you can leverage the purchase of stocks and bonds through stock options, futures, and puts, your risk is far greater—you can literally lose all of your principal—and a great deal more. Leveraging the purchase of real estate is a far safer investment. Even if the market completely collapsed, at most you would lose only your down payment. And in the midst of a real estate boom, you can't find a better investment.

Another bonus of this kind of investment is that the more you are leveraged in your rental property purchase, the more funds you have available for *additional* real estate investments. In the example above, a $50,000 down payment generates a 14 percent return. But that leaves you with $200,000 or so yet to invest, minus the real estate

PURCHASING A $250,000 RENTAL PROPERTY

	100% Cash	50% Cash	20% Cash
Rental income	$24,000	$24,000	$24,000
Estimate expenses (taxes, association fees, etc.)	$6,000	$6,000	$6,000
Mortgage payments (6.5%, 30-year)	0	$9,481	$15,169
Closing costs (3% of loan balance)	0	$3,750	$6,000
Net gain (loss)	$18,000	$4,769	($3,169)
Price appreciation (5%)	$12,500	$12,500	$12,500
Principal accumulation	0	$2,380	$2,380
Total gain	$30,500	$17,269	$11,711
Initial investment	$250,000	$125,000	$50,000
Return on investment	12%	14%	23%

commission. You could purchase additional properties, each generating high returns. This is what I mean by "multiple trade-downs"—the leveraging factor in buying real estate enables you to trade down in such a way that you increase, rather than decrease, your real estate holdings. If you were to buy five rental properties, each costing $250,000, and each financed with a $50,000 down payment (assuming no other costs, for the sake of simplicity), generating 23 percent annual return on your investment, you would have gone from owning one large home with a great deal of "frozen" equity to owning six properties (your trade-down smaller home and five cash-generating rental properties).

In other words, you would have transformed one home valued at $700,000 into a $450,000 house and five $250,000 rental properties, for a total real estate portfolio of $1.7 million. That is the power of using the multiple trade-down strategy.

Trading down can be a powerfully effective way to take your unused, stored-up equity and, exploiting the leveraging capacity of that stored equity, purchase many more properties. Moreover, while your mortgage costs stay fixed (assuming a fixed-rate mortgage), the return on your traded-down multiple investments increases signifi-

MULTIPLE TRADE-DOWNS
(Initial Cash from Home Sale: $700,000)

	Down Payment	Market Value
Trade-Down Purchase	$0	$450,000
Rental Property 1	$50,000	$250,000
Rental Property 2	$50,000	$250,000
Rental Property 3	$50,000	$250,000
Rental Property 4	$50,000	$250,000
Rental Property 5	$50,000	$250,000
Total Value		$1,700,000

cantly with time, since rental income usually grows over time (the historical annual average is about 3 percent).

Retiree Households

If you are retired, your situation is different from that of an empty nester. You are likely in the "over-sixty-five" segment of the population and probably can no longer depend on a steady income from working. Instead you are living on your savings, income from investments and pensions, and Social Security. Like most retirees, you are probably risk averse. Rather than looking for opportunity to gain wealth, you are more likely looking for ways to preserve capital. You want to avoid risk at all costs. If you originally purchased your home for $200,000 and sold it for $700,000, making a gain of $500,000, your real estate investment strategy will be quite different from that of the empty nester. Assuming you purchase a $450,000 trade-down home, I would recommend a more conservative approach with your $250,000 in remaining funds. To take advantage of the real estate boom, I would suggest using the $250,000 to purchase shares in REITs, real estate mutual funds, and real estate partnerships, while also diversifying some of these funds into dividend-paying stocks, bonds, and bond/equity mutual funds. I discuss such indirect real estate purchases in Chapter 11 in detail. Unless you are inclined to take on the risks and management responsibilities of rental property, indirect real estate investing offers a safer way to invest in the boom with greater cash liquidity. Because the real estate markets are expected to expand into the next decade, the returns on such real estate investments should perform admirably vis-à-vis the general market of stocks and bonds.

The Trade-Down Marketplace

In trading down, you are involved in multiple real estate transactions. Use this to take advantage of your market power with real estate agents and lenders. In a simple trade-down, you are selling one home and purchasing another. By working with the same real estate agent on both sides, you may be in a strong negotiating position to lower the real estate commission down a bit, and perhaps ask for a discount on the commission percentage.

If you are engaged in multiple trade-downs, your negotiating position strengthens even more. In the multiple-trade-down example I gave above, the original owner was involved in seven real estate transactions—selling his or her original home, then purchasing a trade-down home and five rental properties. That gives you a great deal of negotiating power. Negotiate with the real estate agent, the lender, the title company, the home inspection company, and so on, for lower fees on each transaction. If you need guidance, talk with your local real estate agent in advance of taking action. If you don't like his response, you're always free to go with another broker. But I think you'll find he will be accommodating and more than happy to advise you in negotiating with the other real estate providers.

INVESTMENT PROPERTIES R US

Owning real estate gives you a real, concrete sense of wealth—and investing in rental property gives you a *visible* investment that generates immediate cash flow. Income-producing property is a far more "tangible" asset than stocks or bonds—"paper" that you never see or touch, investments made through markets you deal with via intermediaries, brokers, or agents who often "manage" those investments for you. Managing your real estate investments can be as "hands on" as you want it to be. And even though your brokerage statements may show a profit, they don't give you the same feeling of actually making money that you get from a monthly rent check.

Yes, sometimes you *have* to be very "hands on" to get your tenant to pay the rent on time—or deal with a leaky roof or a major plumbing or heating disaster, problems that those late-night infomercials don't dwell on when they try to sell you courses on how to make a million dollars with no money down. Following the advice in this book is not necessarily going to make you a millionaire overnight—but if you use common sense and good judgment, and put in some hard work, you can make real estate investments in rental properties that build real wealth. You have to learn how to acquire a rental property and manage it effectively, or pay a professional property manager to do the job. But as you will see, if you buy a house or condo and then rent it out, you probably won't be saddled with problems you can't handle. The bottom line is that this is a tremendous way to take advantage of today's real estate boom.

Why Today Is the Best Time to Invest in Rental Properties

If you could acquire a $200,000 rental property by putting only $40,000 down, financing the purchase by taking out a 30-year mortgage at 6.5 percent interest, and knowing that the value of the property will increase 5 percent per year for the next 5 years, thereby generating a $55,256 gain in value on the original purchase price, would you do it? Before you answer, what if I told you that the monthly rent payments from the property will cover your mortgage payments, property taxes, and maintenance costs? Moreover, what if you know that the monthly rent payment is projected to grow by 3 percent per year? By the third year, the total rental income will be paying you $200 in cash each month, after expenses. Who could pass up such an investment?

But the example above is not an exaggeration; it is reality in today's market. It shows why you should seriously consider investing in rental property. There is no better time to be investing in rental properties than during a real estate boom that is driven by a growing economy, constantly rising housing prices, and relatively low mortgage rates. A healthy economy creates steady demand for rental units as people move out from their parents' homes to find their first apartments. In a booming economy, demand tends to outpace supply (the total number of rental units available). The more people earn more money, the more rent you—the landlord—can charge. As long as interest rates remain historically low, the mortgage loan you take out to buy a rental property is a bargain. Most economists (including myself) are projecting 30-year mortgage rates to stay below double-digit territory for at least the next several years. Low-cost financing means a growing profit margin for you as your rental income increases over time while your locked-in mortgage expenses don't. You're using the power of leverage to buy rental property and build wealth.

Don't Confuse Rental Property with Commercial Real Estate

There is a big difference between investing in rental properties and investing in commercial real estate. Unless you know a great deal about the complexities of commercial real estate properties, I suggest you leave investing in commercial real estate to professionals. Instead, I would focus on residential rental property—single-family residential homes and condominiums. (By commercial real estate, I am referring to multifamily apartment buildings, office buildings, warehouses, and retail property such as shopping centers and hotels.) Sophisticated and experienced professional investors purchase commercial real estate. Don't compete against them head-on—you will lose. Stick to what can make you money.

Interestingly, today's real estate boom isn't really translating into a boom in commercial real estate. The record-breaking home sales and dramatic price appreciation we've experienced over the past several years have taken place in the residential real estate markets, not in commercial real estate. From 2001 to 2003, commercial real estate values were basically flat—a direct result of the post-9/11 2001 recession and widespread job losses in 2002 and 2003. But during that same time period, residential real estate soared. In fact, along with consumer spending, residential real estate sales and appreciation drove the American economy.

The Types of Rental Property

I suggest investing in single-family detached homes, condominiums, and maybe manufactured homes for your rental property purchases. There are also cooperatives (properties), but they are common only in certain areas, like New York City, Chicago, and Washington, D.C., and the "cooperative" concept is not as favorable for property investors as condos. Cooperative members own *shares* in a corporation that owns or controls the building(s) and/or property in which they live. Each shareholder is entitled to occupy a specific unit and vote on the corporation's decisions and is able to block absentee and investor ownership. A condominium, on the other hand, has become a very popular property purchase among investors. There are fewer constraints and restrictions in the way that a condominium is organized. Let me give you an overview of what's involved in investing in condominiums and manufactured homes.

Condominiums

A condominium is a building in which the units (e.g., apartments) are owned by individual condo owners while the common parts of the property, such as the grounds and building structure, are jointly owned by all the apartment owners. Owners pay monthly carrying charges (called condo or association fees) for the operational costs of the common areas and grounds. Condominium owners usually elect a board of directors made up of residents who oversee the overall management of the building—keeping repairs and maintenance up to standard, hiring agents to handle owners' short-term rentals, making sure that new washing machines are installed in the laundry room, and initiating necessary renovations of things like elevators and lobby areas, as well as landscaping improvements.

Sales of condominiums have been extraordinary during the current real estate boom. Almost 1 million units were sold in both 2003 and 2004. In fact, condo prices have been appreciating at a higher pace than single-family homes in recent years. They were up 14 percent (my estimate) in 2004 over 2003 prices, compared to an average of 7.5 percent for single-family homes during the same period. For many singles and married couples, a condo acts as an affordable "starter home."

Today's condominium boom owes its success to several market factors:

- Low mortgage rates have lowered the monthly carrying costs.
- An increasing number of boomer households are downsizing to condominiums as they become empty nesters, increasing the demand for higher-priced condominiums.
- An increasing number of echo boomers (the boomer children) are becoming first-time buyers, raising the demand for lower-priced condominiums.

- Condominiums are very attractive to real estate investors, which drives increasing demand and price increases for these units.

Condominium Versus Single-Family Detached

What are the advantages and disadvantages of investing in single-family homes versus investing in condos? On the plus side, condos are easier to manage and maintain. You usually have lower maintenance costs for the building (fixing leaks, painting, and making other repairs) and landscaping than you do with a house. And the favorable future condo demand from a growing retiree/empty nester population group, combined with a growing demand from the large echo generation group, bodes well for price appreciation. On the minus side, condos have a high monthly association fee that could range from a few hundred dollars to well over one thousand dollars, compared to a small or no fee for a single-family detached property. Finally, rental income from condos, compared to total expenses (mortgage, property tax, condo fees, and maintenance fees) is typically, on average, less than the rental income versus expenses ratio on renting out a single-family detached home.

Over the past several decades, single-family homes have been far and away the most popular rental property investment in America. Nonetheless, in recent years, with condo sales and prices soaring, condominium investments have become much more attractive and are gaining ground. In fact, the real estate boom has benefited condos more than any other type of residential property. And favorable demographic trends are going to continue to make them attractive investments for years to come. But be selective, as some local condo markets are approaching their limits. In some areas of the nation, rents are flat and condo prices are soaring, turning good investments into marginal ones. Unlike purchasing a primary residence, condo investing can become somewhat speculative in select markets.

Manufactured Housing

Manufactured housing refers to homes and dwellings that are not constructed at the site. These properties are usually built in a factory and trucked to the lot where they are assembled. Manufactured housing includes precut, panelized, modular, and mobile homes. They are built according to HUD code, which regulates the home design and construction, strength and durability, fire resistance, and energy efficiency. According to the Manufactured Housing Institute, there are about 24 million Americans living in manufactured homes today, and the average sales price of a new manufactured home has hovered in the $50,000 vicinity.

Manufactured housing is especially attractive to seniors and low-income folks. You buy a premade unit that comes on a wide-load truck and gets plunked down on a piece of land you own or in a "park" or development where basic amenities are available—water, electric, and sewer connections, for example—and the home owners may or may not own the piece of land on which their wide loads sit. Another reason why you may want to consider investing in a manufactured home is that construction costs per square foot are about 10 to 35 percent less than those for a comparable site-built home, excluding the cost of land. Furthermore, the quality of construction has improved, and manufactured homes have more modern amenities than those of just a decade ago.

Most manufactured homes are sold through retail centers and not by real estate agents, unless you are purchasing an existing manufactured home. If you are planning on investing in a manufactured home, make sure that you understand the warranty (usually 1 to 5 years) on the home and what company is servicing that warranty. In addition, the retailer can usually assist you in arranging financing and insurance coverage on the home.

As an investment, manufactured homes should appreciate in value like any other residential real estate. The data is sparse on price appreciation for manufactured homes, but these properties appear to have benefited from today's real estate boom. The same price factors apply: inventory of site-built and manufactured homes in a local community and demand for both home types in a local community. For more information on manufactured housing, contact the Manufactured Housing Institute at 703-558-0400, or visit their Web site at www. manufacturedhousing.org.

How to Buy Rental Property

Investing in rental property requires a strategy quite different from the one employed in purchasing a home. The acquisition of a rental property is a business decision, and it has to be made in a businesslike way. Once you've identified a property that *could* be a good investment, you have to estimate the property's current value, project its future value, and make a realistic assessment of how much rental income you can expect to get from the property, versus anticipated expenses, in order to arrive at the property's profit potential. You want to get expert advice about the benefits of depreciation and tax write-offs. Your calculations must be based on how long you plan to own the property and what it will take to manage the property over that period of time. Your calculations should also reflect whether you think you can personally manage the property or will need to hire a professional manager to do the job.

It is essential that you understand the risks involved in rental ownership. If your tenant doesn't renew the lease and the rental market turns sluggish, you may be stuck paying the mortgage and the operating expenses without any rental income coming in for months. Do you have the financial resources necessary to cover those costs? How can you protect yourself?

You can hedge against the risk of lost rental income by building up a contingency reserve, or obtain rental-loss insurance when you purchase rental property. There is no certainty when it comes to obtaining and holding on to tenants. They are here today and gone tomorrow. You may get lucky and keep the same tenant for five years, or you may have to replace a tenant every year. There is no magic formula for obtaining tenants quickly—it really depends on market conditions: the demand for and supply of rentals. I recommend that you start out with funds in a reserve that will cover a minimum of two months of rent, then gradually build up the reserve over time, until you accumulate funds to cover four to six months of rent. You can invest them in an interest-bearing savings account or money market fund. You can also invest these funds in a mutual fund that specializes in real estate.

Just make sure that your invested reserve funds remain liquid so that you can draw on them without penalty when necessary.

There is also the risk that economic conditions could turn sour in your area—a large corporation may announce major job layoffs, for example—sending property prices plummeting and rents spiraling downward. And, of course, you may discover a nightmare repair problem that has to be dealt with immediately—a roof or furnace that needs to be replaced, burst pipes and water damage, structural damage to the basement. Even if insurance covers some of these unanticipated problems, the cost of your time and the worry such problems cause remain high.

Try to anticipate how you would handle a worst-case scenario. This is all the more reason to choose a property carefully—get the advice of an experienced real estate agent, bring in an engineer to make a thorough inspection of the house, the roof, and the structure. Do as much research as possible on the neighborhood and economic environment in which the property is located. Realistically assess your ability to handle potential problems, psychologically as well as financially.

Working with Real Estate Agents and Lenders

If this is your first rental property, you will probably feel more comfortable if the property you are buying is located nearby so you can keep a close eye on it. The real estate agent you work with will help you identify the appropriate neighborhoods for rental property. Work with a lender to "prequalify" for financing. You need to know up front what interest rate you will be charged and to have a lender on call ready to provide you with a Good Faith Estimate of the closing costs (origination points, application fees, title insurance, etc.) before you place a bid on a property.

I cannot emphasize enough how you will lean on both a real estate agent and a lender for advice and direction in purchasing rental property. But remember that the real estate agent and lender are not investing in a rental property—you are. Neither of them has an obligation to identify the best investment property and financing strategy for you. You are relying on them to be truthful, objective, and considerate of your interests. They are both licensed and professional. Find a real estate agent you feel you can trust, and establish a buyer relationship with him or her.

Here is a step-by-step guide on how to use a real estate agent and a lender when you purchase a rental property:

Step 1: *Select a Real Estate Agent with Investment Property Experience*
Contact two or three local real estate offices (from different companies) and ask if the company performs property management services. If the answer is yes, ask to speak to an agent who specializes in investment properties. Make an appointment and interview these agents, then decide which one is well informed and right for you.

Step 2: *Clearly State Your Investment Objectives*
Sit down with your real estate agent and explain exactly what you are looking for. Be precise about your investment objectives: Do you want to build wealth over time? Or are you more interested in securing a steady positive cash flow from your investment? Be frank about how long you want to own. Are you planning on a five-year investment, or do you want to hold it for ten years or longer? What type of risks are you willing to take on with the property? Can you afford to pay for expensive repairs or loss of tenant rent? Finally, be frank with your agent about how much you can afford to pay for the property and how long your resources will allow you to meet expenses if rental income dries up.

Step 3: *Discuss Property Management Issues*
Have a candid discussion with your real estate agent about property management issues. He or she has been on both sides and understands your needs. If you don't have the time to manage your property or the enthusiasm to do so, research how much property management fees will run you.

Step 4: *Get a Lease from a Real Estate Agent*
Ask your real estate agent to give you a copy of the form of a standard lease for the sort of property you are thinking about purchasing

for investment purposes. You can also get one online. There are several sites that offer sample leases for every state in the nation. Remember, laws vary by state with regard to rental property and tenant rights. Visit www.lease.com.

Step 5: *Ask Your Real Estate Agent to Recommend an Accounting Services Firm*

If you choose not to assume the accounting responsibilities of property ownership, your real estate agent should be able to recommend property management companies (often the agent's company) or independent accountants to provide these services.

Step 6: *Ask Your Real Estate Agent to Recommend a Lender*

Your real estate agent is in an excellent position to recommend a number of banks or other lending institutions that will make you a loan to purchase rental property. He or she can also guide you to using other settlement services companies (e.g., title insurance).

Step 7: *Meet Your Lender*

Once you have selected a lender, request a Good Faith Estimate of the proposed transaction. Even if you have not yet bid on a property, you may request your lender to provide you with a GFE of a hypothetical purchase. This will give you some idea of how much you will pay in closing costs when the property is legally conveyed to you. This will help you determine how much you are willing to bid on the property.

Step 8: *Preparing to Bid on a Property*

You will probably not make money the first year on a rental property—more of your cash will go out than comes in. (Cash that comes out of *your* pocket is *negative* cash flow.) It is rare to find a property that is priced low enough so that your rental income more than covers your mortgage and operating expenses (assuming a 20 percent down payment or less). But what makes rental property such an attractive investment is that your rent income will grow over time, while your mortgage payments are fixed and your other costs, such as property taxes, generally increase at a far slower rate. Moreover, rental property gets favorable tax treatment, so you will reap significant tax savings, increasing the real return on your investment.

Again, when bidding on a rental property, approach it quite differently from the way you handled purchasing your house. You aren't looking for cash income from the place in which you live, but you are in a rental property investment. Let's examine how you do a potential income/cash flow analysis.

Let's assume that a one-bedroom condo in downtown Washington, D.C., is being offered for an asking price of $195,000. Your investment strategy is to put 20 percent down and finance the remaining balance with a 30-year, 7 percent mortgage loan. How much do you bid for the condo? Do you bid the asking price? Do you underbid or overbid? Of course, the price you eventually pay has a great deal to do with market conditions (is the market tight or sluggish?). But to make an intelligent, informed investment decision, you need to run the before-tax cash flow calculations and then estimate the tax benefits from rental property ownership.

Before-Tax Cash Flows

You need to calculate and compare the before-tax annual and monthly cash flows of the condo over a range of bid prices. As you begin the bidding, have a firm idea of how much you can afford to pay out to "carry" the property. For example, you may be willing to pay up to $300 per month to own the rental property. So the maximum price you can bid will be a price that generates a negative monthly cash flow of $300. Prices lower than the maximum will generate lower negative cash flows, which improves your investment position.

In effect, the negative $300 cash flow represents what you are willing to pay for the privilege of owning the property, knowing that sometime in the near future rental income will eventually grow and turn a negative cash flow into a positive cash flow. Of course, the big payoff is the price appreciation and principal accumulation on the property, which eventually creates substantial wealth gains.

To calculate before-tax cash flows, let's assume that you bid the asking price, $195,000, for the condo. Your real estate agent tells you that the rental unit can earn $1,400 per month in rent, generating $16,200 in annual rental income (it's relatively expensive to live in our nation's capital). Now net out the expenses to finance, operate, and manage the property. With 20 percent down, you will obtain a 30-year $156,000 mortgage loan paying 7 percent interest. You will pay $12,454 in annual mortgage payments. Property taxes are estimated at $1,723 for the year (assuming the D.C. tax rate per $100 = .96 and property assessment of $179,525). Hazard insurance (protection from fire, wind, flood, etc.) costs $200 per year, and the condo fees are assumed to run $300 per month, or $3,600 for the year. Finally, you need to put $2,000 (assume about 1 percent of the bid price) aside in a reserve for repairs and maintenance (R & M) of the property. Adding the mortgage payment, property tax, insurance, condo dues (these dues are paid to the condominium association, which pays for repairs, maintenance, and improvements to the shared property, including the building, any amenities—e.g., a pool, landscaping—insurance, etc.), and repair/maintenance totals $19,977 in expenses. Netting expenses from rental revenues results in a negative annual cash flow of $3,177 and a negative monthly cash flow of $265.

Cash Flow Before Tax

Bid price	$200,000	$195,000	$190,000	$185,000
Rental income	$16,800	$16,800	$16,800	$16,800
Expenses				
Mortgage payment	$12,774	$12,454	$12,135	$11,815
Property tax	$1,723	$1,723	$1,723	$1,723
Hazard insurance	$200	$200	$200	$200
Condo dues	$3,600	$3,600	$3,600	$3,600
R & M reserve	$2,000	$2,000	$2,000	$2,000
Total expenses	$20,297	$19,977	$19,658	$19,338
Annual cash flow	($3,497)	($3,177)	($2,858)	($2,538)
Monthly cash flow	($291)	($265)	($238)	($211)

The asking price of $195,000 is pretty close to what you are willing to bid, given that the $265 monthly cash outlay is a bit below your $300-per-month limit. You are now able to bid the seller's asking price. But before you do, let's run some other cash-flow scenarios around the $195,000 asking price to establish a range of prices that may be acceptable to you in case market conditions dictate that you bid something other than the asking price. Let's run the cash flows for $200,000, $190,000, and $185,000. At $200,000, the monthly cash flow rises to $291; at $190,000, the cash flow drops to $238; and at $185,000, the cash flow drops further to $211. You are now presented with the following choices:

YOUR FINANCIAL LIMIT: $300 PER MONTH

Bid Price	Monthly Negative Cash Flow	Annual Negative Cash Flow
$200,000	$291	$3,497
$195,000	$265	$3,177
$190,000	$238	$2,858
$185,000	$211	$2,538

If market conditions are sluggish, you, in consultation with your real estate agent, may decide to underbid by offering $185,000 or $190,000, bringing your monthly costs closer to $200. On the other hand, if conditions are tight and your real estate agent anticipates multiple bids on the property, you certainly can afford to pay $291 per month and raise your bid to $200,000. Whatever you end up bidding, if you use the above cash-flow analysis, you will be bidding intelligently. If the price of the property rises beyond your cash-flow limit, it's probably time to move on to another property.

Of course, there are times when you'll want to put less than 20 percent down, and other times when you'll want to put down more than 20 percent down. If so, just plug in the new mortgage payment numbers in the above cash-flow analysis to see how sensitive the cash flows are to different loan balances. There will be times when a property's value will work with a lower down payment and a higher mortgage amount, and there will be times when you may need to allocate more funds to a down payment in order to make the cash flows work for you.

The Tax Benefits of Rental Property

Fortunately, there are some favorable tax consequences of rental property investments that improve the real return on your investment. Let's assume that you purchased the condo for the asking price—$195,000. To calculate the taxable income or loss from the property, subtract all deductible expenses from the rental income. For tax purposes, there are three types of expenses: mortgage interest expense, operating expense, and depreciation.

According to the 30-year amortization schedule, you can deduct $11,148 in mortgage interest expenses in the first year. Deductible operating expenses include $1,723 in property taxes, $200 paid in hazard insurance, $3,600 paid in condo fees, and $2,000 paid in repairs and maintenance. This gives you $7,523 in total deductible operating expenses. You are also permitted to deduct depreciation on the property. Because you purchased a condominium, there is no land involved, so the full cost of the condominium can be depreciated. (Land does not depreciate.) You are permitted to spread depreciation expense on the property over 27.5 years. This gives you $7,144 in depreciation expenses every year ($195,000 divided by 27.5). (If you purchased a single-family property, you would have to allocate some of the cost to land, so the entire purchase price would not be depreciable.) Subtracting your total deductible expenses of $25,815 ($11,148 plus $7,523 plus $7,144) from rental income of $16,800 results in an annual rental loss of $9,015.

There are several ways you may use the rental loss, depending on your ownership and financial situation. If your adjusted gross income does not exceed $100,000 and you actively participate in the management of the property, the rental loss (up to $25,000) can be deducted from your other income, such as wages, interest, and dividends. In the above example, you would multiply the $9,015 rental loss by your federal income tax rate (assume it's 31 percent), resulting in $2,795 of tax savings. If your state also has an income tax, that rate multiplied by the $9,015 loss would generate additional tax savings.

After-Tax Cash Flow

Purchase price	$195,000
Rental income	$16,800
Deductible expenses	
Mortgage interest	$11,148
Operating expenses	
Property tax	$1,723
Hazard insurance	$200
Condo dues	$3,600
R & M reserve	$2,000
Total operating expenses	$7,523
Depreciation	$7,144
Total deductible expenses	$25,815
Reported loss on property	$9,015

For households that earn less than $100,000 in adjusted gross income, your after-tax cash flow improves significantly due to the $2,795 in tax savings. Remember, the monthly before-tax cash flow was a negative $265. By adding the $2,795 tax savings to your rental income, you are left with only a $32-per-month negative cash flow, making this rental property a very attractive investment! Not only are you essentially breaking even in your first year, but your rental income eventually rises over time (property taxes, as noted earlier, also rise, but only slightly), you are building equity in the property as you pay down your mortgage, and as the property appreciates in value, your return on investment begins to soar.

According to the IRS rules, households with adjusted gross income between $100,000 and $150,000 can deduct passive losses up to a phased-out portion of the $25,000 cap. The phase-out begins with a $25,000 deduction against ordinary income for households reporting an adjusted gross income of $100,000 or less and gradually phasing out to zero deductions for a reported adjusted gross income of $150,000 or more. If you had an adjusted gross income of $125,000 in

Before-Tax Cash Flow

Bid price	$195,000
Rental income	$16,800
Expenses	
Mortgage payment	$12,454
Property tax	$1,723
Hazard insurance	$200
Condo dues	$3,600
R & M reserve	$2,000
Total expenses	$19,977
Annual cash flow	($3,177)
Monthly cash flow	($265)
Tax savings	$2,795
After-tax annual cash flow	($382)
After-tax monthly cash flow	($32)

our example, passive losses would be deductible up to $12,500. Therefore, the $9,615 rental loss would be fully deductible. For households whose adjusted gross income exceeds $150,000, the taxable rental loss cannot be deducted in the current year. These households will be unable to reduce the $265 monthly negative cash flow.

Property owners are permitted to carry forward their suspended rental losses, subject to the passive activity loss limitations. Each year, rental losses can be carried forward until the property is disposed (sold). (This means you accumulate the losses rather than deducting each year's loss from your income.) In the year of disposal, the cumulative suspended rental losses are subtracted from your taxable income, saving you thousands of dollars in income tax. Let's look at an example.

Suppose every year for five years you were carrying forward $10,000 in rental losses from a rental property that you own. At the beginning of year six you choose to sell the property for a $250,000 gain (selling price minus the adjusted cost basis, which is the original cost of the property plus improvements). Your wages, dividends, and other income totaled $200,000 in year six. You are now able to take a $50,000 loss in that year ($10,000 a year for the previous five years), resulting in only $150,000 in taxable income. If your tax rate were 31 percent, you would have saved $15,500 in taxes (31 percent × $50,000). Note that you will also pay a capital gains tax on the $250,000 gain from sale of the property, which as of this writing is taxed at 15 percent (however, the depreciation component of the gain is subject to a 25 percent tax rate).

The loss carry-forward delayed the benefits of rental investing. In effect, you earned another $15,500, which spread over the five-year ownership period provides you with another $3,100 of tax savings per year, improving your cash-flow position—after the fact. As you accumulate more rental properties (building a portfolio of properties), the loss carry-forward becomes more effective. As you sell properties, you will be experiencing tax savings that can help blunt the negative cash flows of your other properties.

Get a Real Estate Accountant

Use the above discussions as a guide only. For individuals with higher incomes or multiple properties, these are complicated calculations. I strongly advise you to consult a certified tax account (e.g., a CPA) for professional assistance in real estate investing.

Many other issues affect the tax consequences of real estate investing. There are times when you can deduct auto mileage when driving to inspect your rental properties. There are times when the costs of placing ads in newspapers and/or the Internet in your search to acquire a tenant for the property are deductible as well. Then there are times when some of the closing costs of obtaining financing can get written off over the life of the mortgage, or be considered additional basis to the property and therefore depreciable. Again, please discuss all of these issues with a professional tax accountant.

Step 9: Managing the Closing Process

A closing for a rental purchase is similar to a closing for a primary residence purchase (covered in Chapter 5). But I want to mention two important tactics that can be applied at closing that favor rental property investors. First, instruct your lender to set the date of the closing toward the end of the month so you can minimize the amount of interest paid up front at closing. Second, if you are purchasing a property that is vacant, try to schedule the closing at least one month after the contract signing to give you more time to find a tenant.

Financing Strategies

It may surprise you to find out that the typical 30-year mortgage rates that lenders quote in the Sunday section of your local newspaper do not apply to investment property. Borrowing rates for property investors are usually a bit higher than those for home owners. Lenders view rental properties as riskier and thus charge investors a higher borrowing rate for their funds. So you have to carefully consider the financing options available to you for purchasing rental property.

Investing in a home to rent out is riskier than purchasing a home to live in, because if times turn bad and you have to choose between paying the mortgage on the home you live in or making a payment on your rental unit, lenders know you will choose your home every time. As a result, lenders consider investment property riskier and will charge a higher mortgage rate than for a traditional mortgage. So much depends on how much you are willing to put down and your credit score. As a general rule, lenders want at least 20 to 25 percent down payment, but they may be willing to accept less if you demonstrate a healthy credit history (i.e., receive a high credit score).

Here are some of the primary financing options available for investing in rental properties—the same, essentially, available for financing home ownership (described in Chapter 5) but with a few strings attached:

Traditional Investment Financing

- A popular financing option for rental properties are long-term, fixed-rate loans—usually 30-year and 15-year mortgages.
- To be eligible for a relatively low investment mortgage rate, you typically need a down payment of at least 20 to 25 percent.

- It is also easier to qualify for an investment loan if the property you are purchasing already has a sitting tenant paying rent. Lenders will allow for a portion of the rental income—50 to 75 percent—to cover part of the mortgage payment. Obviously, purchasing a property that is vacant will not help you qualify for an investment loan, since there is no offsetting rental income.

- Sometimes the carry costs (negative cash flow) for a rental unit are too high given the asking price. Rather than walk away from the deal, you may want to consider obtaining an adjustable-rate mortgage (ARM). One-year adjustable-rate mortgages are usually offered at 2 percentage points below a 30-year fixed-rate loan. For the $195,000 condo purchase in the illustration used throughout this chapter, switching to a 1-year ARM would reduce the monthly mortgage payments by $200! That would lower the negative cash flow from $265 per month with a 30-year fixed-rate mortgage to only $65 per month, making the condo investment very attractive.

- If you have a short-term investment horizon, balloon financing may be an appropriate financing option. Balloon loans represent a reasonable financing option for investors with a 5- to 7-year time horizon. If you are planning on selling your rental property within five years, it makes sense to take advantage of the relatively low balloon rates vis-à-vis paying up for longer-term rates. An increasingly popular financing option is a 5-1 adjustable loan, locking in a low-cost, 5-year mortgage rate and assuming a variable rate thereafter.

Nontraditional financing for rental property purchases includes buy-downs, seller financing, interest-only loans, and builder incentives. These financing options are discussed at length in Chapter 5.

Managing Rental Property

As part of your real estate investing plan, a decision you have to make is whether or not you will manage your property personally. If you don't want to be a "hands on" manager, then you should shop around for the lowest fee that a property management company will charge for taking on that responsibility.

If you are inclined to be your own property manager, good for you. However, if you wish to avoid any direct responsibility for or involvement in property management, you will probably have to pay a property management company a hefty fee. This will reduce your profit and, in the early years of the investment, increase your negative cash flow. But using a property management service may be the right answer for you. It takes skill and experience to manage rental properties, and "on-the-job training" in property management can be more than a little stressful and expensive—you need to have the financial (and emotional) resources to cope with problems that can crop up, problems caused by your tenants or circumstances beyond your control. And it is all too easy for an investor to buy a property and, through lack of experience or sufficient resources, run it into the ground and end up selling it in foreclosure, sometimes for a considerable loss.

I recommend that you take on some responsibilities that you can handle with little effort (and little expense) and let a professional manager handle those that require a great deal of time and effort.

Property Management Responsibilities

Let's list the responsibilities involved in managing rental property so that we can identify which ones you can handle and which ones should be put in the hands of a professional. Bear in mind that a full-service property manager may cost you between 5 and 10 percent of your monthly rental income.

- **Finding the right tenant.** This is perhaps the most difficult and time-consuming task of property management. Finding a quality tenant in a timely manner is critical to the success of your investment. If you take on this responsibility and fail to secure a good tenant in fairly short order, you will be stuck with a vacant property that yields no rental income to offset all of your expenses. Property managers have access to many different ways to advertise your property. The property manager is also in a better position to show your property. Are you going to leave work every time someone wants to look at your rental? You also need to verify a potential tenant's employment history and conduct a credit check. For these reasons, I strongly recommend that you hire a property management company. Property management companies typically charge one month's rent to find and sign a tenant for your property.

- **Getting the lease properly executed.** Unless you are an attorney, you probably should have a property manager, real estate attorney, or real estate agent provide you with a legally bound lease for your tenant. You can always obtain a copy of a lease contract by going to the numerous Web sites that provide real estate contracts (just type the word "lease" on Google). But I recommend that you ask your real estate agent, if affiliated with a property management company, to provide you with a lease that they have used for other rental investments similar to yours. Seven out of ten times, your real estate agent will provide you with a copy of this lease for no cost. It is certainly worth asking before you go out and pay for a professional property manager to provide it. It would also be a very good idea for you to consult a real estate attorney about what is the required disclosure in a tenant/landlord arrangement and what are the tenants' rights and the landlords' rights.
- **Communicating with your tenant.** This is not always as simple or easy as you might think. Sometimes tenants can take up a great deal of your time with complaints, violations of rules, and so on. On the other hand, if you have an easy tenant who pays the rent on time, you won't have to be in touch with him or her until a problem crops up—something that needs to be repaired or a power outage, for example. This is a job you can take on yourself. If it becomes too much of a drain on your time (or you find that you just don't like doing it!), you can always hire a property manager.
- **Collecting rent.** This task is not as difficult as you might think. Again, if you have a responsible tenant who pays on time, just instruct him or her to send the rent check to your home address.

If you run into a situation where there is some delinquency in payments, you will have to send a late notice and possibly make a phone call. If the situation gets out of hand, you can always turn over these responsibilities to a professional property manager.

- **Arranging for maintenance and repairs.** If you already decided to handle communications with the tenant, I think it may or may not make sense for you to take on the responsibility of arranging for maintenance and repairs. In some cases, all it takes is a phone call to the neighborhood maintenance man; he returns your call, comes by the property within twenty-four hours, and fixes the problem. But in other cases, a call to a maintenance person may be nontrivial. We have all been through the repairman cycle: You call the repairman, he calls you back the next day, you set up an appointment a week from now, and he stops by between the hours of 2:00 P.M. and 4:00 P.M., when you or your tenant are not available because both of you work. The cycle goes on and on until, two to three weeks later, the repairman finally repairs the problem. Of course, if there is some serious damage and/or repair to the property, then you may not have much choice—it may be best to turn the responsibilities over to a professional.
- **Inspecting your property periodically.** Unless you live far away from the property, this should not be a problem. In fact, it is reasonable to inspect your property on a periodic basis. If it is a house with recurring maintenance or other problems, once a month is appropriate. If it's a condominium that requires little upkeep (no flooding in the basement, no outside landscaping, etc.), maybe two to four times per year.
- **Handling accounting and recordkeeping.** You need to set up and maintain a monthly accounting report of money received and disbursed. You also need to keep records on all expenses related to inspecting, maintaining, and repairing the property. Here is an example of a simple, basic cash-flow report. If you aren't good at handling accounting and record-keeping tasks, then you are better off using the services of a property management company or a professional accountant.

RENTAL PROPERTY A
Cash Flow Report

	Current Month	Previous Month	Annual
Rental income			
Expenses			
Mortgage payment			
Property tax			
Hazard insurance			
Condo dues			
R & M reserve			
Total expenses			
Monthly cash flow			

Property Management Recommendations

When deciding whether to hire a property manager or go it alone, first look at the money involved. For example, if you own a $200,000 condominium that generates $1,400 per month, it may cost you $100 per month (assuming a 7 percent management fee) to hire a professional property management company. If you choose not to hire a property manager, you have to calculate whether or not the time you will spend on property management is worth $100 per month. You will also find that, as you acquire more rental properties, you will experience an increasing need for outside management. Unless you become a full-time property manager, at some point there will simply be too many properties for you to manage on your own. The following property management recommendations are based on my own experience in rental property ownership as well as advice from a number of real estate professionals who offer property management services.

If you own three or fewer rental properties, I recommend the following:

- Employ the services of a property management company and/or real estate agent to find and secure a tenant for your property and to facilitate the signing of a lease agreement between landlord and tenant. This service should cost you one month's rent.

- Handle most of the property management tasks personally.
  a. Arrange to communicate with your tenant. An exchange of phone numbers will suffice.
  b. Tell the tenant to send the rent payments to your mailing address and notify the tenant if payments are late.
  c. Make a standing arrangement with a reliable maintenance person or service with an established practice in the neighborhood of your property. To identify the right maintenance company, ask your real estate agent. The agent should know reliable maintenance people who have a very good track record with property maintenance and repair. The tenant should be instructed to call you when there's a repair problem. It's then your job to get the maintenance person or service to do the job in a timely fashion. All billing goes from the maintenance company to you. As part of your standing arrangement with a maintenance provider, you should build in some form of cost control—a schedule of charges for small or routine services and a provision for obtaining an estimate before you grant approval to proceed with any major repairs or renovations.
- If you are good with numbers, disciplined, and organized, do the accounting services yourself. If the description above does not apply to you, employ the record-keeping services of a property manager, or hire a third-party accountant.

Rental Boom Purchase Strategies

There's no better time to take advantage of the benefits of rental property ownership than in the middle of a real estate boom. There are a wide variety of strategies that can be employed for successful rental property investing. These strategies are usually successful whether you are in the middle of a real estate boom or not.

One Purchase Per Year

The most general strategy is to commit to purchasing an investment property every year. Many professionals in the real estate business have employed this strategy, so why shouldn't you? These are real estate agents who specialize in brokering investment property. What they do (and how successfully they do it) with their personal investments gives one a good idea of what they can and will do for their clients. It is not uncommon to find real estate agents with ten to thirty properties in their personal real estate portfolio. These agents provide convincing examples of how successful real estate investing builds real wealth.

A "one purchase per year" commitment is an excellent strategy for expanding your real estate reach in today's real estate expansion. Every year, you must commit to purchase one rental property. If you are not in the financial position to raise down-payment money every year, consider buying a new property every other year. It is the commitment that is important, not the frequency.

Trade-Downs/Multiple Trade-Downs

There is no greater opportunity for investing in rental properties than when you trade down to a lower-priced home. As demonstrated in Chapter 5, the federal government allows a $250,000 capital gains exemption for individuals and a $500,000 exemption for married couples upon the sale of a primary residence. These are great opportunities for purchasing rental property (see Chapter 8). If buying more than one property in one year is too much for you, put the capital gains funds into an insured money market account and/or bond fund, where you can earn interest on your funds without fear of loss of capital. Each year, take out the appropriate amount of funds for a down payment on another rental property. Essentially, these measures will help you implement the "one purchase per year" strategy outlined above.

Converting Your Home into a Rental Property

If you are struggling to make ends meet in your own household and believe that you will be unable to raise enough funds to purchase a rental property, you may want to consider turning your home into a rental property. You can take cash out of your primary residence via a cash-out refinancing or with an equity line. Use these funds as a down payment on a new primary residence. There are two huge benefits with this approach: (1) There is little risk in your rental property investment—it's your own home! You know the maintenance and repair history of this property, you know what appliances need repair, and you know the neighborhood. (2) By purchasing a primary residence rather than a rental property, you will avoid paying the higher investment mortgage rates.

Preconstruction Purchases

If you can identify the really hot real estate markets (see Chapter 12), there are opportunities for investors to purchase preconstruction real estate. A preconstruction strategy involves identifying a local market that is expected to experience meaningful price appreciation over the next 12 months. Put down a deposit (usually $5,000) on a unit (i.e., a condo, villa, or single family) as a commitment to purchase and make a down payment (e.g., 10 to 20 percent) at contract signing. The objective is to lock in to a "price" on the property before construction, so that 12 to 18 months later when the property is ready for closing, you will own a property that is worth considerably more than the preconstruction price. This strategy is particularly popular in resort areas, where demand for preconstruction is so great that investors regularly enter a lottery to determine admittance to purchase.

Selling Strategies

If you own rental properties, at some point you are going to need to sell them. If you sell the property, you will have to pay taxes on any gain from the sale. When rental property is sold, any long-term gain (held longer than 12 months) is taxed at the capital gains tax rates, which ranges from 10 percent to a maximum of 20 percent, depending on your tax bracket. Capital losses are deductible from capital gains and, to a limited extent, other income. The gain will be the difference between the cost basis of your property and the selling price.

There are items that during the period of ownership are added to your cost basis, such as improvements and/or additions to the property. And when you sell your property, all the accumulated losses on the property—depreciation and negative cash flows—can be counted as losses against your income. A professional tax accountant and/or an accountant specializing in real estate transactions is the best source to learn more about the tax implications of a property sale.

The purpose of this section is to identify strategies that will help you either circumvent or postpone the tax consequences of a rental property sale. Here are some selling strategies that you may want to consider:

Sell and Pay Taxes Now

This is really no strategy at all. Sell your property, calculate your cost basis, and determine your capital gain, which will be subject to a capital gains tax. At the same time, the losses and depreciation expenses accumulated over the ownership period will be registered as losses against your income.

A Like-Kind 1031 Exchange

Section 1031 of the Internal Revenue Service code permits a property owner to sell a property and then reinvest the proceeds in ownership of like-kind property and defer the capital gains taxes. This exchange is available only for properties held for investment purposes. A personal residence does not qualify.

If you are a rental property investor, you should consider a 1031 exchange, particularly if your rental property has experienced substantial price appreciation and/or you have substantially depreciated the property for tax purposes—resulting in a substantial capital gain subject to taxation. The properties involved in the exchange must both be held for investment purposes and like-kind. The proceeds from the sale must go through a qualified intermediary. All the cash proceeds from the original sale must be reinvested in the replacement property. Any cash proceeds that you retain will be taxable. After selling your property, you have 45 days to find a like-kind property. You must receive the replacement property within 180 days after the date on which the taxpayer sells the original property or by the date in which your tax return is due for the year of the sale. To identify other property owners willing to participate in a like-kind exchange, see your real estate agent or go to Web sites offering contact information (e.g., www.for1031.com or 1031 Exchange Services at www. vestastrategies.com). This exchange has a great deal of tax implications. I strongly recommend seeking advice and counsel from the appropriate real estate professionals.

Another option available to rental property investors that is a sophisticated variation of a 1031 exchange is a tenants in common transaction or more popularly known as TICs. A TIC is a co-ownership structure in which investors own undivided fractional interests in an entire property and participate in a proportionate share of the net income and tax benefits. If you purchase a fractional interest in a TIC, you will receive a deed and title insurance corresponding to your ownership interest. The advantage of TICs over 1031 exchanges is that they are pre-packaged investments with property management and financing already in place. As with 1031 exchanges, seek advice and counsel from the appropriate real estate professionals before entering a TIC transaction.

A Seller-Financed Sale

If you have substantial equity in your rental property, you may want to consider seller financing when disposing of it. The benefits of seller financing are many. A seller-financed property will bring more investors to the table, giving you the opportunity to raise your asking price in the course of the bidding process. Since there is no third-party lender involved, the closing process is accelerated. Since seller-financing rates are a bit higher than conventional home loan rates, you will be earning a competitive return on your real estate. In essence, seller financing gets you into the mortgage lending business, which is the other side of the moneymaking equation in real estate. There is nothing wrong with participating in both sides—rental property ownership and the financing of rental property. If you believe in the real estate boom, there is money to be made on both sides, not to mention the benefits of diversification: owning and lending.

Most important, you may avoid—delay—paying a large capital gains tax on the sale of your property. The government could take at least 20 percent of your gain, depending on your financial situation.

Seller financing spreads the gain over time, because taxes are paid as payments are received.

Capital Gains Sales Exemption

This might sound crazy, but if you move into your rental property and live there for at least two years, you will be able to take advantage of the tax exemption designed for home owners who live in their homes. Actually, you could rent out your primary residence and move into your rental property. In effect, your rental property becomes your primary residence, and your former primary residence becomes a rental property—an exchange that will yield a terrific tax advantage. Through this exchange, you will be able to sell what was a rental property (and is now classified as your primary residence) and be exempt from paying taxes on the first $250,000 gain on the sale for an individual and $500,000 for a married couple. It may sound crazy, but there are a number of investors who follow this strategy. If your current living arrangements permit you to swap your owner-occupied and rental properties, it will help you avoid paying taxes.

Sell to a Family Member

If you want to keep your properties in the family, you could always sell a rental property to members of your family—say, one or more of your children—and seller-finance the transaction. This is a particularly smart move if you are concerned about estate tax issues. According to current tax law, you can give, as a gift, up to $11,000 per person per year of the outstanding balance of the funds owed to you by that person or persons. For example, let's assume you sold a rental property for $200,000 to your children and seller-financed the entire transaction. As seller transactions work, your children will sign a $200,000 promissory note, and there will be a mortgage on the property in this amount. If you have two children who now own the property, you can gift them (tax-free) $11,000 each, totaling $22,000, which would come off the loan balance every year. Of course, if you are married, your spouse can make the same $11,000 gift to each child. Together, you will be able to take $44,000 off the loan balance every year. After the first year, your children owe only $156,000. By the fourth year, you would have paid off the entire balance tax-free.

Cash-Out Refinancing

There is a strategy employed by active rental property investors that offers a fantastic opportunity to shield real estate gains from taxes: cash-out refinancings. If you are fortunate to be in a falling-interest-rate environment, a cash-out refinancing provides an opportunity to take cash (your profits) out of your properties without selling them. For a presentation of this strategy, please visit the end of Chapter 3, which provides a numerical example of this strategy.

Investing in Foreclosures and Fixer-Uppers

There is another world of property investing that I haven't touched on because of its unique nature—foreclosures and fixer-uppers. These property investments have great upside but also possess greater risks. I do not recommend that most readers invest in foreclosures and fixer-uppers. Not everyone is equipped to handle them. But there are certainly people who are comfortable with the risks and equally comfortable with working with properties that have problems. A foreclosure property may be in poor physical condition and require repair and/or renovation. A foreclosure could also involve some financial risk, since the original property owner gave up his or her rights on the property to the lender in question. A fixer-upper property definitely requires a meaningful amount of repair and/or renovation work. The buyer must be willing to assume all of these responsibilities.

Essentially, purchasing foreclosures and/or fixer-upper properties is the practice of purchasing real estate property at below-market prices. Let's look at both foreclosures and fixer-uppers more closely.

Foreclosures

A foreclosure is a home that has been repossessed by the lender because the property owner failed to pay the mortgage. When the property owner is late on three successive payments, the lender/bank will record a notice of default against the property. If the property owner fails to pay his delinquent debt payments, a trustee sale is held, and the property is sold to the highest bidder. The financial institution that has initiated the foreclosure proceedings usually will set the bid price at the loan amount. Thousands of homes are foreclosed every year due to job loss, credit problems, or unexpected expenses or death.

Where to Find Foreclosure Properties

There are many places to look for foreclosed properties to purchase. I suggest you visit the Web sites of the Department of Housing and Urban Development (www.hud.gov), Fannie Mae (www.fanniemae.com), and Freddie Mac (www.freddiemac.com). All have links to listings of foreclosed properties across the nation. Another useful Web site is www.homesdirect.com, a unit of eBay. You can also visit the Web sites of some of the nation's largest financial institutions, such as Bank of America and Wells Fargo, to look at their foreclosure offerings. And finally, you can find foreclosure properties in your local newspapers. In most states, a foreclosure notice must be published in the "legal notices" section of a local newspaper where the property is located or in the nearest city. Also, foreclosure notices are usually posted on the property itself and somewhere in the city where the sale is to take place.

Advantages of HUD Foreclosures

HUD acquires properties from lenders who foreclose on mortgages insured by FHA and VA. These properties are available for sale to both owners and investors. However, you can only purchase HUD-owned properties through a licensed real estate broker. HUD will pay the broker's commission of up to 6 percent of the sales price.

Purchasing an FHA/HUD foreclosure has its advantages with regard to down payments. The amount you have to put down varies depending on whether the property is eligible for FHA insurance. If the property is not eligible for insurance, the down payment may range from 5 to 20 percent. HUD homes are sold "as is," meaning limited repairs have been made but no structural or mechanical warranties are implied. If the property is eligible for FHA insurance, you may be eligible for a no-down-payment loan. When you bid on a foreclosure, you must put down what we call "earnest money." Earnest money is usually about 5 percent of the bid price, not to exceed $2,000 but not less than $500.

The VA also offers foreclosure properties, which can be purchased directly from HUD. VA properties are usually offered below market value, with a down payment as low as 2 percent for owner-occupied properties but 10 percent for investors.

Buyer Beware

Be careful when considering investing in a foreclosure. You may want to hire a foreclosure expert to take you through the process. Because it is a foreclosure, you need to have the house inspected. You also need to make sure that there are not any liens, undisclosed mortgages, or court judgments attached to the property.

There are other potential problems with purchasing foreclosure properties. For instance, if you are purchasing a foreclosure at what is called a legal sale, the sale may require all cash, and you may need to check the title of the property before the bid. Inspecting the interior of the property may not be possible before the bid in some situations. Further, the law may protect the financial institution or the heir (in case of an estate sale) from state disclosure laws, so you may not have recourse against the seller if there was misinformation about the property.

You also need to be careful bidding against professionals. A number of professional companies purchase foreclosure properties, and it would be difficult to compete against them with regard to a bid price and ability to turn around the property. Some professional investors work with the bank that is in foreclosure proceedings and restructure the loan on behalf of the troubled homeowner (borrower). For this service, the investor takes a percentage of equity (e.g., 30 percent) in the property and arranges a lease situation until the borrower is financially able to service the mortgage alone.

Financing a Foreclosure

It may be difficult to get financing for foreclosures. In many cases, you need to bring cash or a line of credit from your bank to the bidding table. If you are bidding on a bank-owned or Fannie Mae– or Freddie Mac–owned foreclosure property, you will have all of the financing options presented in Chapter 5 available to you.

Fix-Up Investing

Distressed properties, or what are commonly called fixer-uppers, are found in most communities, even in wealthy neighborhoods. A distressed property is one that has deteriorated over time and whose value has fallen below the market compared to other properties in the local area.

If you are looking for a quick return on your investment, purchasing a fixer-upper may get you there. Of course, everyone wants to find the worst property in the best neighborhood so that just a few cosmetic changes before resale will be extremely profitable. This is not a likely scenario. In actuality, there are two types of fixer-uppers: light and heavy.

Light and Heavy Fixer-Uppers

A light fixer-upper needs some minor (i.e., cosmetic) repairs. The expenditures to "fix up" a light fixer-upper are relatively modest. But upon completion, the property's value will rise, and more important, the property's rental income potential will rise as well.

A heavy fixer-upper needs some major repair and/or renovation work. This requires a significant investment of funds and time to accomplish the rehab. You will need a large borrowing capacity or on-hand cash to accomplish this. You will need to put money down to purchase the property, pay the carry costs, and pay for the improvements. Not everyone is prepared to take on these financial and resource responsibilities.

Evaluating and Targeting Fixer-Uppers

First off, I can't tell you how to evaluate a fixer-upper; I am not an expert in this field. If you are equally inadequate, I suggest you retain a general contractor and have him inspect and evaluate the targeted property. To develop a strategy for a fixer-upper purchase, I suggest the following:

A Six-Month Rehab Project

Purchase price	$150,000
Down payment	$ 30,000
Mortgage loan	$120,000
Rehab loan	$ 25,000
Total debt owed	$145,000
Closing purchase costs	$ 3,600
Property carry costs	$ 4,200
Rehab carry costs	$ 760
Selling costs	$13,500
Total costs	$22,060
Sales price	$215,000
Total costs	$22,060
Loan paybacks	$145,000
Original down payment	$ 30,000
Total outlay	$197,060
Profit (gain)	$ 17,940
Annualized return on investment	120%

- If you have little experience in rehabs, look for a light fixer-upper needing cosmetic work, such as a refurbish with paint, wallpaper, landscaping, and new appliances.
- Estimate the price differential between the light fixer-upper and properties in the neighborhood that are desirable. This will give you a sense of your profit potential.
- If you are looking for a heavy fixer-upper, avoid deteriorated properties that need major structural repairs; leave this up to the professionals—general contractors, and so on.
- If you identify a heavy fixer-upper that you believe you can handle, estimate the required expenses needed to bring the property value up to its full market potential to determine if it is within your own budget.
- Work with a real estate agent familiar with the neighborhood and get a sense of the bid range for the property.

- Evaluate the property with some professional guidance. If you are unable to do a walk-through, look at the surrounding neighborhood and comparable properties carefully.

Profit Analysis on Fixer-Uppers

Fixer-upper properties can bring you substantial profits because of the leveraging properties of real estate. Consider the following example: You buy a property in need of repairs for $150,000, knowing that if you bring this property up to speed, the comparables in the neighborhood are selling for about $215,000. You project that it will take you six months, from start to finish, to purchase, rehab, and sell the property. You estimate that it will cost you $25,000 for the rehab. Here is how the financial sequence will unfold: You will purchase the property for $150,000, with a $30,000 down payment, closing costs of $3,600, and a $120,000 loan (we assume a 1-year ARM at 4.5 percent). You will use your equity line at 4.5 percent for the $25,000 rehab expenditures. The mortgage and taxes payments will total about $4,200 for the six months. The interest paid on the equity line (rehab loan) totals $760 for the six months. When you sell the property, I assume you will pay a 6 percent commission, totaling $13,500. The debt-service costs plus closing and selling costs total $22,060. After selling the property for $215,000, you must subtract the $22,060, plus the retirement of the $145,000 of debt, plus the original $30,000 down payment to arrive at a profit gain of $17,940 for a six-month project. The annualized return on your original $30,000 investment is 120 percent! Not bad for a six-month project.

Financing Solutions

Heavy fixer-uppers (rehabs) are short-term projects that require short-term financing, usually no longer than one year, to cover the time to complete the renovations and sell the property. The financing option and down-payment requirements depend largely on the magnitude of the renovation and the projected time to completion. Keep in mind that in a rehab, when you first begin a project (maybe tearing down a portion of the property), the value of the property drops. The bank and/or lender worries that if you are unable to complete the project, they are left with an unfinished property with substantially less value. To be compensated for the added risk of a rehab, they may require a larger down payment, depending on the scope of the project. Rehab financing is usually based on the bank's prime lending rate, as well as an origination fee (1 to 2 percent), depending on the financial strength of the buyer. The buyer's experience in residential renovations always figures prominently in the financing terms. It pays to have experience in rehabs to get more favorable lending treatment.

Light fixer-uppers are usually projects that last less than three to six months and where the borrowed funds needed are a lot less than those for the heavy fixer-uppers. In fact, you could probably use your equity line of credit on your primary residence to finance the light fixer-upper improvements.

Both Fannie Mae and Freddie Mac offer rehab loans. For instance, you can qualify for a Fannie Mae long-term rehab program called a HomeStyle loan. It allows buyers to roll rehab costs into their mortgage, putting the money into an escrow account that a contractor can draw from to perform the work. However, the rates are a bit higher than a regular mortgage. Visit both www.Fanniemae.com and www.Freddiemac.com for more details on their rehab loan offerings.

Again, another financing option is for a buyer to use the equity in his own home for a credit line. This gives you flexibility to use the funds as you see fit.

Government Programs for Fixer-Uppers

There are government programs available to assist in fixer-upper purchases. The most popular is the HUD Section 203(k) loan program, which is designed to facilitate major structural rehabilitation of houses with one to four units that are more than one year old. Condominiums are not eligible. A 203(k) loan is usually done as a combination loan to purchase a fixer-upper property as is and rehabilitate it, or to refinance a temporary loan to buy the property and do the rehabilitation. It can also be done as a rehabilitation-only loan.

203(k) loans require a 15 percent down payment for investors (owner-occupants' down-payment requirements are only 3 to 5 percent). To be eligible for this loan, HUD requires that you spend a minimum of $5,000 on improvements. Other requirements are that you get two appraisals and submit work plans/specifications and cost estimates for the proposed work. Visit the HUD Web site at HUD.gov or call 202-708-2720 for more information about 203(k) loans.

The Veterans Administration (VA) also provides rehab loans to veterans who qualify.

For properties that qualify as historic rehabs, the government provides tax breaks/incentives. Qualified rehab buildings and certified historic structures currently enjoy a 20 percent investment tax credit for rehab expenses that qualify. A historic structure is one listed in the National Register of Historic Places or so designated by an appropriate state or local historic district also certified by the government. For more information, call the National Trust for Historic Preservation in Washington, D.C., at 202-588-6000.

Property Flipping

Both foreclosure and fixer-upper properties are a short-term investment for most property investors. You purchase the property at a discount (i.e., below market value) and "fix it up" and sell it at the market price. In many situations, your short-term transaction may be considered "property flipping." A house is considered "flipped" if it is bought and sold on the same day for a higher price, or sold at least at a 50 percent higher price if resold within six months. Often, these properties are sold to low-income home buyers.

Flipping has received a great deal of negative press and attention because some property investors have committed fraud, often through the use of faulty appraisals that improperly push up the value of the property. In many cases, the investor did no meaningful rehabilitation to the property in a flip. An investor who does put value back into the property via home improvements/rehab can justify reselling it at a higher value. The government is more concerned with fraudulent flippers who add no value to the property but sell it at an extraordinarily high profit margin, taking advantage of low-income households. There are times when the FHA will deny FHA insurance on properties that they considered to be flipped.

As an investor, you need to be aware when there is a high level of flipping in a particular local market area. A market highly concentrated in flipping could push home prices higher than they might otherwise be without flipping, suggesting that you may overpay at times. For example, it is thought that there was an excessive amount of property-flipping in Texas during the 1986–1992 period, which contributed to overpricing of some properties. Today, we are observing increased flipping transactions in some of the hot vacation markets, where an investor purchases a property for, say, $500,000 and within three months flips it for $600,000. But if flipping is done honestly, it is a legal transaction. The strategy is to identify underpriced properties whose prices can be reasonably marked up after some improvement/rehab is made. That is the essence of investing in foreclosures and fixer-uppers. Foreclosed properties are especially popular targets for property flippers, since the owners—the banks or other investors—often are looking to get whatever they can for the homes.

If you flip a property within one year, your gains will be subject to regular income-tax treatment. However, if you hold the property for more than one year, you are subject to the capital gains tax rate, which is currently 15 percent.

CHAPTER 10

TAKING ADVANTAGE OF THE
VACATION HOME BOOM

Today, one of the fastest-growing sectors of the real estate market is vacation homes. In 2003 (data is not yet available for 2004), Americans bought approximately 450,000 second homes, of which most were vacation properties. A vacation property, given favorable demographic trends, is a powerful, long-term investment, one that will significantly increase your ability to profit from today's real estate boom. In the most popular vacation markets, properties are appreciating at more than twice the rate of homes in the national housing market, suggesting that vacation purchases could be the most rewarding of all residential property investments.

In almost every resort area across the nation, vacation property sales and price appreciation are soaring. I predict that they will continue to rise, particularly in the most popular locations for second homes—places such as Hilton Head and Myrtle Beach, South Carolina; Park City, Utah; Naples, Florida; and Sunriver, Oregon. But there are thousands of locations where you can find the vacation home of your dreams. Many (aside from the hot spots) offer you the opportunity to purchase a property at a bargain price today, which means you can look forward to a strong return on your investment tomorrow.

If buying a home is the most important investment in your life, then buying a vacation home may well be the second most important investment in your life. In this chapter, I'll show you how to find the right vacation home for you—one whose value will grow. Sales and price appreciation information on second homes is difficult to come by, but I will provide you with a sense of the robust performance of the vacation property marketplace in the next section.

The Vacation Market Is Booming

Data is scarce on the performance of the vacation-home marketplace. The most recent national survey on second homes was conducted by the National Association of Realtors® back in 2002. There have been smaller second-home surveys conducted by NAR and others since, as well as a great deal of anecdotal local information. (There will be another national survey conducted in 2005.) Putting all of this together, I can confidently say that the vacation property market is booming. Second-home buying has become increasingly popular. As of 2003, there were approximately 6.6 million second homes in the United States, and most of these homes were classified as vacation properties. Vacation properties make up about 80 percent of the second-home sales (the remaining 20 percent are rental properties).

Second homes typically account for 5 to 6 percent of total home sales per year. More important, sales of second homes have risen steadily during the past twenty-five years. Second-home sales totaled 288,000 in 1989 and rose to 359,000 in 2001. They are estimated at 445,000 in 2003. I believe second-home sales will have approached 500,000 in 2004. Over the past fifteen years, sales of second homes have been explosive, increasing by 50 percent during the 1991–2004 period.

Getting a handle on home price appreciation for second homes is difficult, to say the least. According to the NAR second-home survey, second-home prices rose by 27 percent during the 1999 to 2001 period. The median second-home price was $162,000 in 2001, compared to a 1999 median home price of $127,800. Since then, we have had to rely on a great deal of anecdotal information from real estate agents across the nation, as well as some smaller surveys conducted by

NAR and others on second homes. The information gathered suggests that the second-home market has experienced brisk sales and strong price appreciation due to strong demand and lean inventories during the past several years. The median home price in 2004 is now probably in the range of $200,000 to $210,000.

A survey by EscapeHomes.com found that home values in ten select markets known to attract second and vacation home buyers rose 22 percent, from $419,000 to $511,000, during the period spanning the second quarter 2003 to the second quarter 2004. The EscapeHomes.com survey examined real estate agent and multiple-listing data from:

Bend, OR
Holden Beach, NC
Incline Village, NV
Myrtle Beach, SC
Naples, FL
Park City, UT
Santa Barbara, CA
Sarasota, FL
St. Helena, CA
Truckee, CA

Although this survey is too small and confined to be of much use to most buyers, it does suggest that the popular second/vacation-home markets can offer a better return on your investment than most primary residential real estate properties.

Who makes up this second-home market? According to the 2003 NAR *Profile of Home Buyers and Sellers Survey*, 78 percent of second homes are bought for recreational use (i.e., vacation). In recent years, there has been an increase in the number of home owners renting out their second homes for periods of time in order to generate investment income. In 2002, the median age of second-home buyers was forty-seven, compared with forty for all home buyers and thirty-two for first-time buyers. The median income of second-home buyers was about $86,000 in 2002, compared to $65,500 for buyers who own only one home.

I expect the second-home market to continue to experience robust growth over the next decade. Another 2003 NAR survey suggests that during the first quarter of 2003, 15 percent of home buyers purchasing a second home already owned a primary home or were buying a new primary home and keeping their existing one as a second home. Most housing forecasters I know expect Americans to purchase more than 4 million second homes over the next ten years, helping drive demand.

Factors Driving Demand for Vacation Properties

The same forces that created the housing boom for primary residences—historically low mortgage rates, a growing economy, and strong demographics—have had a major impact on the vacation-home market. Not surprisingly, the demographic trends are even stronger for the vacation market than they are for the primary market over the next decade, because of our aging population. Add to this a tight supply of vacation homes (particularly waterfront property) and you have the makings of a vacation-home explosion.

Here are the market factors that explain why the vacation-home market should continue to boom (barring an unforeseeable event such as a major war or a terrorist attack or, for some coastal shorelines, a heavy dose of hurricanes and tornadoes):

Single-Digit Mortgage Rates. Mortgage rates are expected to remain in single-digit territory for the remainder of this decade, providing relatively low-cost financing and therefore making vacation homes more affordable.

A Growing Economy. The U.S. economy is now in full expansion and promises to experience healthy, steady growth for the remainder of this decade. A growing economy generates jobs, increases paychecks, and bolsters consumer confidence, all essential ingredients driving demand for vacation getaways.

Healthy Home Price Appreciation. Home price appreciation has been robust throughout the past decade, creating an enormous amount of stored equity in our primary residences. In the past two years alone, price appreciation averaged about 7.5 percent per year. And numerous metropolitan areas have experienced double-digit price growth. Households are cashing out some of their stored equity through home equity loans and refinancing, using the proceeds as down payments for vacation homes. If you believe, as I do, that the overall real estate expansion will continue into the next decade, home price appreciation will also continue, providing further opportunities for households to have the financial wherewithal to purchase vacation homes.

Limited Supply. As demand for vacation homes continues to grow, thanks to the increasing number of retirees, the inventory of vacation homes continues to tighten. For example, only a finite number of vacation homes can be built on the waterfront property available. From the New England shores to the Carolina and Florida beaches, vacation-home construction has been slowing for lack of available space. Demand now exceeds supply in the most popular vacation spots, driving prices upward in the hottest areas. New vacation homes are being built farther and farther away from the most popular vacation locations. By purchasing a home in the prime vacation locations listed on page 186, you are likely to see a healthy price appreciation into the foreseeable future.

Baby Boom Demand. Aging boomers will create the greatest wave of demand for vacation property over the coming years. Today, many households of the baby boom generation are in their peak earning years and, as their kids finish college, can afford a second home. Boomers fall into an age group where their kids are getting older, their house is often paid off, and their incomes are high. And they are looking for a future vacation/retirement home. I expect boomers to drive the vacation/resort marketplace for the next five to ten years.

Retirees Are Living Longer. Because of improved health care, the retiree population is living longer. That means that retirees are staying in their homes longer, further depleting the inventory of available homes for sale in key vacation areas.

Capital Gains Tax Incentives. The capital gains exemption on $250,000 for individuals and $500,000 for married couples, a result of the tax code changes in 1997, provided a boost to vacation-home buying that continues today. The exemption has prompted many empty nesters (boomers with children moving out) to downsize to a smaller primary home and use some of their profit to buy a second home.

Information Technology. Thanks to the miracle of technology, we are able to spend more time in our vacation homes while still working, via the phone, fax, the Internet, and e-mail. Connecting with the office via high-speed modems and telecom service enables us to communicate with colleagues and customers and access company e-mail and voice mail systems, no matter where we are.

Investment Opportunities. The historically strong performance of real estate as an investment has also helped to drive up demand for second homes. More and more households are looking for ways to expand their real estate holdings, helping to increase demand for second homes.

Safe Haven. In a terrorist-sensitive world, the safety and security of real estate investments' risk/return ratio, as compared to the greater value fluctuations of stocks and bonds in an unpredictable time, is a factor that increases the demand for and the valuations of second homes.

Is It a Vacation Home—
Or a Rental Property Investment?

A vacation home is usually a property where you plan to spend a significant amount of time away from your primary residence. Many people use their second home for recreational purposes, as a way to fold into their lives something that they otherwise can't get—a peaceful rural setting, a nearby golf course, a mountain slope for skiing and summer recreation, a lakefront view, or an oceanside retreat. Some people buy a vacation home for the future, as a place to which they plan to retire. Some rent it out when it is not in use, helping to subsidize the cost of owning and maintaining it. But by definition, a vacation home is not a rental property—it is used primarily by the owner. If you own vacation property and rent it out for less than fourteen days, you are allowed to treat the property as if it were a primary residence for tax purposes. Since a vacation home generates a negative cash flow for most owners (the expenses of ownership almost always exceed any rental income it brings in), you will be able to deduct property and mortgage interest. You are allowed to deduct the interest associated with the first $1 million of debt used to purchase, build, or improve your principal residence and one vacation home. These deductions, however, are reduced for high-income taxpayers, as with any deduction. At a certain income level, the IRS no longer permits you 100 percent of itemized deductions; it begins a small phase-out of these deductions—including mortgage interest. (Please see your accountant for more information.) If you do not rent out your vacation home for more than fourteen days per year, you pay no tax on rental income. However, you cannot deduct rental expenses.

If you rent your vacation home for more than fourteen days per year, you have to treat your second home as rental property for tax purposes. The rental income less expenses and depreciation must be included in your taxable income. However, you may deduct property taxes and mortgage interest and all other rental expenses associated with the property, including depreciation. To the extent that rental expenses are not deductible in the year they are incurred, they can be carried forward to future years.

More and more households look to rent their vacation property to help defray costs. With vacation property values rising, this rental strategy makes sense. Nonetheless, for most vacation properties, particularly in the "hot" vacation locations, rental income will likely not cover your property expenses (including mortgage payments). One alternative is to look for a vacation property in a less desirable, less expensive market (e.g., Myrtle Beach, South Carolina). You may not have to rent your property as many weeks per year in a less expensive area for you to be able to financially carry the property.

Vacation Property Types

For purposes of expanding your real estate reach, vacation real estate falls into only two categories: single-family homes and condominiums.

Single-Family Detached Homes

A single-family vacation home is far and away the most popular kind of second home. A single-family property gives you far more privacy than a condominium, although it will cost more in maintenance and repair. Moreover, it has the potential to become your primary residence in the future, or your retirement home.

Condominiums

In recent years, condominiums have gained favor as a second home. First, they are relatively cheap compared with single-family houses, allowing more people to buy second homes. And the process of purchasing a unit in a condominium complex is less complicated and expensive. Some condominium associations have rental programs, helping you rent your condo when you are not using it. (However, there may be restrictions on the rental terms. For example, some developments only permit an investor to rent on an annual basis, not month-to-month.) Condos are a great way of getting into a vacation property without overstretching your financial resources.

But condos do come with other responsibilities and expenses. Condo fees (association fees) can be a significant part of your monthly expenses even if you are not using the property. If you are renting the property regularly, the association adds property management fees on top. You need to know what you will have to pay for things like finding renters, providing maid service, and extra maintenance costs. If you plan to rent your condominium, be conservative with your rental income projections. Request a copy of the financial statements showing the unit's rental income over the past three years.

Time-Shares

Time-shares became popular in the 1980s because most households could not afford a full-time vacation home. American developers got the idea of shared ownership from European developers, who success-fully used the time-share concept in the 1960s. Shared ownership reduces the costs for each owner, allowing developers to successfully market and sell properties to a greater number of people.

Time-shares are defined as buying the right to occupy a unit (one or more rooms with varying amenities) for a limited period of time (usu-ally one, two, or three weeks) during a certain time each year at a certain location. I don't regard time-shares as genuine real estate investments. Buying a time-share gives you the right to use the property for a specific period of time each year, but you have no real equity in it. You don't actually own the physical property in which the unit you use is located; you own a certain amount of time during which you can occupy a unit.

Time-shares are an investment in *vacation activities*, rather than an investment in real estate. As a result, I will not spend any more time on time-shares in this book.

The Benefits of Owning a Vacation Home

A vacation home is not for everyone. If you don't have the funds or income to carry the expenses of owning a vacation home, now is prob-ably not the right time to invest in one. Remember, if you own a pri-mary residence as well as a vacation home, you will be making *two* monthly mortgage payments, *two* property tax payments, payments on *two* sets of utility bills, and so on. But if you can afford the cost of own-ing a second home, vacation properties can provide you with a great opportunity to take advantage of the real estate boom. Perhaps more than any other property type, vacation homes offer the potential for considerable price appreciation over the long term. But there is no such thing as a free lunch. Vacation properties are expensive to purchase and expensive to maintain. In most cases, you are spending a good deal of money each month to carry the property. The payoff could be signifi-cant in the end, but the costs of getting there are not small. Vacation property ownership is not for everyone. But if you can afford to take this step, here are some of the benefits of vacation property ownership:

Tax Deductions. As I noted earlier, vacation property rented out for less than fourteen days is treated as if it were a primary residence for tax purposes, with all the tax benefits associated with home ownership.

Capital Gains Exclusion. If you sell your vacation home, it will qualify for a one-time capital gains exclusion of $250,000 ($500,000 in a joint return) if you live in it and use it as a principal residence for at least two of the five years before the sale. If you rent your vacation home, you may be able to defer tax on the sale by purchasing another investment property under a Section 1031 exchange. (See your accountant for more details.)

Building Wealth Through Amortization. Just like your primary residence, you can build wealth through the amortization of your vacation-home mortgage loan. As you pay off the principal balance on your second-home mortgage loan, you are in effect increasing your equity (wealth). Over time, you build equity in your home while paying down the outstanding loan, until you eventually own the home entirely. Amortization by itself cannot make you wealthy, but combined with price appreciation, it can increase your wealth significantly.

Given the continuing real estate boom, price appreciation is perhaps the greatest financial benefit of purchasing a vacation home. It can be one of the most secure investments you can make with regard to price appreciation vis-à-vis other real estate investments. As already mentioned, vacation-home price appreciation in many areas of the nation is significantly greater than the appreciation of non-vacation-property real estate, particularly in the coastal vacation spots. Even though data is scarce, the NAR survey on second-home properties suggests that price appreciation on vacation homes has been hovering in the double-digit range for the past several years (it was 27 percent in 1999 to 2001, and anecdotal evidence suggests more of the same in 2002 to 2004).

The Happiness Factor. A second home, if considered and chosen carefully, in addition to being a sound investment, offers home owners years of enjoyment and an opportunity to get away from the often hectic environment of their everyday community and home, in a setting that is often more rural, private, and scenic, and that offers different amenities than their primary residence.

The X Factor. There is another potential savings as well. Do you keep records of expenses for some of your previous vacations—airfares, costs of rooms in hotels, resorts, condominium rentals, meals in restaurants, tips to (seemingly) virtually everybody at the places you stay and eat, and all the other big and little costs, from rental cars to taxicabs? If you do, you know how much money such vacations cost—thousands to tens of thousands over the years. Owning a vacation home—especially if it's close enough that you don't have to fly to get to it—will save you a lot of money on travel and accommodations over the year, a factor not everyone considers.

Leveraged Investment. The investment you made in a vacation home is the cost of the down payment plus the monthly expenses. At some point during the life of the mortgage loan, your costs turn into income if you are renting the property out part time. The greater the cash flow, the greater your leveraged return on investment.

A Retirement Option. Some home owners purchase a second home with the expectation that the property will eventually become their retirement home. Such advance planning puts them way ahead of where they would be on their payments and equity investment if they waited until their retirement years to buy. Again, prices are sure to rise in the succeeding decades as 76 million baby boomers reach retirement age—especially in the hottest markets. By buying now before the first wave of baby boomers reaches retirement, you'll essentially be able to buy your future home at a discount. Bear in mind that the 1997 federal tax law changes allow couples to avoid paying capital gains taxes on profits of up to $500,000 on the sale of a primary residence.

Investing in a Vacation Home

Here are the six steps I've developed to help in evaluating and choosing a second home:

Step 1: *Define your second-home objectives.*

Step 2: *Select a vacation environment.*

Step 3: *Identify the prime (high-growth) vacation markets satisfying your environment criteria.*

Step 4: *Contact a real estate agent to work with to find the right house for you.*

Step 5: *Select a lender and financing vehicle, and obtain preapproval.*

Step 6: *Make an offer on a property.*

Step 1: Define Your Second-Home Objectives

Before you make a decision to purchase a vacation home, I suggest you define your goals. Write them on a sheet or two of paper. You should be able to categorize your objectives in one of two ways: Are you buying a second home for personal reasons or for financial reasons? If you are considering buying a second home for personal reasons (to have a getaway in a beautiful setting), ask yourself the following questions:

- Where do you want your vacation home to be located? (On the waterfront? Near the beach? In the mountains? Near a golf course? Are you looking for a warmer or a more seasonable climate?)
- How far are you willing to travel to a vacation home? Are you expecting to drive or will you have to fly to get to it? Are you willing to put up with the hassle of getting to and from the house every weekend/month/year if it is located far away?
- How big a vacation home do you want (both in square feet and in number and types of rooms, and the amount of property you hope to obtain)? How much maintenance and repair work are you willing to take on?

- Are you looking for special features, such as a swimming pool, a boat dock, easy access to ski lifts, or an outdoor deck?
- Is this a home that you will live in when you eventually retire?

If you are thinking of a second home primarily as a financial investment, ask yourself the following questions:

- How much can you afford to pay monthly on a vacation home in taxes, maintenance and upkeep, and mortgage?
- How long do you expect to hold on to the property?
- How much do you hope to eventually profit from this purchase? What is the expected price appreciation in the area you've chosen?
- Are you planning to rely on rental income to help carry some of the annual costs?
- What type of financing do you expect to obtain?
- Can you afford to carry two mortgages and pay for extra utilities and maintenance costs for the period of time you intend to own the house? How does this investment fit into your total personal finance portfolio?
- Have you considered the tax consequences of owning a vacation home?

Step 2: *Select a Vacation Environment*

Decide what type of vacation setting you desire and identify a number of locations that meet your environment criteria. Step 3 will then help you to rank these locations by popularity and future supply and demand.

Select the kind of location you wish and then establish what kind of home you're looking for. We all have different criteria for choosing the best place to vacation and live. For example, say you want a beach vacation environment. Your criteria might be something like this:

- A small beach town filled with single-family beach homes, a main street with quaint stores and a few restaurants, and some scattered beach activities like parasailing, snorkeling, and jet skiing.

Or your criteria might be:

• A large beach-vacation market, like Myrtle Beach, South Carolina, filled with single-family beach houses and condos, with a great deal of shopping, amusement parks, beach activities, golf courses, and so on.

I would categorize vacation (geographic) locations in the following manner:

1. Beach
2. River
3. Lake
4. Mountains
5. Rural
6. City
7. Close to home
8. Other

From these vacation locations, you need to identify the type of vacation resort/activity you desire. You might characterize the vacation resorts/activities in the following manner:

1. Beach activities
2. Boating
3. Skiing
4. Fishing
5. Mountain climbing/rafting
6. Golf
7. Tennis
8. Other sports
9. City activities (plays, movies, etc.)
10. Other

Selecting a vacation location is a personal decision that only you can make. No one can help you with these decisions. When you finally select the kind of vacation spot you want (e.g., a vacation home on a lake or river with golf/tennis nearby), there are several resources you can utilize to find your dream vacation location. First, there are many real estate companies that specialize in resort/vacation properties. Visit their sites. One of the top sites is EscapeHomes.com. You can input your search criteria into their property listings database and identify some areas (regions, metros, counties, etc.) across the nation that satisfy your environment needs. Or visit the largest residential property site for home listings, REALTOR.com, and input your criteria for a vacation location and property type as well.

Step 3: Identify the Prime (High-Growth) Vacation Markets

Once you decide what type of vacation living you desire—beach, ski resort, mountains, and so forth—identify the high-growth and, more important, the future high-growth vacation locations that appeal to you. This will take some time, energy, and resources on your part.

Hot Market Characteristics

What factors determine a hot vacation market? Why are some markets hot and others not? Once you decide what type of vacation environment you desire (golf community, skiing, etc.), there are several factors that I recommend when determining whether a particular vacation area is hot and will remain hot:

1. Migration trends
2. Supply of vacation homes
3. Price appreciation
4. Home sales growth

This is not difficult information to obtain for a particular vacation area. Local real estate agents should be able to provide you with most of this information.

Monitor the Hot-Market Lists

After typing vacation properties into the Google search engine (Google.com), you will find many magazine articles on hot vacation markets, with some of them offering a top vacation-market list. In addition, two of the more closely followed lists on vacation markets are offered by EscapeHomes.com and NeighborhoodScout.com. EscapeHomes.com created a list of the top ten second-home markets based on the quantity of site visitors' requests for information about locales, plus research and conversations with chambers of commerce and real estate agents. NeighborhoodScout.com pinpointed thirty emerging vacation-home markets from 23,000 coastal and mountain communities, based on six criteria: affordability (relative to surrounding area), peace and quiet, safety, educated neighbors, a mix of rental and owner-occupied homes, and excellent public schools.

EscapeHomes.com compiled its own list of the top ten emerging second-home markets nationwide:

Darby, MT
Fairmont, MN
Fergus Falls, MN
Gualala, CA
Kern River, CA
North Fork Valley, CO
Pinetop-Lakeside, AZ
Sisters, OR
Sitka, AL
Spearfish, SD

The following are NeighborhoodScout's top ten communities on the Atlantic/Gulf Coasts, the Pacific Coast, and in the Rocky Mountain region from north to south:

Atlantic/Gulf Coast Region
Bristol, ME
Narragansett, RI
Clinton, CT
Somers Point, NJ
Leonardtown, MD

Blufton, SC
Englewood, FL
Cape Coral, FL
Daphne, AL
Ocean Springs, MS

Pacific Coast Region
Juneau, AK
Oak Harbor, WA
Gold Beach, OR
Ferndale, CA
Gualala, CA
Los Osos, CA
Aliso Viejo, CA
Cambria, CA
Kaunakakai, HI
Captain Cook, HI

Rocky Mountain Region
Phillipsburg, MT
McLeod, MT
Craigmont, ID
Wallace, ID
Ten Sleep, WY
Saratoga, WY
Hanksville, UT
Woodland Park, CO
Bailey, CO
Pena Blanca, NM

My advice is to continually monitor these hot-vacation-market lists. Call the real estate agents (or e-mail them) in these markets and request some of the hot-market characteristics, such as home sales volume, home price appreciation, and the inventory of homes in that local vacation market. The markets may be hot now, but do they have staying power over the next five to ten years? No one has the definitive answer to this question, but the more information you gather, the more comfortable you will be when deciding on purchasing a vacation property.

EscapeHomes.com is perhaps the best-known and largest site devoted to helping buyers find vacation homes. Input the criteria that matter to you: lifestyle, price, type of vacation home, location. You'll then be shown numerous listings that fit your specifications. It is an excellent way to begin a vacation home search before contacting a real estate agent. And again, you can always visit the nation's largest home listings Web site—REALTOR.com—to identify vacation locations and property types.

You may also want to contact local chambers of commerce and/or local governments to gather additional information about their economies. They can provide you with a great deal of material, particularly your target location's overall economic health, including employment, household growth, and housing starts.

Step 4: Contact a Real Estate Agent

Once you've picked the towns you're interested in exploring more seriously, it is time to contact a local real estate agent. Most likely, you will be purchasing a vacation property in a location with which you are not intimately familiar. How do you identify a real estate agent to work with? There are several ways. First, ask friends if they can recommend a real estate agent. If the vacation location is within driving distance, visit the town and drop by several real estate offices. For example, if you are seeking to purchase a beach home, drive toward the beach—there should be several real estate offices close by. They expect you to drop in and discuss potential vacation purchases. Or you can visit REALTOR.org and input the selection criteria for the vacation location you desire. As you look at the different property listings, there will be real estate agents associated with each listing, with their phone numbers and/or e-mail addresses.

A real estate agent can provide valuable information for you on the market, the town, the resort community, and more, as well as find suitable properties for you to consider. Outline your personal and financial objectives to your agent. Armed with that information, he or she can go to work for you. I suggest that you:

1. Travel to your desired vacation location and meet with the real estate agent who most favorably impressed you. Drive around with him or her and get a feel for the area and neighborhoods. Review your personal and financial objectives together.
2. Let your agent recommend several potential neighborhoods in the area that satisfy your criteria.
3. On an ongoing basis, ask your agent to suggest vacation properties that satisfy your criteria with regard to size, price, quality, and so on. Ask your agent to e-mail you the property listings in detail, including potential rental income and virtual tours, where available.
4. Together, identify a number of properties to consider and then visit each one with your real estate agent. If the houses fall short of your expectations, sit down with your agent again and refine what it is you're looking for.

Step 5: *Select a Lender and Financing Vehicle*
1. Ask your real estate agent for a referral to a local lender who finances vacation properties in the area. Compare the lender's terms with those of one or two other lenders in the area, as well as a lender back in your hometown.
2. Request a Good Faith Estimate from the local lender for the financing of a hypothetical vacation home in your price range. This will give you a good idea of the closing costs (up front) that you will have to pay to purchase the property and reassure you, and your prospective lender, that you have the necessary resources to afford a second home in the price range you've targeted. In today's market, I suggest you get preapproval for a loan up to a certain amount, to give yourself an edge with the buyer if the house you are interested in receives multiple bids.
3. Review financing solutions with your lender. Obtaining financing for a vacation home is more difficult than buying a primary resi-

dence. Vacation home loans tend to require more money down and carry higher interest rates. This is because buyers are more likely to default on a second home or vacation home than their primary residences if they run into hard times. Underwriters are looking for people with good credit and greater assets than someone purchasing a primary residence, because they know the buyer will be making two mortgage payments.

Generally, for a vacation home, borrowers will have to pay at least 20 percent down to get the best interest rates. Thanks to home equity loans, reverse annuity mortgages, and other financing opportunities, raising money for a down payment and/or securing a mortgage on a second home, however, is easier and less costly than it used to be.

Since you are responsible for paying off two mortgages, your lender may require you to show that you have funds in a reserve (at least two to four months of payments) to cover your payments, in case you are faced with unanticipated financial or other problems. And if you plan to turn the vacation home into a rental property (renting the property for more than fourteen days a year), the lender will treat the purchase as an investment and charge you a higher mortgage rate (it could be at least ¼ percent higher). The type of loan (fixed-rate, adjustable, or balloon) you select will depend on your financial situation and your financial objectives. (Are you looking for the lowest possible monthly payment, or are you more interested in paying off the loan in a shorter period of time? Do you plan to own the house for the foreseeable future or sell it for a profit within the next five years?) Most vacation-home owners take out 30-year or 15-year mortgage loans. But an increasing number are obtaining adjustable-rate mortgages to keep the monthly payments down.

In the vacation market, some households are cash-rich and can pay for their vacation home entirely in cash. This way, they are not burdened with the monthly mortgage costs of a vacation property. But the majority of investor/buyers of vacation homes take out mortgages to finance their home. Read Chapter 5 for a full discussion of financing options available to you. Be sure to discuss them in detail with your lender.

Step 6: *Make an Offer on a Property*

On a cash basis, you will probably not make money during the early years of vacation-home ownership. But over the longer term, you may earn a substantial profit. To help you in evaluating and bidding on a second home, I will assume that you are treating this property purely as a vacation home and will rent the property for less than fourteen days per year. If you decide to rent out the property for a significant amount of time during the year, you must consider this purchase a rental property. I suggest you read Chapter 9 to learn the ins and outs of buying rental property.

When you are ready to make a bid on a vacation home, keep in mind that your objectives are different from those in buying a primary residence. Valuing a vacation property should be based on two criteria: (1) Can you afford to carry the property every year (can you pay the monthly carrying costs)? and (2) What price appreciation do you expect in the years ahead?

To begin, let me illustrate the cash flows of a simple vacation home. Unlike rental property investments (where investors try to leverage their acquisitions with low down payments), the down payment on vacation properties is usually higher and can vary a great deal. This is because most people purchase vacation properties for enjoyment rather than for investment. They are willing to put more money down toward the purchase to keep their monthly mortgage costs down.

Let's assume that you want to purchase a two-bedroom, two-bath vacation condominium in Naples, Florida, for an asking price of $250,000. Your purchase strategy is to put 20 to 40 percent down and finance the remaining balance with a 30-year, 7 percent mortgage loan. How much do you bid for the condo? Do you bid the asking price? Do you underbid or overbid? Of course, the price you eventually pay has a great deal to do with market conditions (e.g., is the market tight or sluggish?). But to make an intelligent, informed purchase decision, you need to follow the procedure below to run the before-tax cash-flow calculations, then estimate the tax benefits from vacation property ownership.

Before-Tax Cash Flows

Before entering the bidding process, you should know how much you are willing to pay to carry the property. If you have fully paid off the loan on your primary home, you may be willing to pay more per month. For example, let's say you are able to handle up to $1,000 per month. So the maximum price you can bid will be a price that generates a negative monthly cash flow of $1,000. Prices lower than the maximum will cost you less per month, improving your financial position.

The $1,000 per month represents an additional investment in owning a vacation property. Of course, the big payoff comes when you sell, in the form of the house's price appreciation and your accumulation of principal as a result of your mortgage payments. But you also should factor in that if you did not own a vacation home, you would be spending a certain amount of money every year on vacation accommodations. Let's assume that in the absence of owning a vacation home, you would spend two weeks of vacation on rent or hotel costs for your family every year, totaling $5,000.

To calculate before-tax cash flow, let's assume that you bid the asking price, $250,000, for the condo. Your real estate agent says you can expect to earn $5,000 by renting out the condo for fourteen days during the year. You will also save $5,000 on vacation expenses by purchasing a vacation home. So your total income and savings comes to $10,000. You now need to add up your expenses in the financing and management (upkeep) of the property. Again, let's do this assuming a 20 percent down payment, a 30 percent down payment, and a 40 percent down payment.

With 20 percent down, you will obtain a 30-year $200,000 mortgage loan—$250,000 minus $50,000 (20 percent) at 7 percent interest. Using a standard amortization table, you will pay $15,967 in annual mortgage payments. Let's say property taxes are estimated at $1,700 for the year. Hazard insurance (protection from fire, wind, flood, etc.) costs $200 per year (in some places it is a great deal more). And the condo fees are assumed to run $300 per month, or $3,600 for the year. Finally, you need to put $2,000 aside in a reserve for repairs and maintenance of the property (usually 1% of the property's value). Adding the mortgage payment, property tax, insurance, condo dues, and repair/maintenance brings us to a total of $23,467 in expenses. Subtract from this amount your rental revenues and vacation expense savings, and that gives you a negative annual cash flow of $13,467, or a negative monthly cash flow of $1,122.

With a 30 percent down payment (and a mortgage loan of $175,000), the annual cash flow is $11,471, or $956 per month. At 40 percent down, the annual negative cash flow is $9,475, or $790 per month.

Assuming you want to keep your monthly costs to $1,000, you are able to bid $250,000 for the condo only if you put down 30 percent or more. At 20 percent down, the $1,122 negative monthly cash flow substantially exceeds your predetermined limit.

However, there are some favorable tax write-offs associated with vacation-home ownership that improve your after-tax cash flow. The write-offs are similar to those you get from owning your own home. Let's continue with the example of the condo used above. You are allowed to deduct mortgage interest and property taxes from your federal income tax. Assuming you are in a 31 percent tax bracket, a 20 percent down-payment scenario will give you a tax deduction of $5,022, reducing the monthly after-tax cash flow to negative $704, well under your limit of $1,000 per month. So on an after-tax basis, you *could* purchase this vacation property with only 20 percent down. (Your monthly costs will be higher than this, but you'll receive the savings with the filing of your tax return.) Of course, you could be subject to the alternative minimum tax under certain financial situations. Consult with a professional tax advisor before making a purchase decision.

CASH FLOW: BEFORE AND AFTER TAX
(With 20, 30, and 40 Percent Down Payments)

Bid price	$250,000	$250,000	$250,000
Down payment	$50,000	$75,000	$100,000
Loan balance	$200,000	$175,000	$150,000
Rental income	$5,000	$5,000	$5,000
Vacation expense savings	$5,000	$5,000	$5,000
Total cash income/savings	$10,000	$10,000	$10,000
Expenses			
Mortgage payment	$15,967	$13,971	$11,975
Property tax	$1,700	$1,700	$1,700
Hazard insurance	$200	$200	$200
Condo dues	$3,600	$3,600	$3,600
R & M reserve	$2,000	$2,000	$2,000
Total expenses	$23,467	$21,471	$19,475
Annual cash flow	($13,467)	($11,471)	($9,475)
Monthly cash flow	($1,122)	($956)	($790)
Tax deductions (31% bracket)			
Mortgage interest deduction	$4,495	$3,875	$3,255
Property taxes	$527	$527	$527
Total deductions	$5,022	$4,402	$3,782
Annual after-tax cash flows	($8,445)	($7069)	($5,693)
Monthly after-tax cash flows	($704)	($589)	($474)

The two tables on the following page illustrate the potential wealth gain from owning the condo in the example above.

If the $250,000 condo averaged a relatively low 3 percent annual price appreciation, it would be valued at $290,000 in 5 years, $336,000 in 10 years, and $390,000 in 15 years. Your capital gains from such appreciation would be $40,000, $86,000, and $140,000 for the 5, 10, and 15 years, respectively. Of course, the 3 percent appreciation is a conservative figure—it may be far higher or, in an extreme case, lower in a given year. If the condo averaged a more robust 10 per-

VACATION HOME PRICE APPRECIATION

Price Appreciation	5 years	10 years	15 years
3 percent	$290,000	$336,000	$390,000
5 percent	$319,000	$407,000	$520,000
7 percent	$351,000	$492,000	$690,000
10 percent	$403,000	$648,000	$1,044,000

cent annual appreciation, it would be worth $403,000 in 5 years, $648,000 in 10 years, and $1,044,000 in 15 years! And in the hottest vacation home locations, this is quite possible. The capital gains from the appreciation if you were to sell would be $153,000 and $398,000 and $794,000 for 5, 10, and 15 years, respectively.

Of course, you need to also factor in the equity you've built up from paying off your principal, according to the 30-year amortization schedule of your loan. After 5 years, you would have accumulated about $14,000 in principal; in 10 years, $32,000 in principal; and in 15 years, $57,000. This equity needs to be added to your appreciation–generated wealth gains to get a true accounting of the total gain on the vacation property. For example, if your vacation home, on average, experienced a 7 percent annual rate of appreciation, the total wealth gain after 15 years would be $497,000 ($440,000 in capital gains + $57,000 in prin-

CUMULATIVE WEALTH GAIN
(From Original $250,000 Purchase Price)

Wealth Gain	5 years	10 years	15 years
3 percent	$40,000	$86,000	$140,000
5 percent	$69,000	$157,000	$270,000
7 percent	$101,000	$242,000	$440,000
10 percent	$153,000	$398,000	$794,000
Paid-off principal	$14,000	$32,000	$57,000

cipal). This is an example of how a vacation home can increase your overall wealth. You turned an initial $75,000 down payment (30 percent) and less than $1,000 in monthly costs into a $572,000 gain in 15 years! Not bad for the opportunity to live in your own vacation home, with 15 years of enjoyment and memories.

Vacation Home Property Management

Many vacation homes are located far from your primary residence—a plane ride away, or an eight-hour-or-more drive by automobile—particularly if the property is at a beach or in the mountains. But even if it is just an hour or two from your primary home, it is likely that you will need some help looking after your property, since you will often not be there to do it personally. If you are planning on renting your property for less than fourteen days, you don't need the full services of a property management company. However, if you are planning on renting out the property for a significant amount of time throughout the year, I suggest you get a professional management company.

A No-Rental Vacation Property

Assuming that you are not actively renting your vacation home (i.e., renting it for less than fourteen days per year), there is no need to hire a full-time professional property management company. This is your home, and just like your primary residence, if something breaks while you are there, you either fix it yourself or call a repairman. If you are away from your home for long periods of time—say, the entire winter—you may want to contact a property management company who would be willing to monitor the home for a small fee and take care of any repairs or emergencies.

A Rental Vacation Property

If you are planning to actively rent your vacation home, you have little choice but to hire a professional property management company. A vacation property management company will charge you between 10 and 30 percent of rental income. The fee is closer to 20 to 30 percent for most beach vacation rentals. Some resort projects that developers manage could hit 50 percent. But you can expect a great deal from a property management company. Make sure to hire one with an excellent reputation—ask your neighbors or your local real estate agent in the area—because you are depending on it to protect and maintain your property.

The most important service that a property management company provides is to find tenants for your property. It will try its hardest to fill up your rental calendar during the peak season and even some months during off-peak. This is because the company gets a percentage of the rental income. A good property management company can attract prospective tenants whom you could never get on your own. The company will list your property in appropriate multiple listing services, vacation magazines, and so on, to find prospective tenants. It will also take applications from and screen prospective vacationers, negotiate and issue lease agreements, and collect security deposits and rent. It will also check the tenants in and out and collect keys upon departure. It will contract with a cleaning service to maintain the property after each tenant has departed. It will also provide emergency maintenance service for unexpected problems, such as plumbing and electrical. And finally, it will usually transfer funds to the property owner on a monthly basis and furnish an itemized financial statement.

Some vacation-home owners avoid the expenses of a property management company, particularly in handling all of the rentals throughout the year. But this is extremely difficult to do if you are far away from the property.

Vacation Purchase Strategies in a Boom

There are not many fancy strategies for purchasing a vacation home, particularly in a real estate boom. You simply identify a hot vacation market that meets your vacation criteria—and then buy and hold. Except in warm climates like Florida, try to buy in the winter, when the demand for vacation homes is at a low (a ski resort would be another exception). After five or ten or fifteen years, you should see a substantial increase in value. The difficult task is identifying what the hot vacation markets will be. Sometimes you can get lucky and simply stumble upon an emerging hot market, but most of the time you need to do your homework.

But a boom environment makes it easier to be successful in buying vacation homes. Again, in recent years, the boom in the vacation-home market has outpaced the primary-home market. And it is likely to last longer. How can you take advantage of the vacation-home boom? Stay ahead of the crowds and follow the boomers.

Stay Ahead of the Crowds

If you play follow the leader, you will find it hard to make significant money in the vacation-home market. There are approximately 76 million baby boomers in America in their peak earning years, headed toward retirement. They are beginning to buy vacation homes in increasing numbers. In the next five to fifteen years, they will be retiring into vacation homes. Millions every year will be looking to purchase a vacation home as a second home. Why? Because they have the money. Millions of other boomers will be preparing to purchase a vacation property as a retirement home during the next decade and a half. Either way, as I've pointed out before, the boomers will drive demand in the vacation-home marketplace during the next five to fifteen years. This is not the time to follow the leader. If you follow, you will pay a very high premium for a vacation home five to ten years down the road. Now is the time to stay ahead of the boomer crowd. My best advice regarding the vacation-home market is to buy now. Here are some suggestions on how to do this:

1. **Purchase a vacation rental property.** If you can't afford to own a nonrental vacation home, purchase a vacation property that you can rent out full-time, to defray your operating costs. Your goal is to begin converting the property to a full-time vacation home for yourself in five to ten years. This strategy can be very successful for households that cannot afford the large monthly cash drain of a full-time vacation home. Renting it out full-time will lower your monthly costs while

building equity over the years. Eventually, your rent income will cover your fixed mortgage costs.

2. **Purchase a nonvacation rental property.** If you cannot afford the monthly costs of even a full-time vacation rental property, take an intermediate step: Buy an affordable nonvacation rental property. (See Chapter 9.) There are many rental properties where the after-tax cash flows are close to zero, or even earn you money each month. If you purchase a rental property today, you are indirectly taking advantage of the vacation market boom by realizing price appreciation in the general real estate boom. After five years or so, you can take your capital gains and principal accumulation and purchase a vacation property.

3. **Use the equity you have built up in your primary home to buy a vacation home.** If you can afford to buy a vacation home now, take advantage of the stored equity in your primary home. A cash-out refinance transaction (see Chapter 3) permits you to use the stored equity as a down payment on a vacation home.

4. **Tighten your family budget.** This requires setting spending priorities. For example, you may decide to forgo an expensive vacation for several consecutive years and save $10,000 or more for a down payment on a vacation home. Or you may hold on to your car for an extra few years, rather than spend $500 a month on new car payments, saving you $12,000 in two years for a down payment. Or you may do both, saving you $22,000!

5. **Empty-nester trade-downs.** If your children have moved out of your home, as an empty nester you have the one-time ability to sell your primary residence and downsize to a smaller primary residence, using the remaining capital gains to purchase a vacation home. Again, you'll avoid paying capital gains tax on the first $250,000 of gains for an individual and the first $500,000 of gains for a married couple.

6. **Obtain adjustable-rate financing.** Taking out a 1- or 3-year adjustable-rate mortgage on a vacation home may reduce your monthly mortgage payments by $200 to $400, depending on the size of the loan. This could be enough to make a vacation home purchase viable. But make sure that you can withstand the increased monthly payments if interest rates rise significantly.

7. **Purchase a vacation home with another family.** Spreading the costs of vacation-home ownership has become increasingly popular in recent years. If you can find another family or relatives that share your personal and financial views of vacation-home ownership, this may be a viable option.

8. **Purchase a less-than-ideal vacation home.** All right, you may need to forgo your dream vacation home. But by lowering your sights, you may be able to buy a perfectly wonderful vacation home in a less-than-red-hot market, or a smaller home in the neighborhood you most desire. Be open to considering other options.

9. **Move cash out of stocks into a vacation home.** This option will be blasphemy for some. But there are an increasing number of households across America who are taking money out of the stock and bond market to purchase real estate. I believe so strongly in the real estate market that I urge you to consider diversifying your investment portfolio by transferring some of your investment funds out of stocks and bonds and reinvesting them in real estate. Using stock/bond investments to purchase a vacation home may be one of the most successful investments in the long run you ever make.

Follow the Footprints

The early boomers who are buying vacation homes now are literally leaving footprints in the sand (beach) and/or dirt and snow (mountains and ski areas). Buy where the boomers are buying and your vacation home will generate strong wealth gains when you are ready to sell. Where and how can you track their footprints? I am able to identify several trends that the boomers appear to be following:

1. **Beach, mountain, and ski resorts.** Boomers are attracted to beach (ocean) resorts, mountain resorts, and ski resorts. These are the three vacation spots in which supply is tight and prices are rising because of steady, strong demand. During the next fifteen years, I expect that an excess demand for these limited-supply vacation resorts will pump up prices to a point where it will become increasingly difficult for many investors to find properties they can afford to purchase. That

means you should look for properties in these areas sooner rather than later.

2. **Affordable towns with double-digit price appreciation.** Some boomers are attracted to towns that are near (within an hour's driving time) beach, mountain, and ski resorts. These towns are more affordable (right now), but boomer demand is driving prices upward.

3. **Close proximity to primary residence.** Some boomers are choosing to purchase vacation homes close to their primary residences. This trend has been observed since the 9/11 terrorist tragedies. A certain percentage of boomers no longer want to travel far away from their primary residence. They want to stay close to their friends and family even in retirement. Rising sensitivity to terrorism has some boomer households desiring to stay near home where they feel comfortable and secure. Boomers also probably make up the majority of households who use their second homes on weekends and holidays throughout the year—if the travel time from primary to secondary home is manageable.

4. **Rural/small-town telecommuting homes.** Boomers are the first generation to take full advantage of the great technological innovations of the past several decades, which has led to increased purchases and use of vacation homes. Boomers who are not yet retiring are purchasing vacation homes earlier in their lives when their job creates an opportunity for telecommuting. These households are attracted to vacation homes in small towns and/or rural areas where they can telecommute to their jobs. Some of these boomers are "consultants" and need just a laptop computer, a cell phone, and voice mail. Others work for companies that permit telecommuting and provide them with the necessary technology to make it happen. As long as they are close to some mode of transportation—airports, trains, or highways—that enables them to reach the office fairly quickly when necessary, they find telecommuting workable. These footprints are more difficult to identify, since they are scattered outside of most major metropolitan areas of the nation. But there will be more and more boomers who will take the telecommuting plunge, driving up vacation property values, so you need to stay ahead of this crowd.

INVESTING IN REAL ESTATE THROUGH REITS, MUTUAL FUNDS, AND OTHER VEHICLES

I f you are still intimidated by the process of investing in real estate beyond the property you live in, there are ways to invest in real estate that do not make any demands on your time or require any special expertise. Known as indirect real estate investing, such investment strategies involve using real estate's two primary investment rivals: stocks and bonds. Depending on how much you have to invest and your investment objectives, you can purchase shares in real estate investment trusts (REITs), real estate mutual funds, or equity shares of real estate and real estate–related companies. You may also purchase mortgage-backed securities issued by Fannie Mae, Freddie Mac, or Ginnie Mae. Or you can purchase shares in a real estate limited partnership.

The Boom Is Residential, Not Commercial

Remember, the real estate boom is in residential, not commercial, real estate. Your real estate purchases, whether direct or indirect, should be confined to the residential side of real estate. Commercial real estate values are highly vulnerable to the ups and downs of the general economy—which explains why investments in this area have not performed well over the past half decade.

So if you are investing in a REIT, choose one that largely confines itself to holdings in residential properties. The same rule applies to investing in a real estate mutual fund. Both types of investments are hard to come by and are limited. For example, most REITs are dominated by commercial real estate investments, as are most real estate mutual funds. But if you look hard enough, you will be able to identify REITs and mutual funds that are residential-dominated.

Be equally cautious in investing in mortgage-backed securities (MBS) or REITs that are holding mortgages. The performance of these types of investments is not only influenced by fluctuations in residential property sales and prices but is also directly linked to the general condition of the economy. For instance, if a borrower defaults on his or her mortgage loan, the performance of the MBS suffers. A borrower default is directly correlated with the performance of the economy, not the housing markets. During a recession, for example, when unemployment rises and jobs are lost, default rates rise.

There are also some REITs, such as those primarily invested in multifamily properties, that are tied to income growth on rental properties. There is a fine line between residential rental properties and commercial real estate properties—so be careful.

A Second-Best Solution

To be sure, indirect real estate investing permits you to take advantage of today's real estate boom, but not as fully. It has its shortcomings as well as its advantages.

Shortcomings

- You are not taking advantage of real estate's greatest benefit—the ability to leverage a down payment, which generates above-normal investment returns.
- You are not fully taking advantage of the tax benefits and government subsidies granted to property ownership.
- You are not building wealth the real estate way—through price appreciation and the amortization of a loan.

Advantages

- Indirect real estate investments permit you to take advantage of today's real estate boom without experiencing the administrative and time costs of purchasing real property. As property values continue to rise, indirect real estate investments, particularly REITs and real estate mutual funds, may outperform non–real estate investments.
- Indirect real estate investments permit you to diversify your overall investment portfolio. Residential real estate is usually associated with a growth cycle different from that of non–real estate investments. Thus, indirect real estate investments reduce risk in traditional stock/bond portfolios.
- Indirect real estate investments are more liquid than real property investments. Although the buying and selling of property has become easier, simpler, and less expensive, real estate still remains less liquid than bonds, stocks, and indirect real estate investments.
- Indirect real estate investments permit you to invest in commercial real estate (when this market is performing). For individuals, direct investing in commercial real estate can be dangerous, since they would be competing against commercial real estate professionals.
- Indirect real estate investing eliminates the operational risks of property ownership. There are no tenant problems, repairs, mortgage payments, or other administrative and operational headaches.
- Indirect real estate investing permits you to diversify your real estate portfolio. You can mix commercial real estate investments with residential real estate investments, bonds with equities, and so on.

Real Estate Investment Trusts (REITs)

Real Estate Investment Trusts (REITs) were established by Congress in 1960 to provide a means of raising capital for companies focused on owning and operating commercial real estate property. (Some REITs are composed of mortgage loans as well.) The primary objective in establishing REITs was to enable small investors to make investments in large-scale, income-producing real estate. The idea was to "pool" funds from average investors so that the REIT could purchase commercial properties that were otherwise unavailable to individuals. REITs played a limited role in the real estate markets for the first thirty years of their existence. They had a difficult time attracting capital because investors preferred to purchase commercial real estate as tax shelters, where interest and depreciation could be deducted against their income. But when the 1986 Tax Reform Act severely limited commercial real estate investments as tax shelters, interest in REITs gained momentum. Between 1978 and 1998, equity REITs had a total annual return of 14.35 percent, exceeding the 8.72 percent return of direct property investments. The number of publicly traded REITs tripled during that twenty-year period. Of course, after 1998, property values began to climb appreciably, making direct property investments preferable.

REITs are attractive for their tax advantages as well as their pooling advantages. A REIT may deduct from its corporate tax bill the dividends paid to shareholders, as long as the trust distributes at least 95 percent of its earnings every year. REITs are well on their way to supplanting pension funds as the primary funding source in the real estate equity markets. Investments in these trusts are similar to investments in mutual funds. Shareholders simply select the REIT that focuses on their investment target. REITs primarily specialize in all kinds of commercial properties: regional shopping malls, warehouses, office buildings, or a mix of all real estate property types. I suggest that you avoid these investments. To take advantage of the real estate boom, you must identify REITs that are primarily invested in residential real estate. There are fewer of these available.

In recent years, REITs have expanded into residential real estate (mostly multifamily properties and manufactured housing) and mortgage loans. Saying that multifamily properties are residential is a stretch, but it is similar to purchasing rental property. As of October 2004, the equity market capitalization of residential REITs was $42 billion, while REITS specializing in mortgage loan purchases totaled $16 billion in market capitalization. These are not huge numbers. But they do give you a chance to invest in REITs.

With regard to rental property investments, equity REITs (those that own real estate) may be the way for you to indirectly invest without the headaches of owning real estate. Though REITs are not able to provide the great leveraging benefits of actual rental property purchases, they do provide some leverage. Most REITs operate with about 50 percent debt. It is equivalent to your placing a 50 percent down payment on a property purchase—not bad for an equity investment. The biggest gain from REITs results from yield on investment, the dividends you receive from the REIT. During the five-year period (1999 to 2003), REITs as a group (using the NAREIT Composite Index) returned 15 percent a year, compared with the Nasdaq's 2 percent loss and a 1 percent loss for the S&P 500. During the ten-year period between 1994 and 2003, the NAREIT index returned 12 percent, still edging out the Nasdaq's 10 percent and S&P's 11 percent returns. (Returns include capital appreciation and dividends.)

Real Estate Mutual Funds

Today a wide selection of real estate mutual funds are being offered to the investment community. Investors can find real estate mutual funds that are heavily weighted toward commercial properties, rental units, apartments, or a mix of all three. Again, I recommend that you focus your attention on mutual funds weighted toward residential properties to take advantage of today's real estate boom. To identify these funds (which could have equity ownership in residential real estate companies), you need to look at the portfolio composition of each fund. Every fund will provide you with this information.

A typical real estate mutual fund will provide the following information for potential investors:

- A profile of the fund: the percentage of funds invested in income-producing real estate assets
- The targeted property types and/or REITs
- The fund manager's biography
- The fund's performance: year to date, over 1 month, 3 months, 6 months, 1 year, 5 years, and life

- Historical performance
- Fees, loads, and expenses
- Price history
- Distribution schedule: dividends and capital gains
- Holdings: domestic and foreign asset allocation
- Major market sectors
- Purchase minimums
- How to order a prospectus

The assets in real estate mutual funds have increased substantially during the past decade, outpacing equity and bond mutual funds growth. Similar to REITs, most real estate mutual funds primarily invest in commercial real estate, so you need to be careful not to "overemphasize" commercial real estate in your mutual fund purchases. Almost every major mutual fund company offers a mutual fund with a percentage of residential real estate. Here are some of the most popular funds (most of them invest in REITs):

- Aetna Real Estate Fund: 888-423-5887
- ABN-AMRO Real Estate Fund: 312-855-7099
- Advantus Real Estate Securities Fund: 651-665-3826
- AIM Real Estate Fund: 800-347-1919
- Alex Brown Kleinwort Benson Realty: 410-347-0600
- Alliance Real Estate Investment Fund: 212-969-2258
- Alpine International Real Estate Equity Fund: 212-687-5588
- American Century Real Estate Investments: 800-345-3533
- Basswood Real Estate Partners: 212-521-9500
- CGM Realty Fund: 800-345-4048
- CRA Realty Shares: 888-711-4272
- Davis Real Estate Funds: 800-279-0279
- Dimensional Fund Advisors: 310-395-8005
- Dreyfus Inc. Real Estate Fund: 800-645-6561
- FBR Real Estate Funds: 800-446-1012
- First American Real Estate Investment Funds: 800-637-2548
- LaSalle Partners U.S. Real Estate Fund: 800-527-2553

- Merrill Lynch Real Estate Funds: 800-637-3863
- Morgan Stanley International Europe Real Estate Fund: 800-548-7786
- Pioneer Real Estate Funds: 617-742-7825
- Principal Real Estate Fund: 800-247-4123
- Prudential Real Estate Securities Fund: 800-225-1852
- Scudder REIT Fund: 800-225-2470
- T. Rowe Price Real Estate Fund: 800-638-5660
- Templeton Global Real Estate Fund: 800-342-5236
- The Vanguard REIT Index Portfolio: 800-662-7447
- Van Kampen U.S. Real Estate Fund: 800-421-5666

Real Estate–Related Securities

Ginnie Mae Securities

Government National Mortgage Association (Ginnie Mae) securities provide a simple way to invest in government-insured mortgage loans. Ginnie Mae securities are relatively attractive bond investments because they are backed by the full faith and credit of the federal government. Basically, qualified mortgage lenders that originate Federal Housing Administration (FHA) and Veterans Administration (VA) loans assign these loans to Ginnie Mae. These loan packages are the basis of securities issued and guaranteed by Ginnie Mae. The Ginnie Mae securities are then sold to investors who market them in minimum denominations of $25,000. (For a more complete description of Ginnie Mae securities, please see Chapter 3.)

Ginnie Maes are essentially mortgage-backed securities that provide investors with monthly principal (due to amortization of the principal of the mortgage loan) and interest payments. Because these securities are guaranteed by the U.S. government, there is little default risk to the investors.

There are two primary risks inherent in Ginnie Mae security investment: (1) reinvestment risk and (2) prepayment risk. Reinvestment risk exists because every month investors have to reinvest the payment of partial principal in new investments that could yield lower or higher returns, depending on the direction of interest rates. Prepayment risk is present when there is an unusually high number of mortgage refinancings. To illustrate these two risks, consider the following example: Assume an investor owns $100,000 in a 15-year Ginnie Mae security yielding 8 percent. His reinvestment risk comes in when he must reinvest the principal he gets back every month. If the Ginnie Mae security were paying only interest, like a bond, the investor would receive about $604 in interest (for an 8 percent coupon) every month, and he would receive his $100,000 investment back at the end of 15 years. But this Ginnie Mae security pays back some portion of the $100,000 principal every month. (Remember, someone is making a monthly mortgage payment in which both interest and principal are being paid.) In the first month, the investor would receive a total of $956, of which $665 is interest and $291 is principal. Thus, he needs to reinvest $291 at the current market interest rate, which could be lower or higher than the original 8 percent. This is his reinvestment risk. With a traditional bond, there is no reinvestment risk on the principal. Investors receive their principal investment back at the bond's maturity. With Ginnie Mae securities, there is reinvestment risk every month.

Prepayment risk just adds to the investment risk. If someone refinances a home mortgage loan, he or she is prepaying the loan before maturity. Thus, the investor in a Ginnie Mae will receive even more principal payments if a lot of refinancing occurs in the pool of mortgage on which the Ginnie Mae security is based. In our example above, the Ginnie Mae security would be subject to a great deal of prepayment risk if mortgage rates suddenly fell to 7 percent. Some of the FHA/VA mortgage loans in the pool of mortgages that backs the Ginnie Mae security would be paying off because borrowers are refinancing their mortgages to the lower mortgage rates. As they refinance their loans, the 15-year Ginnie Mae investment term may be shortened considerably, leaving Ginnie Mae securities holders with the problem of reinvesting a large sum of money in the marketplace at a lower interest rate. Thus, investors face both reinvestment risk (investing cash flows at new market-determined interest rates) and prepayment risk (households refinancing their mortgages, and in effect, returning their principal back to the investor).

Fannie Mae/Freddie Mac Securities

Perhaps the most prominent "quasi"-government bonds are Fannie Mae and Freddie Mac securities. They are similar to the mortgage-backed Ginnie Mae securitites in that they provide investors with monthly principal (due to amortization of the principal of mortgage loans) and interest payments.

Fannie Mae is the Federal National Mortgage Association, the largest company, as measured by assets, in the United States. Freddie Mac, the Federal Home Loan Mortgage Corporation, is smaller than Fannie Mae but is still one of the largest corporations in the United States. Both of these companies are called government-sponsored agencies, which gives an impression that the United States would financially support them in times of need. They were conceived by the federal government, but both companies are publicly traded on the stock exchanges and have private boards of directors. Fannie Mae's and Freddie Mac's primary mission is to purchase mortgage loans orig-inated by mortgage-lending companies and then securitize these loans by selling mortgage-backed securities in the financial marketplace. Fannie Mae and Freddie Mac compete against each other for provid-ing funding to the thousands of mortgage lenders across the nation.

The attraction for investors is that both Fannie Mae and Freddie Mac guarantee payment of interest and principal to investors, even if a home owner misses his or her mortgage payments. The key here is that the markets believe that both Fannie Mae and Freddie Mac are as close as a private company can get to being backed by the full faith and credit of the U.S. government, up to $3.5 billion in case of default. For investors, Fannie Mae and Freddie Mac bonds represent relatively safe investments (almost, but not quite, as safe as U.S. government bonds), but the real kicker is that these bonds have a higher return than Treasury bonds. So if you are looking for an investment that is almost as safe as U.S. federal debt but pays higher returns, Fannie Mae and Freddie Mac securities qualify.

Real Estate–Related Company Investments

This list can go on and on and on. . . . There are literally thousands of publicly traded companies that are available for you to invest in, including: mortgage-lending companies, homebuilders, real estate brokerage companies, title insurance companies, appraisal companies, Fannie Mae, and Freddie Mac, to name a few. Be careful to distinguish between the refinancing business and the purchase-origination business when investing in real estate companies. For example, a lending company that is heavily dependent on refinancing loans is probably not a wise investment if you are looking to take advantage of the real estate boom.

The real estate boom lifts all housing boats, so most of the categories mentioned above will show positive price performance during the boom period. However, there are no guarantees for specific company performance, since there are many factors that influence stock price movements (such as management, competition, etc.). But if you are looking to indirectly invest in residential real estate, I recommend that you look to invest in companies in the following categories:

- Fannie Mae/Freddie Mac
- Mortgage banking companies (e.g., Countrywide Credit Industries)
- Real estate brokerage companies (e.g., Cendant, which owns a number of large franchises)
- Settlement service companies: title insurance, appraisal, etc. (e.g., First American)
- Homebuilders (e.g., Pulte)
- Home improvement companies (e.g., Home Depot, Lowe's)
- Furniture/appliance companies (e.g., Basset, Circuit City)

Limited Partnerships

Limited partnerships consist of individual investors (partners) and a general partner. The purpose of the partnership is to invest in real estate properties. The individual partners are classified as limited partners because their liability is limited to their initial investment. The general partner(s) usually manages the portfolio of properties and earns management fees while also sharing in the cash flows and capital appreciation of the properties. In recent years, the popularity of limited partnerships has markedly diminished. Many of the earlier tax advantages have been stripped away during the past decade, so there is less incentive to form partnerships.

However, there are companies that offer limited partnerships, particularly in commercial real estate ventures. These companies usually specialize in acquisitions, mergers, and development of commercial real estate. For investors who prefer to limit their participation in the direct purchase of properties such as apartment buildings, hotels, office properties, and shopping centers, limited partnerships remain an attractive option. The general partner will usually perform the following tasks in the partnership: create the new limited-liability company; acquire properties; conduct due diligence on new acquisitions; manage the debt and equity placement; and provide asset management services and eventual disposal of the properties.

There are some limited-partnership deals that are specific to residential real estate, but you have to conduct an extensive search to find them. Sometimes, a developer will offer limited partnerships in their residential housing project (multifamily). For example, you may be able to invest $25,000 in capital with a developer so that the company can develop an apartment building in Chicago. The developer would offer you a guaranteed higher-than-market return for a specified period of time (usually the time it takes to complete the construction of the apartment building).

12

HOW TO NAVIGATE THE REAL ESTATE BOOM

In 2004, forty-five metropolitan areas in the United States experienced double-digit home price appreciation for the year (third quarter 2004 over third quarter 2003), led by Las Vegas, Nevada, with an incredible 54 percent appreciation. Naturally, the question on every real estate investor's mind is: Are the housing cups in these metro areas half full or half empty? Or in Las Vegas's case—has the cup runneth over?

These are fair questions. Would you purchase a property in Las Vegas that just rose in value by 54 percent during the past year? Are the best days of Las Vegas real estate behind us? But on the other hand, a 54 percent price appreciation could be just the beginning (or the middle) of the housing boom in the Las Vegas housing market, one you would not want to miss. Which is it: half full or half empty?

Your decision on whether or not to buy should have nothing to do with being an optimist or pessimist. Your decision must be an objective and analytical one. It has to do with knowing how to navigate the real estate boom. By conducting some research, you will learn that Las Vegas still has incredible upside potential. Navigating the boom requires that you gather some data and know how to evaluate it to help you make an intelligent property purchase decision.

You need not do the research on your own. Conducting research is not for everyone. In fact, you do not need to read this chapter to be a successful real estate investor. You need only rely, like everyone else, on the relationships that you make with real estate agents and lenders. Utilize their talents, experiences, and expertise. Part of their job is to gather the data and do the research for you.

Nonetheless, you can do a lot of the data gathering that the experts offer on your own. It is much like investing in stocks. Most large Wall Street companies offer in-house research on companies, providing performance data, analyses, and an earnings outlook, so that you can make intelligent investment decisions on these companies. If you are so inclined to do the research on your own, the Internet provides you with that capacity—it has most of the data, reports, and so on. But you have to be responsible and do your homework.

With real estate investing it's the same—the data is out there on the Internet. You can gather it, analyze it, and review research written by the experts and then make informed decisions on property purchases. The remaining pages of this chapter will provide you with the road to real estate research: what data to look at; what the important indicators of current and future real estate activity are; what factors influence real estate values, and so forth. I will put it all in the context of today's current real estate boom.

My advice is to rely heavily on real estate agents and lenders for information and guidance in purchasing and financing real estate. Nonetheless, reading this chapter will help you become a more intelligent real estate investor. And depending on your own skills and ambitions, you may do all of the research on your own, some of it, or none of it. Either way, this chapter will help you become a more savvy buyer and seller of residential property.

Important Economic/Housing Data

Let me paint a picture of what makes the real estate (housing) market tick. It is really quite simple. Housing activity has only two components: the demand for housing and the supply of housing. Taken together, they generate home prices, home sales, and so on. So if you want to measure the health of the nation's housing market or your local housing market, you need to first understand and measure demand and supply conditions.

Demand Conditions

Housing demand depends on a number of social, economic, and housing factors. I have divided demand into four areas: population influences, the cost of purchasing property, consumer wherewithal, and ease of financing.

Population Influences

By far the most important factor that influences the demand for housing is population growth. Without it, the demand for future property purchases stagnates. Household formation and demographic and migration trends also play crucial roles in determining the demand for housing, both nationally and locally.

- **Population growth.** Simply stated, population growth is the primary fuel for home buying. The total population in the United States is projected to grow by 5 percent during the next decade. That should add about 15 million more people to the existing population. Statistically, the nation's home ownership rate tells us that about 69 percent of households will eventually purchase a home.
- **Household formation.** The real estate business considers a household, rather than an individual, when measuring who is purchasing property. Households could range from a person living by him- or herself, to a married couple, to a mother or father living with children, and so on. Household formation is important, because when it changes, it impacts the demand for housing. For example, a married couple is considered one household because they will live in a home together. But if this couple divorces, they are now considered two households because they will be living

separately. Thus, divorce rates influence household formation. The higher the divorce rate, the greater the number of households demanding home purchases.

- **Demographic trends.** Changing demographics are perhaps the best-known influence on the demand for home buying today. I have discussed demographic trends in other chapters. Focus on the life cycle trends of the five major population groups: retirees, boomers, bust, immigrants, and echo boomers.

- **Migration trends.** Even if the total population stagnates, the magnitude and pace of migration will keep certain housing markets active. For example, one of the primary reasons Las Vegas is experiencing substantial price appreciation is its high migration rate. Over 50,000 people moved to Las Vegas last year alone, creating greater demand for local home buying.

The Costs of Purchasing Property

Demand for any product usually is inversely related to the cost of purchasing it. If costs rise, demand falls. This holds true for property purchases. There are two major areas of the cost of property ownership: mortgage rates and settlement costs.

- **Mortgage rates.** Property is still the most interest-sensitive purchase in our economy. This is because the majority of property purchases are financed. A rise in borrowing costs can make the transaction cost prohibitive. I have estimated that a one percent rise in mortgage rates, on average, prices out about 250,000 households from purchasing property. Conversely, a one percentage drop in mortgage rates motivates an additional 250,000 households to purchase homes.

- **Settlement costs.** As I mentioned in the chapter on financing, settlement costs at closing can be quite substantial (2 to 6 percent of the loan balance). A rise in settlement costs can inhibit home buying, especially among first-time buyers, while a drop in settlement costs can motivate home buying.

Consumer Wherewithal

Do consumers have the financial wherewithal and confidence to purchase big-ticket items like homes and autos? That is what this category is all about. You need job security, steady income, and confidence to be in the financial and emotional position to purchase property. Of course, for many households, saving enough funds for a down payment is the most difficult task in purchasing a home.

- **Personal income.** The typical home owner spends about 20 to 30 percent of disposable income on housing and housing-related goods and services (e.g., furniture, landscaping). The growth in income and the mortgage debt service (your monthly mortgage payments) as a percentage of disposable income are useful measures to evaluate housing demand.
- **Job security.** If you don't have a job, or if your job situation is unstable, you will have a difficult time qualifying for mortgage financing.
- **Stored wealth.** In addition to income, households have stored wealth either through savings, inheritance, existing home equity, investments, or gifts. The amount of your perceived wealth may influence your demand for housing. For example, if the value of the home you currently reside in jumps 50 percent, giving you a $200,000 unrealized price gain, you may feel a bit wealthier and may be more inclined to purchase a larger home in the near future.
- **Consumer confidence.** There are two primary consumer confidence indices that are available on the Internet: the Conference Board's Consumer Confidence Index and the University of Michigan's Consumer Sentiment Survey. Both provide a measure of current and future confidence levels of consumers with regard to purchasing big-ticket items such as homes and automobiles.

Ease of Financing

One of the least discussed but most influential determinants of the demand for home purchases is the many ways that consumers finance their property purchase. Certainly, the ease, availability, and costs of financing play a major role in determining the costs of purchasing a property.

- **Menu of mortgage products.** The greater the number of available mortgage loan products, the easier it will be for households to identify a mortgage loan that is right for them. Thus as lenders create (offer) more and more mortgage loan products, the demand for home purchases tends to increase.
- **Government assistance/low-down-payment programs.** The more low-down-payment loan products/programs and/or government assistance that are available, particularly to low-income/moderate-income families, the greater the demand for home buying.

Supply of Homes

Housing supply depends on a number of factors in the marketplace, including builder and material costs, local growth restrictions, and builders' response to demand conditions.

Builder and Material Costs

- **Lumber.** Prices of lumber vary a great deal and can influence the construction and, thus, the supply of homes. The United States imports a great deal of lumber from Canada, and you need to be aware of the tariffs and quotas between the two nations that may influence the price of lumber imports.
- **Steel and other materials.** All the other materials that go into the production of a residential property influence the costs of building a home and thus the number of homes that are built. In recent years, steel and other material prices have risen significantly, partially contributing to the relatively tight supply of homes.
- **Labor and other nonmaterial builder costs.** Labor costs and other nonmaterial builder costs also influence the supply of homes. If the local housing market is hot, a general contractor will have a difficult time getting the prices he needs from subcontractors

(such as electrical work, framing, etc.). In some local areas, sub-contractors are busy, which limits the total number of homes that can be constructed in that area.

Builder Activities/Response to Market Conditions

- Housing starts/permits (i.e., construction projects) are gathered by the government on a monthly basis. A high growth rate in starts reflects builders' response to healthy housing conditions, while a slowing in the starts' growth rate reflects builders' lack of confidence in the housing markets. The government gathers building permit information to gauge future construction activity, as well. Construction companies have to get approvals via permits for their construction projects from local governments. By tracking permits, you can get a sense of how builders are responding to market conditions.

Growth Restrictions

- **Local municipality building growth restrictions.** In some local areas, builders struggle to get land and construction permits to develop/construct residences on land. Monitoring local growth restrictions provides some insight on the tightness or looseness of the local inventory of homes.

Housing Indicators

Now that you have an understanding about demand and supply conditions and their influences in the housing markets, it is useful to identify a short list of indicators of housing activity that are readily observable by home buyers. These measures of housing activity will provide you with information on current and/or future housing activity on a national level. Some of these measures are also available on a local level (we will look at local measures next). They are useful tools for navigating the real estate boom.

Useful Tips on Housing Data

Before I begin, there are some nuances about the housing data that you need to know. First, home sales are divided into three categories: existing home sales, new home sales, and condominium sales. Existing home sales comprise about 75 percent of total homes sold, while new home sales comprise 14 percent and condo sales the remaining 11 percent. Here is where it gets a bit confusing. Condo sales are existing sales but are gathered only on a quarterly basis, while existing home sales are gathered on a monthly basis and so are reported separately by the National Association of Realtors®. Both condo and existing home sales are based on closings, which means the sale is recorded at the closing table where the actual transfer of property from seller to buyer formally takes place. However, new home sales, reported by the U.S. Census Bureau, are recorded when a buyer signs a contract to purchase a new home. So there is a timing difference between new home sales and existing home sales. For instance, after signing a contract to purchase a home, the closing may not occur for another month or two. This creates an apples-to-oranges comparison when contrasting existing home sales data with new home sales data.*

In addition, home sales and home prices are subject to seasonal variations. For example, there is a greater demand for home buying in the springtime than any other season of the year. This is because families with children typically look to purchase homes in the spring so that they can move into the home during the summer months when the school year is over and prepare their children to enter a new school in the fall. Because of this seasonality, it is very difficult to compare home price appreciation from month to month. For example, if there are more families with children purchasing homes during the spring season, these homes, on average, will be bigger in size and higher in price than homes purchased during the other three seasons

*By the time this book is published, the National Association of Realtors® will have released a major revision to the existing home sales series. In addition, condo sales will now be combined with existing home sales on a monthly basis to create a new existing home sales series.

of the year. This is because families with children, on average, require larger homes than households without children. This is why the real estate industry always employs year-over-year home price appreciation comparisons, so that it can contrast home prices in the spring of this year with home prices in the spring of last year, and so on.

The Top Housing Indicators (in no particular order)

1. **Existing Home Sales.** The National Association of Realtors® gathers sales of existing homes on a monthly basis from a large number of multiple listing services boards (MLSs) across the nation. Again, existing home sales are recorded at the closing of a home purchase transaction. It is useful to look at the growth in existing sales from the previous month to obtain a sense of where the home sales market is headed. Year-over-year comparisons are also useful. Home sales data is seasonally adjusted. This data is easily accessible on most real estate Web sites, including that of the National Association of Realtors®.

2. **New Home Sales.** The U.S. Bureau of Census reports new home sales on a monthly basis. This data series is somewhat erratic from month to month and is sometimes subject to substantial revisions. Month-to-month changes in sales volume as well as year-over-year comparisons are useful to home buyers and owners.

3. **Condominium Sales.** Sales of condominiums are reported by the National Association of Realtors® on a quarterly basis. (It will be reported on a monthly basis beginning in January 2005.) NAR began tracking the condo/co-op market in 1981; prior to the late 1970s, condos were not an important segment of the nation's housing market. Condo sales comprise about 11 percent of total home sales. Month-to-month changes in sales volume as well as year-over-year comparisons are useful indicators of condo activity.

4. **Housing Starts/Permits.** The Commerce Department gathers data on housing starts and permits from a pool of about 19,000 towns, cities, and metropolitan statistical areas. The housing starts report includes single-family and multifamily units and is the most reliable indicator for residential investment and building activity. Housing permits are also

gathered by the Commerce Department and represent the permit approvals for homebuilders to commence construction projects.

5. **Mortgage Applications.** The Mortgage Bankers Association conducts a weekly survey of mortgage application activity at the thirty to forty largest mortgage-lending companies in the nation. The survey produces two important indices for real estate purchasers to monitor: the purchase index and the refinancing index. The purchase index measures weekly mortgage application activity to purchase homes, while the refi index measures weekly mortgage application activity to refinance mortgage loans. The purchase index is a reliable leading indicator of future home sales. A purchase index greater than 300 reflects a strong home purchase market, while an index below 200 represents a weakening purchase market.

6. **Pending Home Sales.** The National Association of Realtors® will introduce a new housing data series covering pending home sales. In March 2005, this series promises to become the most reliable leading indicator of future home sales in the nation. Pending home sales are contracts pending on existing homes (similar to new home sales). Monitoring both monthly changes and year-over-year changes should prove useful. Pending sales have been estimated to be a one-to-two-month leading indicator of existing home sales.

7. **Mortgage Rates.** The direction and level of mortgage rates continue to be the most important influences on housing activity today. Single-digit rates are favorable, while double-digit rates are a yellow flag in any housing market. Mortgage rates climbing by at least two percentage points in a given year raise a yellow flag for all housing markets, while rates dropping by two percentage points or more in a given year suggest very favorable housing activity ahead.

8. **Housing Affordability Index (HAI).** The National Association of Realtors® housing affordability index measures whether or not a typical family could qualify for a mortgage loan on a typical home. A typical home is defined as the national median-priced, existing single-family home as calculated by NAR, and a typical family is defined as one earning the median family income as reported by the U.S. Bureau

of the Census. Along with the prevailing mortgage rate, these components are used to determine if the median-income family can qualify for a mortgage on a typical home. A value of 100 means that a family with the median income has exactly enough income to qualify for a mortgage on a median-priced home. An index above 100 signifies that a family earning the median income has more than enough income to qualify for a mortgage loan on a median-priced home, assuming a 20 percent down payment. For example, a composite HAI of 120.0 means a family earning the median family income has 120 percent of the income necessary to qualify for a conventional loan covering 80 percent of a median-priced existing single-family home. An increase in the HAI, then, shows that this family is more able to afford the median-priced home. (All calculations assume a down payment of 20 percent of the home price and a qualifying ratio of 25 percent, which means the monthly principal and interest payment cannot exceed 25 percent of the median family monthly income.)

9. **Months' Supply.** The National Association of Realtors® monthly existing home sales report also includes data on the supply/inventory of homes. The months' supply measures the number of months it would take to deplete the entire housing inventory of homes at the current sales pace. Historically, demand and supply for homes are in balance when the months' supply hovers in the 5.5 to 6.5 months range. A 5 or less months' supply reflects lean housing inventories, while a 7 or greater number reflects an excess supply of homes.

10. **Price Appreciation.** There are several sources of home price appreciation available to potential home buyers and property investors. They include the National Association of Realtors® (existing home sales), the U.S. Bureau of the Census (new home sales), Office of Federal Housing Enterprise Oversight, and the Federal Housing Finance Board. Some of the price series are really intended for housing economists and researchers and not for individual buyers. My recommendation is to focus on NAR's existing home prices, if you are purchasing an existing home and/or the Census Bureau's new home prices—if you are purchasing a new home. Both existing and new homes have historically

hovered in the 5 to 6 percent price appreciation range. Any appreciation that is above that range reflects very healthy price appreciation, and any appreciation that falls below that range reflects a softening of prices.

Real Estate Is Local

The one basic truth in real estate investing is that real estate markets are local. That is, property values are determined by local demand and supply conditions. Understanding the national real estate market is helpful, and the top housing indicators will provide you with very reliable information about the direction of real estate values. But if you are about to purchase a specific property in a specific location, you will need some local real estate information as well. I strongly suggest that you request the following housing measures from your real estate agent and/or mortgage lender:

- **Metro existing home sales.** Metropolitan-area existing home sales volume is reported by the National Association of Realtors® on a quarterly basis. However, your local real estate agent should be able to provide you with some local home sales data—maybe by county or zip code.
- **Metro home prices.** Metropolitan-area existing home prices are also reported by the National Association of Realtors® on a quarterly basis. Again, your local real estate agent may be able to provide you with some local home price data—maybe by county or zip code.
- **Local inventory/months' supply.** Real estate agents should be able to provide you with the months' supply of homes in the local marketplace (e.g., county or metro level). The months' supply measures the amount of months it would take to exhaust the current supply of homes in your local marketplace at the current sales pace. Historically, a normal range for months' supply is between 5.5 and 6.5 months. Anything less is considered a lean inventory, while anything greater is considered an excess supply of homes.

- **Days on market.** Your local real estate agent should be able to provide you with the days-on-market average for homes in your metro area and/or county. Days-on-market measures how long the property that you are considering for purchase has been on the market. Days on market depend heavily on local market conditions.

- **Local pending sales.** You may request from your real estate agent the trend in pending sales on a weekly or monthly basis. This will give you a sense of future local sales activity.

- **Lender mortgage applications.** You may be able to obtain regional and/or metro mortgage application trends from the Mortgage Bankers Association. You should also request that your lender provide you with the latest numbers of purchase mortgage applications from his or her company.

- **Local housing starts/permits.** Virtually every metro area provides housing starts/permit data. High growth in local housing starts/permits reflects a healthy local housing economy, while low growth in housing starts/permits may reflect some weakening.

- **Local economic reports.** It is important that you obtain information about the local economy when you are considering purchasing real estate. You should request from your real estate agent local employment and personal income numbers.

- **Local population/demographics.** Obtaining information about the local population and demographic trends is also important. Local migration reports are available by metro area (see the National Association of Realtors® research page on REALTOR .org). These reports will tell you how many people are migrating into the metro area versus how many people are leaving the metro area. In addition, knowing the composition of population groups and their trends in a local area is helpful. For example, what percentage of retiree, boomer, bust, and echo population groups are in a metro area and what are the projections during the next ten to twenty years for this composition? The changing face of America is very important to future demand for home buying at a national level and should be equally important on a local level.

Navigating the Boom

The real estate market will always experience geographical and periodical ups and downs. It is also important to acknowledge that property values do not experience double-digit appreciation every year—even in a boom. Similarly, home sales cannot go up endlessly. You cannot register record home sales year in and year out—even in a boom period. As interest rates fluctuate, so will property values and home sales. And as you now well know, real estate is subject to local economic conditions, so some areas of the nation will be more influenced by boom conditions than others.

What I have observed over the years is that a real estate boom cannot touch every town, city, and rural area in the nation. Some regions of the nation benefit more than others. The boom is distributed unevenly, and this makes it particularly important for you to take great care in identifying property that will directly benefit in boom times. Today's boom has created a division of haves and have-nots in America's housing markets.

As you can see, a household purchasing a home in Las Vegas at the beginning of 2004 earned 52 percent appreciation, while a household purchasing a home in Dallas, Texas, basically earned nothing. Are both metro areas experiencing the same real estate boom? Obviously, Dallas did not enjoy a real estate boom in 2004. The contrast between the haves and have-nots is presented in the tables on page 240, treating the haves as a group and the have-nots as a group. The average median home price for the haves is $370,000 versus only $131,400 for the have-nots. Home values rose by 31 percent on average for the haves, while rising by a meager 2 percent for the have-nots. Upon closer inspection, there were two primary reasons for these differences: net migration and employment growth. The haves averaged in-migration (number of people moving into the metro area) of 24,600, while the have-nots averaged only 8,300. Job growth was a robust 1.9 percent for the haves but only 0.1 percent for the have-nots.

Of course, being a have or a have-not depends on your perspective. If

THE HAVES

Metro Area	Median Home Price	2Q 2003–2Q 2004 1-Year Appreciation (%)
Las Vegas	$269,000	52
Anaheim (Orange Co.)	$655,300	38
Riverside/San Bernardino	$294,500	38
San Diego	$559,700	37
Los Angeles	$438,400	30
West Palm Beach	$294,000	26
Miami	$271,900	26
Washington, DC	$352,400	23
Portland, ME	$231,200	23

THE HAVE-NOTS

Metro Area	Median Home Price	2Q 2003–2Q 2004 1-Year Appreciation (%)
South Bend, IN	$93,800	3.1
Syracuse	$94,700	2.0
Little Rock	$109,400	4.0
Columbia, SC	$120,700	−1.8
New Orleans	$137,500	3.2
Greensboro/Winston-Salem	$140,300	−0.4
Detroit	$141,800	5.5
Dallas	$141,000	0.8
Columbus, OH	$150,400	0.3
Austin	$158,900	−1.3
Atlanta	$156,800	3.6

you are looking to purchase a home in the high-appreciation metro areas, the median income is $33,776, while the median income for the low-appreciation metro areas is $30,775. Certainly, the median income in the

	Haves	Have-Nots
Median home price	$370,000	$131,400
Price appreciation	31%	2%
Net migration	24,600	8,300
Job growth	1.9%	0.1%
Income (per capita)	$33,776	$30,775

low-appreciation metros will go a lot farther when purchasing a home. You may not build wealth as fast as the high-appreciation areas, but you can get into the home with a lot less money.

The earlier tables should demonstrate that you need to do your homework when navigating the boom. The real estate boom does not raise all boats alike. You need to dig deep, evaluate the housing data, and then select the right boats.

Targeting Properties in a Boom

There are many signs in the housing marketplace that indicate whether a particular location or property is positioned to perform well in the future. The previous sections provided you with the pertinent data and indicators (e.g., the top housing indicators) for monitoring whether the nation and/or a particular geographic region are enjoying a healthy real estate expansion. A summary list of these indicators, titled "Boom/Bust Indicators," is provided at the end of this chapter.

As a real estate purchaser, your objective is to purchase property that will rise in value, not fall. After monitoring the national and local housing indicators, your attention should be turned to identifying what geographic locations are expected to benefit from a real estate boom. And then your attention should turn to what property types will benefit from the boom within each location.

It might prove useful to look at some of today's major boom locations to confirm the important market factors that have created a

METRO AREAS EXPERIENCING BOOM TIMES

	3-Year Price Appreciation (%)	Wealth Gain	Months' Supply	Net Migration	Job Growth
Las Vegas	183	$122,600	1.7	55,100	38,300
Anaheim	186	$302,600	1*	4,200	3,000
Riverside	187	$137,000	NA	108,700	25,900
San Diego	188	$261,400	3.8	3,300	20,700
Los Angeles	187	$204,000	NA	11,600	21,400
West Palm Beach	199	$146,400	4.8	27,300	10,700
Miami	170	$112,200	NA	9,900	12,800
Washington, DC	170	$145,000	1.2	37,900	80,600
Portland, ME	149	$76,200	NA	1,700	1,600
Group Average	185	$180,000	2.9	25,000	21,000

Source: National Association of Realtors®

boom environment. The table above shows some of the top price-appreciation metros across the nation.

Certainly, all of the metros in the table satisfy the primary boom conditions: tight supply and healthy demand. As a group, the 2.9 months' supply is alarmingly low, creating excess demand for a limited inventory of homes, exerting a great deal of upward pressure on prices. Strong home buying demand is supported by healthy economic and population growth, led by 21,000 job gains and a favorable net migration of 25,000.

Boom Properties

It is equally important to look at how each property type behaves in a boom period.

- **Starter homes.** The neighborhood or local area that you are targeting needs to have a healthy growth rate of echo boomers (i.e., boomer children) and immigrants. Both population groups have a high demand for starter homes, placing upward pressure on the value of starter homes.

- **Trade-up homes.** Look for healthy appreciation in starter homes and/or middle-priced homes in your targeted metro area, because trade-up buyers will use their equity gains in their current homes to trade up. Also, look for a healthy composition of boomers, since they are still trading up to larger homes.
- **Vacation homes.** There are two types of vacation-home types— pure vacation properties as a second home and vacation properties used solely for retirement. The coastal vacation properties obviously will stay in demand because of limited supply, but be careful on other vacation properties. Vacation properties sometimes get trendy. Follow the boomer population. Where are they vacationing and/or retiring? Today, states such as Oregon, Colorado, and Arizona are hot retirement locations, but what about tomorrow?
- **Rental properties.** Rental properties experiencing a boom environment are usually located in metro areas experiencing healthy economic growth. Look for healthy job and income growth in local areas. High growth in young households translates into upward pressure on rental prices. Also, high immigration growth exerts upward pressure on rents, which in turn exerts upward pressure on rental property values.

When Booms Go Bust

Now that you can identify conditions for a real estate boom, it is equally important to know when a bust is coming. So much has been made in the media about the possibility of a "housing price bubble" bursting. For an individual property investor and/or home buyer, a price bubble bursting means a drop in the value of your property. This is a situation all of us want to avoid. But a housing boom going bust does not necessarily mean that home prices will fall everywhere. A contraction in the housing markets means that home sales will fall, which eventually softens home price appreciation. Whether home prices grow slowly, stay flat, or actually fall depends on local supply-and-demand conditions. What you are likely to find is that national home price appreciation may slow from 7.5 percent to 4 percent. The air is "coming out" of the balloon, so to speak. But during a housing contraction, there could be some local real estate markets that experience price declines, and that is what individual investors need to look out for.

As I have stated many times throughout *Are You Missing the Real Estate Boom?*, there is a big difference between national versus local real estate markets. The local influences on home values always dominate the national factors influencing home values. Real estate is local and highly influenced by local supply-and-demand conditions. So let me address the price bubble debate on both a national and local level.

National Bubbles

Nationally, there has not been a drop in home values since the Great Depression. The closest this nation ever came to home prices dropping on a national scale was back in 1989, when home price appreciation registered a meager 0.2 percent. That was a time when the housing markets experienced a double-digit drop in home sales, leaving the nation with an excess supply of homes (9.2 months' supply).

There have been times when "real" home prices turned negative, particularly in the 1980s, when inflation reared its ugly head. Real home prices are the nominal price (observable price) minus the inflation rate. No one is claiming that real prices cannot decline. Real rates of return for stocks and bonds also decline when inflation rates are high. It is clear from the table on the following page that with regard to long-term property values there is nothing worse than rampant inflation.

Real home price appreciation averaged only 1.4 percent during the 1970–1994 time period. Nominal home price appreciation averaged a very healthy 6.1 percent during the period covering 1970–2004. Given the leveraging properties of real estate (returns are based on the down payment), 6 percent price appreciation generates returns that are substantial and, in most years, greater than comparable stock and bond returns.

The price bubble debate has to do with nominal prices dropping, not real prices. Those who believe that there is a national house price bubble about to pop point to the fact that home price growth has outpaced family income growth during the past five years (2000–2004), making it increasingly difficult for households to afford the higher-

HOME PRICE APPRECIATION
(Median Price for Existing Homes)

Year	Nominal Price Appreciation (%)	Real Price Appreciation (%)	Year	Nominal Price Appreciation (%)	Real Price Appreciation (%)
1970	5.3	NA	1988	4.2	0.2
1971	7.8	3.5	1989	0.2	−4.4
1972	7.6	4.2	1990	2.7	−2.5
1973	8.5	1.9	1991	5.4	1.3
1974	10.7	−0.3	1992	3.0	−0.4
1975	10.1	1.1	1993	3.0	0.4
1976	8.0	2.0	1994	4.1	1.3
1977	12.3	5.8	1995	2.7	0.3
1978	13.9	5.5	1996	5.2	1.8
1979	14.1	2.8	1997	5.1	2.8
1980	11.7	−1.6	1998	5.4	3.8
1981	6.6	−3.3	1999	3.9	1.6
1982	2.4	−3.8	2000	4.1	0.9
1983	3.1	0.5	2001	5.8	3.4
1984	3.5	−1.3	2002	7.6	5.3
1985	4.2	0.7	2003	7.3	5.1
1986	6.5	4.3	2004	7.5*	4.3*
1987	6.6	2.9	Average	6.1	1.4

*Projected

priced homes. Home prices appreciated by 7.5 percent in 2004, compared to only a 3 percent growth in family income. Eventually, they claim, households will have to "cry uncle" and stop purchasing homes because they can no longer afford to purchase. In turn, home sales will plummet, bursting the bubble, sending home values falling.

I believe this scenario is flawed for several reasons. First, if we take a more historical view of home prices and family income, we find that recent home price growth partly reflects a "catch-up" with the high-income growth of the 1980s and 1990s. In most years during the

HOME PRICES GROWING FASTER THAN INCOME

	Family Income Appreciation (%)	Home Price Appreciation (%)
2000	3.6	4.3
2001	1.3	6.3
2002	1.4	7.0
2003	2.6	7.5
2004	3.0	7.5

1980s and 1990s, income growth exceeded home price growth. In fact, from 1980 to 2002, the growth in income and home price growth both totaled 138 percent!

Second, focusing on family income growth not keeping pace with home price growth is misleading. The real estate boom really has little to do with evaluating whether households can "afford" to purchase homes that are rising in value. A more appropriate measure is mortgage debt service as a percentage of household income. Why do I say that? Most households finance the purchase of a home. As a result, their ability to purchase a home depends not on their income level but on whether they can afford the monthly mortgage payments. Because mortgage rates have hovered near historic lows for the past several years, the debt servicing as a percentage of income is now close to a cyclical-low 18.1 percent. That is, a median-income household purchasing a home at the median price would have a mortgage debt servicing cost as a percentage of income at 18.1 percent. Low mortgage rates are making homes more affordable. The dramatic rise in home prices has been offset by the dramatic decline in borrowing costs via monthly mortgage payments. As you can see from the chart on the following page, the mortgage debt/income ratio was well over 30 percent during the 1980s. I estimate that this ratio would have to rise to 22 percent before home sales growth stalled.

Third, there are a number of mortgage loan products, such as adjustable-rate mortgages, that help lower debt servicing costs. As I have stated earlier, ARM loans, on average, are about 2 percentage

MORTGAGE DEBT PAYMENT
(As a Percentage of Median Income)

Year	Mortgage Debt Payment	30-Year Mortgage Rates	Year	Mortgage Debt Payment	30-Year Mortgage Rates
1970	17.0	NA	1988	22.0	10.34
1971	16.5	NA	1989	22.2	10.32
1972	16.2	7.38	1990	22.0	10.13
1973	16.9	8.04	1991	21.4	9.25
1974	19.2	9.19	1992	19.3	8.40
1975	20.2	9.04	1993	18.1	7.33
1976	19.9	8.86	1994	18.5	8.36
1977	20.7	8.84	1995	18.9	7.96
1978	22.4	9.63	1996	18.8	7.81
1979	25.7	11.19	1997	18.7	7.60
1980	31.3	13.77	1998	17.7	6.94
1981	36.3	16.63	1999	18.0	7.43
1982	35.9	16.08	2000	19.3	8.06
1983	30.1	13.23	2001	18.4	6.97
1984	28.2	13.87	2002	18.5	6.54
1985	26.2	12.42	2003	17.8	5.82
1986	23.0	10.18	2004	18.1	5.9
1987	22.0	10.20	Average	21.58	9.5

Source: National Association of Realtors®

points lower than fixed-rate loans. Whenever mortgage rates begin to rise, the market share of ARMs obtained by home buyers typically doubles shortly afterward (about 3 months).

Fourth, home owners trading up to a larger and higher-priced home are using the increased equity they accumulated by selling their existing homes at substantially higher prices as a down payment toward the trade-up home. What we are seeing in the data is that the loan-to-value ratio has sharply declined during the past five years. That is, home buyers are purchasing homes with more down-payment money than we've seen since the early 1980s. Households, on average, have more equity in the higher-priced homes they are now purchasing—undercutting the general belief that households are struggling to purchase today's higher-priced homes.

Finally, I would claim that there is little speculative buying in real estate, unlike the stock market. Most households purchase real estate to live in (first-time buyers, trade-up buyers, and vacation property buyers), not to speculate on price increases. I do recognize that there currently exist some local rental markets where investors may be purchasing residential property at above-market prices hoping that home values will continue to rise. But this activity is too small to impact national prices. And even if property buyers wanted to speculate on residential real estate, it would be difficult, since there are relatively high transaction costs (compared to stocks) associated with the buying and selling of property (closing costs, etc.). Even in a boom period, speculative buying is difficult, because property is just not as liquid as stocks and bonds.

During a boom period, however, there could be a number of households that could purchase property earlier than they otherwise would, if they believe that prices will continue to rise. This is called "fence jumping" in real estate jargon. Fence jumping occurs for two reasons: (1) when households purchase real estate earlier than they would like because they believe that if they don't, the price will be higher when they are ready to enter the market; and (2) when households believe that mortgage rates will be rising, and they purchase property at today's lower mortgage rates rather than tomorrow's higher mortgage rates.

Fence jumping is a rational response to expectations of future prices and/or mortgage rates. Both involve the future costs of purchasing a home. But there is no irrational exuberance in the real estate markets. For the overwhelming majority of Americans, a home is the largest and most expensive asset they will ever purchase. And again, most households purchase property to live in, not speculate.

Local Bubbles

Now that I've presented what I think is a compelling case for why it is unlikely that there will ever be a national price bubble, I must admit

LOCAL BUBBLES THAT BURST
(Due to Job Losses and Oversupply)

	Home Price Decline (%)	Months' Supply	Job Losses (%)
Boston	7.2	16	12.7
New York	10.0	12	10.9
Los Angeles	21.4	15	10.0
San Francisco	3.8	14	7.3
National	No decline	9	1.6

to the possibility of local bubbles. Local bubbles are very real, and you must avoid potential local bubble situations when possible. There have been a number of large local bubbles that burst over the past thirty years worth reviewing. Understanding the conditions that led to the dramatic drops in the value of homes in these areas should help you avoid similar situations in the future. The table above presents four major local housing bubbles that burst during the last time the housing markets contracted in the 1989–1991 period: Boston, New York, Los Angeles, and San Francisco.

Local price bubbles swelled in these four metro areas because they were all negatively affected by a substantial loss in local jobs, while housing inventories built to unacceptable levels. The nation as a whole experienced a 1.6 percent drop in jobs during the recession/sluggish period (1990–1991). The metro areas experienced job losses in the range of 7.3 to 12.7 percent. Similarly, the months' supply for these metro areas ranged from 12 to 16, compared to a 9 months' supply for the nation.

History suggests that concentrated job losses, combined with an oversupply of homes, will pop a price bubble. For the nation as a whole, today's housing boom conditions are just the opposite—we have a lean inventory of homes (months' supply is under 5), and the economy (although sluggishly) is creating jobs (unemployment rate is below 5.5 percent). But you need to look closer at your local economy to see if your local housing is vulnerable to a popping of a bubble—if good times turn bad. As of this writing, 45 metro areas across the nation experienced double-digit price appreciation during the past year. Upon closer inspection, all of those metros possessed relatively lean inventories of homes. The months' supply in these areas was less than 6 and in most cases less than 4.

Boom/Bust Indicators

Whether you are purchasing real estate in boom times or sluggish times, you need to constantly monitor housing, population, and economic trends in each target property location. Below is a brief list of some of the indicators that you should be tracking that suggest either boom or bust conditions on the horizon. Most of these indicators have already been discussed. There are no trigger points in the data that tell you if a local boom is going to burst. Use these indicators as a green flag to purchase properties, a yellow flag to proceed with caution, or a red flag to avoid property purchases in a particular location.

BOOM/BUST INDICATORS

	Boom Indicators	Bust Indicators
Home sales	Rising	Falling
Price appreciation	Exceeds historical average	Double digit
Housing inventory	Less than 5.5 months	Greater than 6.5 months
Days on market	Falling	Rising
Local job growth	Rising	Falling
Mortgage rates	Falling	Rising
Net migration	Positive	Negative
Housing starts	Rising	Falling
Economic growth	Positive	Negative
Inflation	Low	Rising
Consumer confidence	High	Falling
Debt service ratio	Less than 22%	Greater than 22%
Loan-to-value	Falling	Rising

CHAPTER

13

REAL ESTATE AND
FINANCIAL PLANNING

I t has always puzzled me why most financial planners treat real
estate holdings separately from a household's investment portfolio, which is typically composed of stocks, bonds, and mutual
funds. Real estate has played second fiddle to traditional stock and
bond investments for far too long. The real estate markets have grown
up—the buying and selling of property is no longer a long, awkward,
and costly process. Property holdings have become more liquid and
their financial rewards have become legendary during this past decade.
Property ownership has generated substantial wealth and income
gains for people across America. Real estate has earned the right to
stand side by side with stocks and bonds in any investment and/or
retirement portfolio.

The remainder of this chapter identifies ways to integrate real
estate purchases into your overall financial planning goals and activities. Financial planning encompasses six primary areas: cash and budget management, investment planning, tax planning, retirement
planning, estate planning, and insurance planning. As you will find,
real estate can be incorporated into all of these planning areas. If you
continue to take advantage of today's real estate expansion and extend
your real estate purchases beyond owning your home, your property

holdings promise to play an increasing role in your short-term and long-term financial plans.

Financial Planning and Real Estate

Planning is never an end in itself. Don't use it as an excuse for not acting. I remember a story about General Douglas MacArthur during World War II, when he asked his Army engineer how long it would take to build a bridge across a river so his troops could get to the other side. The engineer told him about three days, and MacArthur told him to draw up the plans right away. A few days later, MacArthur asked the engineer when he thought the bridge would be ready. The engineer said that the bridge was completed and safe for his troops to cross, but if the General wanted to wait until the plans were done, it would take longer.

Hopefully, none of us will go to that extreme. You always need to be planning as you go through life, but there is no such thing as a perfect plan. Financial planning is a process of addressing the financial challenges that life presents by developing a "personalized plan" to achieve your financial goals. The ultimate goal in financial planning is to help you deal with the financial pressures of life by achieving greater wealth and financial security.

My intention is not to present a complete discourse on financial planning (I do not have the expertise to do so) but to paint a picture with a broad brush so that you can begin to learn where to integrate real estate purchasing into the planning process.

Let's begin with outlining the basic steps in the planning process:

- Identify goals and objectives
- Gather the necessary financial data and information
- Conduct a situation analysis (i.e., evaluate your present financial situation)
- Develop and implement planning strategies
- Monitor performance and revise your plan periodically

There is nothing new or different in these steps. Any planning process, whether it involves a financial plan, a strategic plan, or a business plan, includes these five steps. I recommend that you follow these steps closely as you develop your own financial plan. Hopefully, you will be working with a professional to assist you in this endeavor. This chapter is not a substitute for a professional financial planner. I recommend you utilize the services of a certified financial planner, or CFA, if you wish to employ one.

Let me review the six primary areas of financial planning and identify a role for real estate for each area.

Cash and Budget Management

Most people do not appreciate the importance of managing your day-to-day cash outlays and budget with regard to your overall financial planning goals. But effective cash and budget management can play a major role in helping you meet your longer-term financial goals. There are many financial products and services available to assist in managing your short-term cash and budget needs, including checking accounts, savings accounts, money market accounts, and money mutual fund accounts. There are also many software programs available for managing a budget as well as a personal balance sheet (assets and liabilities and net worth).

For most households, a large portion of cash and budget management activities involve the liability side of the balance sheet—in other words, borrowings. All of us use credit cards, lines of credit, and consumer loans to assist in managing our daily, monthly, and annual cash needs.

Real estate holdings play a major role in cash and budget management in two ways: (1) property equity enhances a household's capacity to borrow and (2) the purchase of your primary residence and how you choose to finance the purchase will have a major impact on your monthly cash needs.

Equity Borrowings

As I've shown throughout this book, property owners can regularly tap their stored property equity for borrowing purposes. Borrowing through equity lines, cash-out refinancings, and collateralized consumer loans are some of the ways property owners can take advantage of their home equity. To accomplish this, your cash and budget management planning needs to identify your total unencumbered real estate equity holdings that could be earmarked to increase your borrowing capacity.

Home Purchase

There are many financial factors involved in the purchase of your primary residence that will significantly impact your monthly cash-flow situation: the price of your home (how much home you can afford); closing costs; down payment; property taxes; mortgage payments; maintenance expenses; furnishings; and landscaping, to name just a few. All impact your monthly cash and budget activities. I estimate that home owners spend between 30 and 40 percent of their disposable income on housing-related goods and services. In addition, the timing of refinancing your existing mortgage loan to lower monthly mortgage payments can greatly improve your cash-flow situation. I suggest you write a list of all the housing and house-related items that impact your budget on a monthly basis and incorporate them into your overall household budgeting process.

Investment Planning

Investment planning brings excitement to the financial planning process. Building an investment portfolio provides opportunities to earn healthy returns on your hard-earned money and sometimes to speculate on a penny stock that may become the next Microsoft. Some households get so taken with investing that they mistake an investment portfolio for financial planning, which could be costly in the long term.

There are a number of steps you need to follow for investment planning that are worth mentioning. These steps help establish the criteria for building an investment portfolio. Included in this portfolio are the usual suspects—stocks, bonds, and mutual funds.

Building an Investment Portfolio

Step 1: *Define Property Investment Goals*
Step 2: *Establish Investment Priorities*
Step 3: *Determine Investment Time Horizon*
Step 4: *Determine Level of Risk Taking*
Step 5: *Determine Level of Diversification*
Step 6: *Determine Acceptable Property Investments*
Step 7: *Determine a Method of Investing/Financing*

I will not spend time explaining the seven steps involved in building an investment portfolio composed of traditional investment vehicles. There is a plethora of investment books, reports, and analyses that provide this information. My focus here is to add real estate to your investment portfolio. To accomplish this, we need to review how these seven steps help establish criteria for building a real estate portfolio within your investment portfolio.

Step 1: *Define Property Investment Goals*
Is your objective to become rich by age forty, or are you willing to wait until retirement age to cash in on your investments? With regard to real estate, your purchase goals depend heavily on age. Young households are just looking to save enough money for a down payment on a starter home, while established households are hoping to trade up into their dream home. But savvy property investors are looking to build a real estate portfolio that will play a major role in both their investment and retirement portfolios.

Step 2: *Establish Investment Priorities*
With regard to real estate, your number-one priority is to purchase a primary residence (probably a starter home). After owning a primary residence, you need to review your property expansion plans by prioritizing the following options: home improvement, trading up, vacation property, and rental property.

Step 3: *Determine Investment Time Horizon*

How long you intend to hold on to a property is an important decision. Depending on the property type, location, and local market performance, a holding period could be as short as 6 months (flipping), 1–5 years (short term), or more than 5 years (long term). Fixer-uppers and foreclosure properties are potential flip opportunities, vacation properties could be a long-term hold, while the holdings horizon for rental properties depends on market conditions.

Step 4: *Determine Level of Risk Taking*

Real estate covers a wide spectrum with regard to risk. You need to determine your level of acceptable risk taking for real estate properties. First, decide on a property type—single-family or condo; vacation property or rental property. Condos usually pose less risk since there are lower maintenance costs, while single-family detached homes pose greater risk due to the higher maintenance costs. Vacation properties pose a great deal of risk, since you are likely to be absent from the property for long periods of time, and there may be little rent to cover the expenses associated with financing and maintaining the property. Rental properties also pose a relatively high level of risk due to tenant uncertainty, maintenance costs, and so on. Within rental properties, you could purchase foreclosures and fixer-uppers, which potentially pose the greatest risk (but highest return) of all property types.

With regard to location, some locations are riskier than others, depending on local population and economic and housing conditions. You need to decide how much risk you are willing to assume with the financing of the property (e.g., variable or fixed-rate loan, size of down payment).

Step 5: *Determine Level of Diversification*

Everyone knows the expression "You don't put all your eggs in one basket." If the basket falls, you may lose all your eggs. Similarly, you don't put all your hard-earned money into one real estate investment. If this investment turns sour, you could lose a great of money. This is why I recommend that households expand their real estate investments beyond their own home.

But diversification is a comprehensive strategy. Diversifying your eggs into many different baskets that are on the same truck transporting them for delivery still poses unwanted risk. What if the truck crashes into another vehicle? You could still lose all your eggs. The lesson learned is to have more than one truck transporting your valuables. The key to diversifying is to invest in a mix of properties or locations whose values do not depend on the same local conditions.

I would recommend that you diversify your property portfolio (i.e., two or more properties) in one of two ways: diversify among property types; or more important, diversify among geographic location. Investing in the same property type brings simplicity and some economies of scale (e.g., if you purchase three one-bedroom condo units in the same building), but you need to be careful not to become too dependent on a specific property type. However, if you have found a successful formula for investing in only one-bedroom condos, do not use diversification as a reason to change direction. Diversifying among geographic locations is preferable, in theory, but sometimes difficult to implement. For example, ideally you would diversify a portfolio of rental properties among different locations across a metro area, but it may be difficult for you to logistically monitor and service those properties.

Another form of diversification is the mix of property holdings compared with stocks, bonds, and mutual funds in your total investment portfolio. In many cases, residential real estate dances to a different drummer than do traditional investment vehicles. For example, the real estate boom continued during the 2001 recession, while stocks and bonds faltered. If you had real estate in your investment portfolio during the past five years, your overall performance would have been significantly better than most people with only traditional investment portfolios.

Real estate holdings are underrepresented in most investment portfolios. A typical investment portfolio may have no property investments (apart from one's primary home). Occasionally, one might find indirect real estate investments, such as REITs and/or real estate mutual funds, and I would argue that your primary residence does *not* belong in an investment portfolio. It is better suited to your retirement portfolio, because the funds on this property will most probably be allocated to your final retirement property.

An investment portfolio with property holdings is a more diversified portfolio. Below is an example of an investment portfolio with real estate holdings:

Investment Portfolio with Real Estate Holdings
- Stocks
  - IBM
  - General Motors
  - Lucent
  - Microsoft
- Bonds
  - CDs
  - 10-year Treasury
- Mutual Funds
  - Fidelity
- Real Estate
  - Rental property 1
  - Rental property 2
  - Vacation property

In the above investment portfolio, the rental properties generate annual cash flow (via rent) and, thus, annual returns, similar to stocks and bonds. The vacation home probably generates little cash flow, if any, but it is housed in the investment portfolio because its value is expected to rise over time. Unrealized price gains from the vacation property raise the overall value of the investment portfolio. The portfolio share of real estate versus stocks and bonds depends heavily on two factors: risk and liquidity. How much risk are you willing to assume in property investments? Rental properties are associated with high returns, but greater risk than most stock and bond investments due to tenant and maintenance risk. Given those risks, you need to determine how many rental properties you are willing to take on in the investment portfolio. In addition, property investments are less liquid than stocks and bonds. Liquidity concerns come into play as your investment time horizon shortens.

Step 6: *Determine Acceptable Property Investments*

Once you develop a property investment strategy, make sure the properties you choose don't leave you stranded. Depending on your investment focus, determine which property type and location is best suited for your needs. The most constructive strategy is to make a list of the acceptable property types for your investment portfolio. Here are some examples:

- **Primary residence.** Obviously acceptable (though, again, I would allocate this to your retirement portfolio).
- **Primary home improvements.** The risk here is under your control since you determine the funds going into it, but you need to be willing to accept contractor problems and a temporary disruption in your daily living.
- **Vacation property.** Somewhat under your control if you can manage the extra financial burdens of a second mortgage.
- **Rental properties.** These are the high-risk investments in your property investment portfolio. You can manage the risks more effectively by purchasing only less risky condos within thirty miles of your primary residence so you can service them on a timely and manageable basis.
- Indirect property vehicles such as REITs and real estate mutual funds.

Step 7: *Determine a Method of Investing/Financing*

This is an important last step. I recommend that you establish some criteria for the method of investing in properties. Let me give you an example of what I mean.

Investment/Financing Criteria for Rental Properties
- Property type: One- or two-bedroom condo units
- Location: Washington, D.C., metro area
- Negative cash flow (expenses minus rental income) not to exceed $400 per month
- Down payment not to exceed 30 percent
- Financing based on 30-year amortization schedule
- Property needs to be tenant occupied
- Condo association fees not to exceed $350 per month
- Price appreciation projections not to exceed 5 percent

Tax Planning

Unfortunately, financial planning and tax planning are joined at the hip. As long as you earn income and/or create wealth, the tax collector will not be far behind. Tax planning in the broader context of financial planning is all about reducing, postponing, avoiding, or eliminating the tax consequences of a financial activity. I urge strongly that you seek tax-planning advice from a professional tax accountant.

As I discussed in Chapter 3, real estate is a favored asset in the U.S. tax code and offers perhaps one of the few opportunities for households to take advantage of the tax system in their financial planning activities. The favored tax treatment on property is a long list and includes: the mortgage interest deduction, property tax deduction, passive loss treatment, capital gains exclusion, deductibility of certain closing (settlement) costs, and 1031 transfers, to name a few. Most of these tax issues are treated somewhere else in this book, but I recommend that you discuss these issues at length with a professional financial advisor and/or accountant.

Retirement Planning

Obviously, the single most important objective of financial planning is to accumulate sufficient funds to satisfy your financial needs for retirement. The risk of outliving your income is a tremendous motivator for any long-term financial plan. Retirement planning, in the overall structure of a financial plan, leans heavily on the accumulation of many sources of funds, including your investment portfolio, 401(k) plans, investment retirement accounts, IRA (Roth and traditional) and other retirement programs, your primary residence, deferred-compensation plans, pension plans, Social Security benefits, and annuities. All of these comprise a household's retirement portfolio.

The real estate connection to retirement planning is strong and essential. For most households, there is no better source for accumulating retirement funds than your primary residence. By the time a person reaches retirement, their primary residence is usually clear of debt obligations, so that he or she has 100 percent equity in the selling value of the property. Retirees usually trade down upon retirement, taking advantage of the capital gains exclusion provision in the tax code ($250,000 for individuals, $500,000 for married couples). A portion of the funds from the sale of property is used to purchase a retirement home (usually smaller and less expensive than your primary residence). The remaining funds are added to your retirement portfolio.

Ownership of other real estate also plays a major role in retirement planning. Households that own a vacation property need to account for the net value (asset value minus any liabilities) of that property in their retirement portfolio. Households that own rental properties also need to account for the net value of each property, as well as any positive cash flow distributed to the property owner. Here is a typical retirement portfolio, including real estate assets:

Retirement Portfolio
    Investment Portfolio
        Stocks
        Bonds
        Mutual funds
    Retirement Programs
        401(k)
        Pension
        Social Security
        IRA—Traditional

IRA—Roth
Annuities
Other retirement programs
Real Estate
Primary residence
Vacation property
Rental properties
Other long-term property

In such a retirement portfolio, you need to monitor the cash flow for each investment, the current market value of each investment, and the percentage it makes up of your total retirement portfolio. The composition of your retirement portfolio—that is, the respective portfolio shares of the investment portfolio, retirement plans, and real estate holdings—depends to a large degree on the dollar amount of the retirement portfolio, the number of years until retirement, the target size of your retirement portfolio, and the level of risk you are willing to assume. All of these questions need to be answered by you and your professional financial advisor.

Estate Planning

Estate planning is the part of financial planning that most of us do not like to think about. But it is extremely important to our heirs. Essentially, estate planning is a well-thought-out plan to transfer your financial and personal assets to your heirs (e.g., children) while trying to maintain its total realized value. Since there are tax consequences associated with transferring your assets, estate planning is very much linked to tax planning.

There are many complex issues surrounding estate planning that only a professional accountant and/or attorney specializing in estate planning can address. For our purposes here, your real estate holdings play a large role in the transfer of estate property. There are many estate issues that involve your real estate holdings, including defining property ownership status, spelling out if a property is encumbered or unencumbered, dealing with "jointly held" clauses, establishing living, testamentary, and revocable and irrevocable trusts, gifting property, and charitable property contributions. These are all issues that you need to discuss with the appropriate estate professionals.

Insurance Planning

If you have not purchased the necessary insurance policies to protect against financial risk, your investment, retirement, tax, and estate planning efforts may be for naught. One devastating loss could wipe out everything you have planned and worked for. Knowing how and when to use insurance removes the uncertainty in a long-term financial plan. To manage financial risk, most households invest in life insurance, health insurance, long-term-care insurance, disability insurance, and property and liability insurance (for auto and home). Selecting the type and amount of insurance coverage is all part of financial planning. The premium costs associated with the menu of insurance options are expenses worth taking in your overall financial planning scheme.

With regard to real estate, there are a host of insurance options for you to consider, including home owner's insurance, hazard insurance, mortgage insurance, condominium insurance, and flood insurance. Home owner's insurance is required by the lender, so you have no choice here if you have a mortgage. Hazard insurance may also be required, and given the recent number of hurricanes that have inflicted great harm on so many properties from southern Florida to the Carolinas, certain property owners should take this coverage seriously. Mortgage insurance is not for everyone. Most condominium owners are covered by their condo association insurance policy, but sometimes that policy does not cover all parts of the building. You need to read your condo association's policy statement carefully before making a decision. And finally, if you are purchasing property near a flood zone, you need to inquire whether the property is located in a federal flood zone. If it is not, you will need to acquire private flood insurance.

A Dynamic Approach to Real Estate Planning

As I stated earlier, financial planning is a process of addressing the financial challenges that life presents by developing a "personalized plan" to achieve your financial goals. Nowhere is this more evident than in real estate planning. More than any other wealth-building asset, real estate is joined at the hip with the life cycle.

Typically, young households purchase small, inexpensive homes; middle-aged households purchase larger, more expensive homes; while retirement households return to small, less expensive homes. There is no avoiding the impact of life's needs and challenges on property purchases.

Integrating the dynamic nature of real estate purchasing into the financial planning process is not difficult—just follow the life cycle. For simplicity, I categorize the real estate cycle into four population groups: young households, thirty-something households, peak households, and retiree households. For each household type, I will list their needs, plans, and objectives with regard to purchasing and investing in real estate. Hopefully, this information will provide you with some extra insight into how to integrate real estate planning into your financial planning goals.

Young Households (20s to early 30s)

The first entrée into home buying occurs when children transition into adulthood and begin to accumulate some funds to purchase a home. Their incomes will likely grow in a healthy manner throughout this decade. Here are some of the dynamics of this household group:

Phase I *Purchase a starter home*
- Learn how to manage debt by cash and budget management.
- Establish a satisfactory credit record.
- Accumulate funds for down payment on a starter home.
- Identify starter home with price appreciation potential.
- Obtain low-down-payment/30-year-mortgage financing.

Phase II *Accumulate equity/wealth for a trade-up home*

- Establish 3- to 7-year goal to accumulate equity to purchase a trade-up property.
- Set a target for accumulated total equity necessary to trade up.
- As income growth permits, make extra mortgage payments to pay off more principal.
- Refinance into a 15-year mortgage loan when economically viable (i.e., when mortgage rates drop and/or when income rises).
- Monitor the value of your home on an annual basis in order to calculate the amount of home equity accumulated (price gain plus principal paid).
- Try to limit equity borrowings during this stage of life. Use your income growth to fund major purchases.
- Prioritize retirement/college savings account by contributing to savings/retirement programs: 401(k), IRA, pension, etc.

Thirty-Something Households (30s to early 40s)

If you fall into this age group, you need to get serious about your investment portfolio, including real estate. You must try to achieve your targeted equity goal so you can trade up to a more expensive home that will appreciate equity more quickly.

Phase I *Purchase trade-up home*

- Achieve equity target goal.
- Identify trade-up home with price appreciation potential.
- Obtain 30-year mortgage financing with down payment of 20 percent or greater.
- Purchase trade-up home—use equity in first-time home.

Phase II *Save for second-property purchase*

- Make extra payments when possible.
- Refinance to 15-year loan when possible.
- Continue to build a retirement/savings account—401(k), IRA, pension, etc.—for college and retirement.

- Home equity is now part of your investment portfolio—integrate it in.
- Utilize equity borrowing capacity by using borrowing for auto, college, home improvements, etc.
- Use accumulated equity to purchase a second property for investment/vacation.

Peak Households (50s to 60s)

These are the best years of your life (no matter what the college generation says). You are in your peak earning years, making more money than you ever dreamed of. You need to take advantage of this by expanding your investments into real estate. This is the time to build a real estate portfolio.

Phase I *Build a real estate holdings portfolio*
- Use accumulated equity to purchase third property for investment.
- Buy real estate as a vacation home.
- Buy real estate as a retirement home.

Phase II *Consider trade-down strategies*
- If you are an empty nester, consider trade-down strategies.
- Take advantage of capital gains exclusion and trade down to a less expensive home and use remaining funds for multiple real estate investments.
- Set up a revocable living trust to protect properties from inheritance taxes.

Retirement Households

As you wind down in life's activities, you must also wind down your relatively high-risk investment portfolio by selling off a significant number of your real estate properties.

- Consider downsizing to a smaller/less expensive home if you haven't already done so during your peak years.

- Use remaining funds to purchase more liquid investment vehicles rather than real estate.
- Begin selling your real estate properties as you transition your portfolio to a more liquid and less risky bond/mutual fund–dominated portfolio.
- Hold on to a select number of properties that could be inherited by your heirs.
- Consider reverse mortgages if you need a cash flow for retirement.

EPILOGUE

LIVING IN THE GOLDEN AGE
OF REAL ESTATE

As I mentioned at the beginning of this book, I believe that in years to come historians will see the beginning of the twenty-first century as the "golden age" of real estate. As you complete this book, my hope is that you will have a greater appreciation for what I believe is America's greatest investment—real estate. For those of you who have not fully taken advantage of what residential properties have to offer—give yourself a swift kick in the rear and then get on with the business of investing in real estate.

Real estate is more liquid today than ever before, making the buying and selling of property easier, simpler, and less costly. As I've shown, the great real estate expansion of the past 13 years is likely to continue into the next decade. However, if you expect the same double-digit price growth/multiple property bid marketplace that we've seen in the past several years, you will be disappointed. Looking forward, the real estate boom will almost certainly soften a bit. Nonetheless, I believe it will create significant wealth gains for those who participate. I expect future home sales to be strong and home price appreciation healthy, thanks to long-term demand and supply fundamentals (e.g., favorable demographic trends). The benefits inherent in residential property should not be ignored. Real estate's ability to leverage your capital, build wealth, provide tax benefits, and attract government subsidies all offer advantages that stocks, bonds, and other income-producing assets do not.

My message is quite simple: Expand your real estate reach—now. Taking advantage of the real estate boom is all about attitude— overcoming the belief that buying real estate is awkward, costly, and a hassle.

Nonetheless, as I've stressed throughout the book, the buyer must beware. Today's real estate boom has not evenly spread its riches throughout America. No one is claiming that the real estate boom is fair and equitable. Some regions boom while others lag. Real estate is first and foremost local. Research the dynamics in your neighborhood, town, or region. The boom can discriminate at times, creating a nation of haves and have-nots. Navigate carefully with this book as your guide and the help of your local real estate experts, and you will select the right properties at the right time in the right places, and reap the rewards.

NATIONAL ASSISTANCE HOUSING PROGRAMS

- **American Dream Down Payment Assistance Act (ADDI).** This act authorizes up to $200 million annually for fiscal years 2004–2007 for first-time home buyers seeking to purchase single-family homes. Individuals qualifying for assistance must have incomes not exceeding 80 percent of area median income. If you believe you qualify for ADDI assistance, request more information from your lender or contact the Housing and Urban Development Department (HUD) at 202-708-1112.
- **H.O.M.E. Program.** This is another program administered by HUD that provides grants to state and localities that partner with local nonprofit organizations. The program covers a number of housing activities, including the building, purchasing, and/or rehabilitating of affordable housing for rent or ownership. The program also provides direct rental assistance to low-income households. For more information, contact HUD at 202-708-1112.
- **Zero Down Payment Act.** This act eliminates the down-payment requirement for households that buy homes with FHA loans. If you are a first-time home buyer and satisfy FHA's underwriting requirements, you will probably qualify for a zero-down-payment FHA loan.
- **Teacher Next Door Program.** Also administered by HUD, this program encourages teachers to buy homes in low- to moderate-income neigh-

borhoods. If you are a teacher and work full-time for a public school, a private school, or a federal, state, county, or city educational agency as a state-certified classroom teacher, you will qualify for this program.

- **Officer Next Door Program.** This is also administered by HUD. To take advantage of it, you must be a full-time, sworn law-enforcement officer who is employed full-time by a federal, state, county, or municipal government, or by a public or private college or university. You do not have to be a first-time home buyer to participate. And you must agree to live in the HUD home as your only residence for three years. Selected officers are permitted to purchase property at a 50 percent discount off the list price. The discount is subsidized by HUD. You may purchase homes only in the HUD-designated revitalized areas.

- **Public Housing Home Ownership Programs.** The Public Housing Authority, PHA, has been created to help public housing residents become home owners. If you are a public housing resident, you may be able to convert your rent into a mortgage payment. The PHA may sell a public housing development (specific units) to eligible residents.

- **State/Local and Community Programs.** There are literally thousands of special assistance programs administered by state/local governments in partnership with community organizations across America. I recommend three excellent sources to help you identify if these programs exist in your community. In most cases, all you will have to do is type in your zip code and these sites will generate a list of assistance programs within your area.
  - Fanniemae.com
  - Freddiemac.com
  - REALTOR.org/housingopportunity

In addition, HUD provides a central source for local home buying programs across the nation. Visit HUD.gov/buying/localbuying.cfm to gain access to these programs. At that site, go to your state and then to your metropolitan area/community. There you will be given the phone number of the local housing authority, which can identify all of the local housing programs available.

INDEX